# BEYOND THE BOUNDARIES

SUNY series in
Afro-American Studies

John Howard and Robert C. Smith

Karin L. Stanford

# BEYOND THE BOUNDARIES

## Reverend Jesse Jackson in International Affairs

*Foreword by Ronald W. Walters*

State University of New York Press

Cover photo: Jackson discussing the release of foreign hostages with Iraqi President Saddam Hussein at Hussein's palace in August 1990.

All photographs by D. Michael Cheers and Courtesy Jesse Jackson Archives. Reprinted by permission.

Production by Ruth Fisher
Marketing by Anne M. Valentine

Published by
State University of New York Press, Albany

For information, address the State University of New York Press, State University Plaza, Albany, NY 12246

**Library of Congress Cataloging-in-Publication Data**

Stanford, Karin L., 1961–
    Beyond the boundaries : Reverend Jesse Jackson in international affairs / Karin L. Stanford ; foreword by Ronald W. Walters.
      p.  cm. — (SUNY series in Afro-American studies)
    Includes bibliographical references and index.
    ISBN 0-7914-3445-1 (acid-free paper). — ISBN 0-7914-3446-X (pbk. : acid-free paper)
    1. Jackson, Jesse, 1941– —Career in international relations. 2. United States—Foreign relations—1981–1989—Citizen participation. 3. United States—Foreign relations—Developing countries—Citizen participation. 4. Developing countries—Foreign relations—United States—Citizen participation. 5. Afro-Americans—Politics and government. I. Title. II. Series.
E185.97.J25S73  1997
327.2'092—dc20                           96-41612
                                              CIP

10 9 8 7 6 5 4 3 2 1

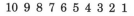

*To the memory of my sister, Toni Monique Grayson*

# CONTENTS

# FOREWORD

Shortly after New Year's Day in 1984, while Rev. Jesse Jackson, then a candidate for the Democratic nomination for president, was in Syria attempting to get Lt. Robert Goodman out of jail, I received a call from a reporter.[1] In the course of a series of questions he asked about Reverend Jackson's activities and motives. There was the clear impression that a conversation the reporter had with a member of Congress revealed the possibility that Reverend Jackson would be charged with violation of the Logan Act upon his return.

I had heard this before, during what was, perhaps, the first significant attempt at private diplomacy by African American leaders. In 1979, when Andrew Young, then U.S. Ambassador to the United Nations, resigned under pressure after it had been discovered that he had been in negotiations with the Palestinian authorities, some members of the press had intimated that blacks were uninitiated in the politics of the Middle East and as such had no right to become involved. This prompted a series of meetings by black political leaders that resulted in their strong assertion of the right to voice opinions and to become involved in international affairs, including those in the Middle East. To emphasize this point, two missions seeking a dialogue on peace were immediately launched to several Middle Eastern countries, one of which was led by Reverend Jackson and another by Rev. Joseph Lowery and Congressman Walter Fauntroy, both leaders of the Southern Christian Leadership Conference. Some members of the press intimated that the leaders of these missions might be charged with violations of the Logan Act.[2]

This subtle intimidation was ineffective, partly because the individuals involved were seasoned civil rights veterans, and partly because of the unique character of American democracy. The Logan Act was named for a Pennsylvania Quaker, George Logan, who, in 1798, went to France at his own expense in an attempt to prevent a war between the United States and France. He was promptly rebuked in a law passed by Congress in 1799, then controlled by the Federalists, who desired such a conflict. The Logan Act ostensibly forbids a private citizen from engaging in unauthorized negotiations with a foreign power with which the United States maintains a dispute.[3]

In practice, however, the Logan Act has never been tested, since it also appears to run afoul of the Constitutional protections of free speech and assembly awarded American citizens as well. Thus, when Ramsey Clark, a former attorney general, visited North Vietnam at the height of the Vietnam War, under explicit prohibitions from the U.S. government, an irate American government nevertheless, did not prosecute him, and when Harrison Salisbury, a journalist, reported from Hanoi in 1966, no action was taken. However, the First Amendment did not protect William Worthy, a black journalist, who was the last American journalist in Communist China whose passport was taken by the State Department in the late 1950s. In any case, this meant that there was no legally enforceable way to restrain the diplomacy of Reverend Jackson since so many citizens had become involved in its practice—but it did become a public issue with his trips to Latin America in July of 1984.[4]

The present volume by Dr. Karin Stanford is exceedingly welcome because it accomplishes two important feats. It contributes to the literature on the generic subject of citizen diplomacy, which is surprisingly sparse considering the private roles other American citizens have played in foreign policy, such as that which industrialist Armand Hammer has played in United States–Soviet relations. This suggests that one of the reasons why so little attention has been given to it is that the intersection between big business and diplomacy would make the Logan Act all but unenforceable if it were taken seriously. Also, it is useful as a conceptual approach with which to review the international activities of Reverend Jesse

Jackson, which have not had the kind of substantive analysis in any of the works about him to date, either scholarly or popular.

As a progressive, the Jackson venture into foreign policy was unique to presidential politics. Although it has been traditional for American presidential candidates to seek to establish their bona fides on foreign policy by travelling to the Soviet Union or the Western allies in the midst of a campaign, the Jackson trips were a blend of his moral and political approach, in line with what I have called elsewhere a "campaign/movement."[5] As his campaign was addressed to the dispossessed in America, the nature of his foreign policy proposals, complimented by his foreign travels as a candidate, were also addressed to issues of concern to those "stuck on the bottom of life" abroad as well. One of the best statements of his general position on international affairs is found in a speech he delivered in London, England, in April 1981, on "The Possibility of a New World Order," in which he said: "Human rights for all human beings is the rallying cry. The human rights and the civil liberties of those struggling for more humane and just societies—in South Africa, Argentina, Chile, Brazil, El Salvador, or wherever in the world—must be protected and defended." With respect to the operational aspect of achieving a humane international order, he suggested: "We must know and not violate the laws of development. We must fight for social change—economic and political equality and parity—but we must also fight for a revolution in moral values and in the quality of life."[6] Urging a global redistribution of resources and humane values, he highlighted the fact that much of American foreign policy was linked to the same economic and political interests in other countries, and, therefore, Americans participated, either knowingly or not, in the economic and political oppression of people whether in major Western industrial countries or in the third world.

Jackson's foreign policy, as Dr. Stanford shows, was decidedly opposed to the Cold War framework and counseled negotiations with opponents from a moral perspective that might insure fairness on both sides. What is important about this approach was that in several of the countries that he visited and proposed such a process, it eventually proved to be the basis for resolving conflict. For example, it furthered the peace process in the Middle East, in Latin America, and in South Africa.

Thus, it was with a considerable sense of satisfaction that Reverend Jackson was present on the White House lawn in 1993 as Menachem Begin, Yasser Arafat, and other leaders came to sign the documents which set out a new framework of living together in that region. As I watched this historic moment from my seat on the White House lawn I was pleased that, despite the substantial rejection of the media and many elements in the American public, the Jackson campaign has persisted in attempting to move America in just this direction.

The same was true with respect to Nicaragua and Cuba. Overtures for peace in Latin America were not directed merely to garner primary election votes at home in the Hispanic American community like those by so many other politicians. Reverend Jackson marched with Hispanic migrant farm workers in South Texas and in California where few votes were present. As Dr. Stanford shows, his motive was to cast light on the failed foreign policy of the Reagan administration which had attempted to isolate the Sandinistas through funding a covert war by the Contras. Thus, when Congress cut off funding for the Contras in October 1984, it became clear that the Sandinistas were the key to peace. The Jackson initiative in Nicaragua was the first to act as a vehicle through which the Sandinistas could signal their willingness to respect church authorities and mount legitimate elections. The action of Congress in thwarting the Reagan administration's policy of forceful pacification of Nicaragua led to a new consensus that allowed the Sandinistas to approach elections with some confidence. Since that time, the democratic process in that country has also been adopted.

The clear implication here is that the overtures made by Fidel Castro through Reverend Jackson's mission to Cuba may also eventually be followed as the basis to normal relations. To this extent, U.S. policy-makers will ultimately have to abandon the last vestiges of the Cold War approach to the Cuban government and negotiate—seriously—with Fidel Castro if a more comprehensive democracy in Latin America is to be achieved. It is important not only in a moral sense that relations with Cuba are normalized, but increasingly, in light of the North American Free Trade Association (NAFTA) this region has begun to assume a critical role in the economic future of the country as well.

Finally, Jackson's early position to oppose and isolate the racist apartheid regime of South Africa was also correct. As Dr. Stanford points out, in the Democratic Primary presidential debates of 1984, Jackson addressed the previously hidden issue of South Africa, challenging the other candidates to take a stand on one of the great moral issues of the day, a constitutional racism which legitimized the economic, social, and political subordination of black South Africans, Coloreds, and Asians. As Jackson's policy helped to initiate a change in American foreign policy, which led to the adoption of the Anti-Apartheid Act of 1986,[7] it was no surprise that Reverend Jackson headed President Clinton's delegation to monitor the truly comprehensive elections in South Africa in 1995.

Dr. Stanford has elaborated the international diplomacy of Reverend Jesse Jackson through the use of the concept of 'citizen diplomacy.' It not only enriches the view that U.S. citizens may often play a useful role in the outcome of foreign policy, but in this case, it helps to illustrate how the civil rights movement has been expanded through the Jackson campaign to the international system.

Nevertheless, Dr. Stanford also sought to define the limitations of citizen diplomacy in the presumptive conflict it establishes between the goals and methods of the state and those of the private actor. Thus, she has shown that when the interests of the actor are congruent with those of the state, citizen diplomacy, is most often successful. Given this finding, Jackson's attempt to expand the human rights movement beyond the control of American political elites, both foreign and domestic, was somewhat successful but severely limited. It attracted some anticipated opposition for the traditional reason that American blacks, as a subordinate group, were not perceived to have the right to substantial roles in foreign affairs without the sanction of institutional elites. This was the case when Martin Delany sought to negotiate land in Africa for black settlement in 1859, when Marcus Garvey sought to do the same in the 1920s, and when Malcolm X attempted to carry the charge of American racism to the Organization of African Unity and the United Nations in 1964.

Overall, this book is an important scholarly treatment of Reverend Jesse Jackson's international activities. The book reveals that several international conflicts were eventually resolved in the direction of Jackson's policy proposals, strongly suggesting that they were the correct basis of policy in areas vital to U.S. interests. As such, the content of Jackson's policies provides a virtual manual for a set of humane priorities in foreign policy. Through this analysis, Dr. Stanford has helped to highlight the kind of foreign policy approach that could successfully address the challenges of living in the multicultural global society of the twenty-first century.

Ronald W. Walters
Howard University

# PREFACE

This project began informally in 1984, during the height of the anti-apartheid movement and Reverend Jesse Jackson's first bid for the presidency of the United States. Reverend Jackson's consistent objections to the United States' policy of "constructive engagement" toward South Africa throughout the campaign raised my awareness of international politics. After completing my undergraduate degree, I became active in the anti-apartheid movement. When I entered graduate school, my research efforts inevitably centered on the role of African Americans in international politics. However, as a student of political science, I found that only a handful of scholars endeavored to locate African Americans in international affairs. I became a student of those scholars. This project is a modest contribution to the small body of literature that situates African Americans as actors in international politics.

This book could not have been written without the assistance and encouragement of numerous people. My greatest intellectual debt is to Ronald W. Walters, my dissertation chair, academic adviser, and mentor. Professor Walters' advice, analyses, and critique were key to the development of this project and also furthered my growth as a progressive-thinking scholar. Special appreciation is also given to Lorenzo Morris whose astute insight and writing advice greatly improved this work. I also owe intellectual debts to John Cotman, Babalola Cole, and Gary Weaver for their wise counsel. I alone take full responsibility for the book's contents and interpretations.

Other professors in the Department of Political Science at Howard University contributed to my growth and development as a scholar. Among them are Jane Flax, Michael Frazier, Mervat Hatem, Michael Nwanze, and Brian Weinstein. Staff members Gwen Sumlin and Rosemary Betha encouraged, inspired, and supported my academic pursuits. Gratitude is also expressed to Kenneth Coleman and David Lowery of the University of North Carolina, Chapel Hill, for reading and commenting on this research project.

A special note of appreciation is expressed to those individuals who assisted with the substantive aspects of this project. National Rainbow Coalition President and Founder Reverend Jesse L. Jackson and International Affairs Director Jack O'Dell both were generous in extending their time and interest. Jack O'Dell especially helped me conceptualize Reverend Jesse Jackson's international endeavors and gave me access to important data. The photographs exhibited in this publication were provided by D. Michael Cheers, Ph.D. Cheers, currently the Managing Editor of *Ebony South Africa Magazine* in Johannesburg, covered Jesse Jackson for eleven years. In particular, Cheers covered Jackson's 1984 and 1988 campaigns and Jackson's foreign trips from Syria in 1983 to 1994 when Jackson led the U.S. South Africa Delegation to observe the first South African non-racial elections. Special thanks is also given to others who provided essential information on Reverend Jackson's missions abroad, especially Frank Watkins of the National Rainbow Coalition, Political Science Professor Armando Gutierrez, Kenneth Bleakly of the State Department, former Rainbow Coalition Deputy Press Secretary Eric Easter, former Washington Office on Africa Director Damu Smith, journalists George Curry of *Emerge Magazine* and Sylvester Monroe of *Newsweek*.

Other colleagues and friends who supported this effort are Daryl B. Harris, Rose Harris, Clarence Lusane, Maurice Carney, Derrick Cogburn, Robyn Willis, Cobie Kwasi Harris, Sahr John Kpundeh, Gary Masoni, Ollie Johnson, F. Carl Walton, Joe Davidson, Valerie Johnson, Deborah Rhodes, Ronald Roach, and Musa A. Musa. I am indebted to them for their advice and encouragement. I am also indebted to James Joseph and Mary Braxton of the Council on Foundations for giving me the time and latitude to complete this work. Of course, thanks to my family, whose support has made all things possible.

Appreciation is also expressed to Clay Morgan of the State University of New York Press and the press's readers for their comments and suggestions. Special appreciation is given to Robert Smith not only for his comments and suggestions but also for his encouragement and friendship.

Finally, the University of North Carolina, Chapel Hill Post Doctoral Scholars Program and the Institute for World Politics/ Dorothy Danforth Compton Fellowship for Minority Group Students in World Affairs Program both provided financial support for this project. My sincere appreciation.

# 1

# Introduction

"But for the grace of God and Jesse Jackson we wouldn't be here," exclaims Lloyd Culbertson, a former hostage whose release was negotiated by Reverend Jesse Jackson after the August 2, 1990, Iraqi invasion of Kuwait.[1] Once again, Reverend Jackson returned from a mission abroad in the company of Americans who had been held captive by a foreign government. In this instance, Iraqi President Saddam Hussein released forty-seven Americans and a large group of other foreigners to Jackson on September 2, 1990, one month after the invasion. At the press conference after the return, Jackson expounded on his visit to Iraq and set forth his proposals for averting a war.

Jackson's five-day mission to the Middle East was inspired not only by the Iraqi invasion of Kuwait, but also by the aggressive acts which followed. One of the most volatile issues was that of foreigners held in Iraq and Kuwait. Iraqi news agencies reported that the thousands of foreign women and children would soon be free to leave the country. However, other reports suggested that the foreigners in Iraq and Kuwait were hostages and could be distributed among potential military strike targets by Hussein as a defensive shield in the event of an attack on Iraq.

In the midst of the crisis, Jesse Jackson obtained a letter of invitation from the Iraqi Embassy to interview President Hussein and some of the foreign hostages for his new syndicated TV talk show. By going as a journalist, Jackson was able to comply with the U.S. advisory against contact with Iraq.[2] Although State Department officials tried to discourage the mission, key members of the organization held a briefing session with Jackson before his departure.

After Jackson publicly announced his intention to visit Baghdad, several American families who had relatives held in Iraq and Kuwait asked him to assist in gaining their

1

release. The State Department gave Jackson a list of American citizens held by Hussein to take with him.[3]

While in Iraq, Jackson held meetings with President Saddam Hussein and Foreign Minister Tariq Aziz. In those meetings Jackson focused the conversation on issues that could lead to a peaceful solution of the Persian Gulf crisis. He inquired about the issues and complications that prevented the departure of the foreigners and expressed his displeasure with Iraqi disruption of operations at the U.S. Embassy in Kuwait.[4] Jackson further argued that those kinds of hostile acts and holding hostages would not help matters with the United States and, moreover, contributed to the lack of focus on Iraqi's initial grievances with Kuwait and U.S. policy.

With Hussein's permission, Jackson traveled to Kuwait and interviewed American, British, and other foreign hostages. It was after his television interview with Saddam Hussein that Jackson began to press for release of the hostages. He submitted the State Department list of American hostages to Hussein, who eventually agreed to the release if Jackson could obtain landing privileges in the United States for an Iraq airplane. Asserting his respect for Jackson's efforts, while continuing to criticize American policy, Hussein declared, "This is in your honor. I'm doing this for you— not Bush! I have no respect for Bush. But for you!"[5]

The Jackson entourage stopped in London first to drop off the European hostages, then flew to Dulles Airport with the remaining Americans. At a press conference afterwards, several former hostages thanked Jackson for facilitating their release. Jackson used this occasion to publicly encourage President George Bush to negotiate with Hussein in order to avoid further conflict. Explaining President Hussein's concerns, Jackson said, "He feels ignored . . . He feels if we can talk to Gorbachev while they're in Afghanistan with missiles pointed at our country he deserves to be talked with. We need a political solution, not war."[6] Also at the airport press conference, the Iraqi ambassador to the United States agreed with the call for negotiations and welcomed the hostages back.

However, others were not as pleased with Jackson's success. British and American newspapers scolded Jackson for exploiting the Persian Gulf crisis for his own publicity. They asked by whose authority was Jackson negotiating with heads of states on important international issues. They further declared that Jackson undermined official efforts. Even the State Department hinted that diplomacy should be left to the professional U.S. diplomats, and not be engaged in by independent private citizens. Other critics argued that Hussein exploited Jackson and used him as a spokesman for his propaganda in the United States.[7] Despite these longstanding and often repeated criticisms of this kind of international activity, intervening in troubled spots throughout the world is not new for Jesse Jackson, nor for many other American private citizens.

Throughout the years, private citizens in various forms, have endeavored to impact United States foreign policy and international affairs. Using "legitimate" channels, the public influences foreign affairs through conventional exercise of its right to free speech, right to petition and assembly, right to protest, ability to vote, and personally contacting officials. When those avenues fail, many private citizens take on roles previously reserved for United States officials and travel to foreign nations to further understand the problem, focus attention on their areas of concern, and intervene when they believe their actions can make a difference. The subject of this book is the latter avenue chosen by citizens—the choice to engage in citizen diplomacy.

## Research Focus

This book assesses the historical and political significance of Jesse Jackson's use of citizen diplomacy during the 1984 presidential election campaign and his 1986 mission to Southern Africa. One central objective is to explain the motivation for Jackson's diplomacy, the strategies employed, and the impact of his initiatives. This analysis also explores how African American politics, political culture, and historical internationalism influenced Jackson's endeavors. This discussion not only is important for historical context, but it also helps dispel the myth that African American international concerns and activities are theoretically insignificant and in practice ineffectual.[8]

Jackson's diplomatic efforts also allow one to ask broader questions about the relationship between private citizens' initiatives in international politics and democratic participation in an elite foreign policy arena. An important question is: To what extent does citizen diplomacy expand the representation of other views and thus enhance pluralism in foreign policy-making? Other critical issues explored are associated with the structure and processes of citizen diplomacy. Does citizen diplomacy provide an alternate approach for citizen participation in foreign affairs and in the international arena? How does citizen diplomacy fit into the foreign policy-making apparatus and process? Does citizen diplomacy represent a significant challenge to the U.S. foreign policy-making process? What factors contribute to the successes and/or failures of citizen diplomacy? How and when does race become a factor in citizen diplomacy?

Jackson's expeditions to Syria, Central America and Cuba during his 1984 presidential election bid and his 1986 trip to Southern Africa are the examples used in this analysis. The results of the examination suggest that citizen diplomacy provides an additional point of access into the political system and foreign policy process and therefore increases democratic participation in U.S. foreign affairs.

Although Jackson had engaged in citizen diplomacy before, his efforts during the 1984 presidential election campaign were of greater import because he was considered a legitimate contender for the presidency.[9] In addition, the fact that Jackson succeeded in making apartheid in South Africa one of his most vocal issues during the campaign requires some discussion of his efforts in Southern Africa in 1986. Although other accounts of Jackson's endeavors are discussed in this book, these three cases best illustrate the various approaches to citizen diplomacy. The following issues were considered in the analysis of each case: U.S. official policy; Jackson's foreign policy agenda and platform; divergence in foreign policy objectives between the government and Jackson; motivation for Jackson's diplomacy; Jackson's specific diplomatic goals and objectives; and the results and effectiveness of Jackson's mission.

Jesse Jackson's diplomatic efforts are important to the discourse on citizen diplomacy for several reasons. First, his endeavors are numerous, and therefore an analysis that incorporates many issues and areas of concern is possible. Second, Jackson's efforts broaden the discussion of citizen diplomacy because concrete benefits often resulted, such as the release of hostages. Henceforth, investigating the effectiveness of Jackson's diplomacy requires one to analyze the causes of his successes and failures. This also makes salient the rationale and motives of foreign governments when they negotiate with and assist U.S. citizen diplomats.

Third, Jackson's efforts help to distinguish citizen diplomacy from ordinary interest group participation in international affairs and provide a line of demarcation between the actions of established interest groups, who utilize formal channels of influence, and private citizens and interest groups who bypass orthodox channels. It must be noted here that sometimes Jackson acted solely as a private citizen and at other times as a representative of the Rainbow Coalition and his foreign affairs constituency. However, the purpose here is not to determine when his constituency's concerns are the basis for his actions, but to focus on the activity itself.

Fourth, investigating Jackson's diplomatic efforts broadens the discussion of where citizen diplomacy is likely to take place. In the past, the majority of citizen diplomacy was directed toward the Soviet Union as a reaction to the cold war, while most other efforts have taken place during times of war. Jackson's energy was directed predominately toward economically depressed and crisis areas in the world, thus examining Jackson's efforts may illuminate when and where citizen diplomacy is likely to take place and who is likely to initiate such efforts. In addition, a more complete picture of the diversity of U.S. foreign policy emerges when examining Jackson's foreign policy agenda and his diplomatic efforts.

Fifth, using Jackson's efforts allows one to discuss how citizen diplomacy can be used in presidential election campaigns. It also expands the discussion of minorities in presidential politics and can contribute to our understanding of the divergence between progressive, liberal, and centrist forces within the Democratic party. And finally, Jackson's foreign policy endeavors raise the question of race and how it affects the efforts of U.S. private citizens who attempt to influence foreign policy.

Because this examination is based on the activity of an individual who represents a particular constituency, one must note that the Rainbow Coalition, which is a broad-based progressive U.S. political coalition founded by Jackson, formed the core of support for his efforts abroad from 1984 through 1986. There were, however, other interest groups who supported or were intricately involved with Jackson's diplomacy such as TransAfrica, the African American lobby for Africa and the Caribbean, and the League of United Latin American Citizens (LULAC). Other private citizens not affiliated with the Rainbow Coalition but who actively supported Jackson's approach to a particular international issue are also considered part of Jackson's foreign affairs constituency.

## Foreign Policy and U.S. Democracy

In conducting U.S. foreign affairs, there has always been a dilemma between broad democratic participation versus participation by a small elite.[10] This dilemma is shaped by the foreign policy roles prescribed in the U.S. Constitution and the American emphasis on expertise.

The constitution divides the making and implementation of foreign policy between the executive and legislative branches of government.[11] The presidency holds the power to command the armed forces, initiate the treaty-making process, appoint and receive ambassadors, and use presidential authority to conduct diplomacy. Congressional powers in foreign affairs are associated with treaty making, war, and control of expenditures. Notwithstanding the passage of the War Powers Act, the congressional role in foreign affairs is largely reactive to presidential lead.[12]

The dilemma of broad democratic participation versus elitism is also shaped by the need for expertise on national security and national interest questions. The emphasis on expertise is based on a longstanding belief that the "high" nature of foreign policy-making requires the talents and skills of America's most qualified individuals. Because of the importance placed on foreign policy issues, expertise is valued over mass participation. In the "national interest" or for the "common good" most Americans support this emphasis and subordinate their specific interests to the interests of the nation. It is for this reason that the formulation and conduct of U.S. affairs are monopolized by the president and his carefully selected advisors.

However, the increasing complexity of the world and a perceived realist bias in foreign policy-making have contributed to the ascension and prominence of nonstate domestic actors. Interest groups, the media, and political parties use a variety of methods, such as lobbying, soliciting public opinion, and directly contacting officials, to gain attention for their international concerns. In *American Foreign Policy Making and the Democratic Dilemmas,*

Eric Uslander and John Spanier use a set of concentric circles to illustrate the hierarchy of power in foreign policy-making and to show the influence of nonstate actors.[13] Within the inner circle of the hierarchical model are the president and key advisors; the second circle consists of bureaucrats and advisers; the third circle is Congress; and the fourth circle consists of political parties, interest groups, public opinion, and "personal diplomacy."[14] Based upon this model, the active citizen fits into the fourth circle, which is peripheral and is considered to play only a minor role in crisis situations. Because of this perceived lack of power that the traditional nonstate actors possess, some U.S. private citizens circumvent the fourth circle and engage in citizen diplomacy, which is a less conventional and frequently considered undesirable method of opening up the elite foreign policy process.

## Citizen Diplomacy: A Model of Private Citizen Activity in U.S. Foreign Affairs

Citizen diplomacy is defined as the diplomatic efforts of private citizens in the international arena for the purpose of achieving a specific objective or accomplishing constituency goals. One of the most distinctive features of this type of diplomacy is that it operates outside of the existing national foreign policy-making system and may not be supportive of official policy.[15] The principles of citizen diplomacy posited here are drawn from various cases and delineate the motivation for engaging in this type of activity, the frequently pursued modes of operation, and the effectiveness of the activity.[16]

Although the diplomatic activities of citizens vary, several themes remain constant. The citizen diplomat is often motivated by a strong desire to make issues of morality salient in world affairs and is usually concerned with peaceful conflict resolution. Citizen diplomats bypass the official foreign policy-making system usually after they have exhausted other measures for influence and when they perceive that policy-makers are insensitive to their concerns. The most frequent concerns relate to issues of peace, war, hostages, business deals, disagreement with government policy, and feelings of nationalism and/or ideological affinity.

The effectiveness of citizen diplomacy is dependent upon various factors, such as the prestige of the citizen diplomat, the willingness of nations to resolve disputes, the political advantages and/or vulnerability of the disputing parties involved, timeliness, and perhaps most important the difficulty of the goal pursued. The least difficult tasks are fact-finding, while the most difficult is to change the policy orientation of a government.

Determining effectiveness is a difficult task. Concerns relate to the question of how one measures effectiveness, considering that many variables can be attributed to policy outputs, and how one measures influence in a situation where the individual is attempting to influence policy when he or she has no official standing. The foremost question concerns whether influence is only measured by policy change, or whether having input and consideration in the decision-making process satisfies influence? Because effectiveness can have various meanings, there are grounds for arguing that if the goal was ultimately accomplished or the citizen diplomat was able to make a "meaningful" contribution to policy formulation or implementation, then the effort can be considered effective.

The discourse on private citizens' initiatives in international affairs usually excludes the activity of those persons who engage in citizen diplomacy. One result of this exclusion has been a concentration on those acts that are homologous with the pluralist model of democracy, thereby highlighting track two activity (a political-psychological approach that also provides an avenue for private citizen participation in the international arena[17]), interest group activity, and people-to-people contact. Consequently, the Dartmouth Conferences (dialogues between U.S. and Soviet citizens of stature) and the work of individuals such as Norman Cousins, who was sent by President Eisenhower to discuss with Soviet leader Nikita Khrushchev what private citizens could do to help ease the tension between the two superpowers, are well documented.[18] Other popular cases concern those seeking international business deals—such as the late Armand Hammer, industrialist and promoter of Soviet trade for over six decades—and the work of church organizations and religious groups seeking to provide humanitarian relief for suffering people. However, the activities of individuals who pursue their own objectives in the international arena and who employ unconventional means of participation are generally dismissed as out-of-the-mainstream and therefore insignificant.

The dismissal of the significance of citizen diplomacy may have come about for several reasons, particularly a belief among scholars that these types of activities are not influential enough to warrant detailed scrutiny. However, this discussion contends that often the efforts of private citizens in the international arena have serious implications for U.S. foreign policy and the policy-making process and are therefore worthy of study. The failure to acknowledge the activities of these sometimes very important international actors and their accomplishments results in a deficiency of information in the field of democratic participation in foreign affairs.

As noted previously, the involvement of the private citizen in foreign affairs has evoked a myriad of criticism. Some critics assert that citizen diplomacy interferes with the foreign policy-making process—which has been primarily reserved for elite participation. Others hold the opinion that citizen diplomacy may endanger national security. Regardless of these denunciations, due to the continual advancement in communication technologies and the breakdown of consensus in society on the goals and strategies of U.S. foreign policy, private citizens will remain zealous in their attempts to influence the direction of U.S. foreign affairs.

## What Is Already Known about
## Private Citizens in International Affairs

The literature on the intervention of private citizens in foreign affairs reflects the conceptual confusion that has dogged this area of study and also reveals the lack of consensus on how to approach this phenomenon. Evident at first glance is the problem of nomenclature. Phrases that are in current use to describe private citizen participation in the international arena are private diplomacy, nonofficial diplomacy, unofficial diplomacy, public diplomacy, supplemental diplomacy, informal diplomacy, demi-diplomacy, and track two diplomacy.[19] Moreover, citizen participation in the international arena, whether it is scientific or cultural exchanges, workshops or seminars on questions of peace, or attempts to impact policy can be found under the rubric of any of the aforementioned terms.

### Track Two

Up until this time, one framework has generally been accepted to guide the discussion on the diplomatic efforts of private citizens. Track two diplomacy as defined by William Davidson, a psychiatrist, and Joseph Montville, a foreign service officer, is nongovernmental, informal, and nonofficial diplomacy conducted by private citizens of a nation-state.[20] Track two diplomacy, though not a substitute for the official track one diplomacy, supports and often parallels track one goals. The goal of this people-to-people contact is to break down psychological barriers between parties and to create an alternate set of relationships that can prevent an escalation of conflict. Track two should result in an identification of common ground between the parties in dispute. Examples of track two diplomacy are leaders participating in workshops with adversaries and cultural exchanges.

Track two diplomacy, though useful as a starting point for analyzing citizen diplomacy, is problematic for several reasons. First, track two lacks boundaries because it suggests that most forms of citizen-to-citizen contact can somehow nullify psychological barriers, without adequately discussing how. Further this construct does not focus on the types of individuals who are likely to engage in citizen diplomacy, nor the types of issues which may induce their participation. Moreover, track two does not attempt to clarify specific acts that may lead to the effectiveness of the citizen diplomat. More important, track two diplomacy remains an integral part of the U.S. foreign policy-making system. The purpose of track two is merely to support official endeavors. Consequently, those individuals who disagree with official objectives find that it is difficult to develop a parallel track and therefore cannot effectively participate in track two diplomacy. It is at this stage that citizen diplomacy originates.

Track two diplomacy, as does interest group theory, is dictated by and operates within an unquestionable pluralist framework.[21] However, this does not mean that there are no similarities in the two forms of international activity. Citizen diplomacy does parallel track two in several ways. Both track two and citizen diplomat initiatives are concerned with impacting foreign affairs and relations. Second, both track two and citizen diplomacy usually result from the concerns of a specific group of individuals, and therefore both have constituencies. Finally, both track two and citizen diplomats interact with other groups in society in order to gain support for their efforts.

The primary distinction between the two forms of activity is that advocates of track two emphasize their support of official efforts while citizen diplomats are independent of an ambition to sustain or bolster official efforts. Hence, those activities that are centered on impacting international politics within the framework of official U.S. policy, or in which the participants operate within the framework of the structures provided for citizen influence are considered separate from citizen diplomacy. In addition, those activities of citizens that seek only to gain an audience with citizens of other nations in order to promote healthier relations between citizens should be considered people-to-people contact, track two diplomacy, or even an aspect of interest group behavior. Viewed in this light, people-to-people contact and other types of international exchanges of information between citizens of different nations should not be analyzed in the same manner as activity that is not officially sanctioned by the U.S. foreign policy establishment, such as high-level negotiations between a citizen and a foreign official. This distinction between track two activity, interest group activity in the international arena, and citizen diplomacy is made in this book. Classifying these activities by their methods and objectives will alleviate the problem of nomenclature and conceptual confusion and help solve the problem of barriers. Accordingly, those contacts between Jesse Jackson and high-level decision-makers from foreign governments that involved discussions adverse to U.S. policy objectives and Jackson's efforts to accomplish specific objectives in the international arena, are the focus of this analysis.

## The Logan Act

In addition to track two, any discussion of citizen diplomacy must include the Logan Act. For it is the Logan Act which limits the rights and activities of U.S. citizens in international politics. The Logan Act (1799) prohibits private citizens, without the authority of the U.S. government from "intercourse with any agent of a foreign government with the intent to influence the conduct of that government in relation to any controversies with the U.S., or to defeat any measures of the U.S."[22] Since its enactment, several arguments for the repeal of the act have been put forth. For instance, it has been argued that the Logan Act should be invalidated because it violates the First Amendment right to free speech, fails to properly inform citizens of the conduct it proscribes, and allows extensive discretion on the part of the executive in determining when violations have occurred. Moreover, the federal government's failure to invoke the Logan Act since its enactment would make application of the act at this juncture in history discriminatory.[23] Despite those objections to its existence, the Logan Act remains viable law and, in certain instances, American presidents have threatened to prosecute citizen diplomats under it in order to prohibit their direct international intervention.

## Book Outline

The book is organized in the following manner. Chapter two highlights two central approaches to citizen diplomacy frequently utilized by African Americans: nationalism/Pan-Africanism and ideological affinity. In addition, it briefly comments on other approaches to citizen diplomacy, such as hostage release, to provide additional context for Jesse Jackson's efforts. A broad-ranged discussion of the international efforts of African Americans is also provided for historical context. Chapter three examines the international efforts of Jesse Jackson prior to his 1984 presidential election campaign. Also addressed in this chapter is an examination of those key factors that help explain Jackson's international propensities. This includes a brief biographical discussion of Jackson and an examination of African American political culture and behavior. Chapter four presents a discussion of the 1984 Jackson campaign for the presidency and sets forth Jackson's and the Rainbow Coalition's perceptions of U.S. foreign policy and their international agenda. This chapter emphasizes that Jackson's longstanding personal views on international politics were reflected in his presidential campaign's international agenda and platform. Chapters five, six, and seven serve as case studies for Jackson's efforts in Syria, Central America and Cuba, and Southern Africa. A significant amount of attention is given to the motivation for each mission, the mode employed, and outcome. The implications for democratic participation in U.S. foreign policy formulation and processes is also set forth in each case study. Chapter eight provides a summary of the major findings. In the postscript, Jackson's international endeavors since his 1988 presidential election bid are highlighted.

# 2

# Approaches to Citizen Diplomacy

In this chapter two central approaches to citizen diplomacy often employed by African Americans will be examined. The purpose is to link the concept to actual practices and to illuminate the motivations for diplomacy, the strategies used, and to explore the outcomes that may result from the efforts of private citizens in the international arena. In addition, a brief overview of African American internationalism will be provided with the objective of offering a basic understanding of the nature of citizen diplomacy when it is conducted by African Americans. Although this book focuses on the citizen diplomacy of African Americans, certainly, the diplomatic efforts of persons outside of the African American community cannot be dismissed. For instance, no one can doubt the importance of the diplomatic work of former President Jimmy Carter conducted through the Carter Center. The former president has traveled the globe to promote human rights within nations and resolve conflicts between governments. The diplomatic efforts of George Logan must also be recognized. Logan's significance stems not only from the fact that his citizen diplomacy was the first to receive critical attention in early U.S. history, but also, it was his actions that led to the creation and passage of the Logan Act. Hence, this discussion will begin with a look at the exploits of George Logan and other important figures in citizen diplomacy.

## George Logan and the Logan Act of 1799

One of the earliest instances of citizen diplomacy occurred in 1798 with the activities of George Logan in Europe. Logan's case is essential to the discourse on citizen participation in the international arena because it was his mission that resulted in the enactment of the Logan Act (1799), which prohibits citizen diplomacy.[1]

George Logan was a doctor, farmer, and politically active Quaker. In the Quaker tradition, during times of conflict between nations, individual members have set forth their concerns before officials of nations and courts. Thus, when France responded to U.S. ratification of the Jay Treaty (1794) with Great Britain[2] by withdrawing its minister from Philadelphia, refusing to receive the new U.S. minister to France, and continuing seizures of U.S. shipping on the high seas, the chance for dialogue between the two nations diminished. George Logan was determined to make a personal effort for peace. He approached his personal friend Thomas Jefferson for a certificate to travel with no discussion of his real intent for the trip.

Logan left for Europe on June 12, 1798, with the objective of persuading the French to demonstrate goodwill to the United States by releasing prisoners and/or raising the embargo.[3] While in Europe he met with various officials of the Executive Directory (the French government in exile), including French Foreign Minister Charles Tallyrand. He introduced himself as a private citizen concerned with the state of affairs between the two nations and spoke with officials on the state of public opinion in the United States and the imminent danger of war. Throughout his mission, Logan reiterated that his purpose was not to speak for the U.S. government nor to criticize France, but only to suggest ways in which the relationship between the two nations could be improved. Minister Tallyrand showed no real interest in Logan or his ideas. However, Merlin Douai, who occupied the highest political office in the French Republic, presented Logan's ideas to the Directory. Although it has been suggested that Logan's actions were not the motive for France's eventual lift of the trade embargo and the release of the U.S. seamen held in French jails, it is believed that his visit provided convenient timing for the implementation of decisions which were possibly already made.[4]

Upon his return to the United States in early November, Logan received a myriad of reactions. The Federalists claimed that his diplomacy interfered with duties reserved for government and called for a law that would prohibit similar activities, while the Republicans praised his efforts. Setting a precedent for future efforts of this sort, Logan contacted high-ranking U.S. officials to report on his endeavors. Both General George Washington and Secretary of State Timothy Pickering regarded his actions with great suspicion. However, President John Adams believed Logan was sincere and listened attentively to his accounts. Nevertheless, on January 30, 1799, President Adams signed the Logan Act into law.[5]

Another important precedent set by George Logan was his refusal to abide by the Logan Act. In his continuing efforts to prevent an outbreak of war between the United States and Europe, Logan embarked upon another private mission to reduce conflict between the United States on one hand, and Britain and France on the other. In that situation, U.S. merchant ships were being stopped and searched on the high seas by British and French warships. In June 1807 British soldiers killed and wounded several U.S. seamen. The United States retaliated by instituting the Non-Importation Act and Non-Intercourse Act, two pieces of legislation designed to strangle the two countries economically.[6]

In response to those events, Logan wrote and traveled to Washington to appeal to the president and other officials to settle the dispute peacefully. When those efforts failed, Logan announced that he would go to England to deliver any messages the president might have for his minister there. President James Madison accepted Logan's offer and directed his minister to resume negotiations. Having other motives, however, Logan met with British officials and other prominent persons to urge them to influence popular opinion, Parliament, and the government to reverse their policies on the matter.[7] Although he failed to obtain a meeting with Prime Minister Spencer Perceval, Logan wrote to him, outlining his concerns and suggesting ways to avoid escalating the conflict.[8] On May 11, Spencer Perceval was murdered as he entered the House of Commons, and by the end of June the new government had suspended their policy of confrontation.[9]

For George Logan, the motivation of obtaining peace was far stronger than the threat of punishment. Logan and those who follow his example believe that bypassing the official foreign policy-making system and becoming personally involved in problem solving is a credible option to reduce the chances for war. Logan's strategy, which centered on written correspondence and face-to-face meetings with foreign officials, is classic citizen diplomacy. Although no one can say exactly how his diplomacy contributed to the outcome of each dispute, it is evident that the information provided by him to the conflicting factions factored into the decision-making process. Logan's legacy is reinforced each time a private citizen travels abroad to meet with foreign government officials to discuss a dispute with the United States.

## Beyond George Logan: Historical Uses of Citizen Diplomacy

The unconventional activities of individuals who disagree with a particular U.S. foreign policy are frequently ignored in scholarly discussions. This leads to a failure to identify all the factors that may have contributed to a specific foreign policy outcome and a lack of information on specific occurrences. However, as illustrated by the cases of citizen diplomacy for hostage rescue, citizen diplomacy can be significant.

Seeking the release of hostages or prisoners of war (POW) is a common motive for citizen diplomacy, most likely because the seizure of foreign nationals is a common occurrence during war. The incentive for citizen diplomacy in cases of hostage rescue are usually humanitarian and often involve the relatives and acquaintances of prisoners. Frequently, in these situations, citizen diplomats find themselves acting out the role of traditional diplomats. Face-to-face negotiations and bargaining with representatives of the captors, foreign governments, and individuals believed to have knowledge of the situation are the norm. The notoriety of the citizen diplomat is usually a good barometer for determining whether or not the diplomat will be granted an audience with captors. For example, during the Vietnam War, Jesuit Priest Father Berrigan, a well-known peace activist and poet, traveled to Hanoi specifically to secure the release of three prisoners.[10] Father Berrigan was granted an audience with the premier of North Vietnam, Pham Van Dong, and various other high-level officials on the basis of his prior public critiques of the Vietnam War and because he had proved his dedication to the antiwar cause by going to prison for his beliefs. Berrigan's success at accomplishing his goals possibly saved the lives of three Americans.

An unusual case of citizen diplomacy for hostage release was demonstrated by the activities of Peggy Say. Say engaged in citizen diplomacy to secure the release of her brother, Terry Anderson, the chief Middle East correspondent for the Associated Press, who was kidnapped March 16, 1985, while on assignment in Beirut. The Islamic Holy War, a Shiite Muslim group, claimed responsibility for kidnapping Anderson. For the first few months of her brother's captivity, Peggy Say "had faith in the Reagan Administration's promises that if the hostage families would wait patiently, their relatives would be freed."[11] However, when the passengers who were hijacked by the Shiite Muslim group from TWA flight 847 were released in the summer of 1985 while her brother remained a hostage, Say began to lose faith in the Reagan administration and went so far as to assert that "if there were more Americans in Lebanese hands, the government would find a way to free them."[12]

Supported financially by the Associated Press, Say launched her own personal crusade to secure the release of her brother. Say traveled extensively, meeting with and urging world leaders, heads of governments, and peace activists to use their influence to help free Anderson. For example, in 1990, Say embarked upon a two-and-one-half-week trip to the Middle East and Europe on a humanitarian pilgrimage with an Associated Press delegation. While there she met with figures such as UN Secretary General Javier Perez de Cuellar, Pope John Paul II, and Robert Runcie, Archbishop of Canterbury. In a meeting with the foreign minister of Syria Farouk Charaa, Say was assured that on his next trip to Tehran he "would work intensely to push for the freeing of the hostages."[13] Palestinian Liberation Organization (PLO) Chairperson Yasser Arafat told Say in an hour long meeting in the Tunisian capital that "he'd like to help but the problem was the fanatics in Iran."[14]

Despite Say's diplomacy to free her brother, Terry Anderson remained a hostage for seven years. Critics charged that Say's crusade caused a serious backlash which not only made her brother very valuable to his captors but was also responsible for the Iran-Contra affair. This line of thinking suggests that her constant pressure on the Reagan administration to obtain the release of the hostages induced the administration to trade arms for hostages. In response to her critics, Say stated in an interview with the *Washington Post*, "I may have erred politically. I may have erred strategically. I've never erred morally."[15] An alternative view is that the extent to which the government put forth any effort to free hostages was directly a result of the work of Peggy Say. Negotiations led by UN Secretary General Javier Perez de Cuellar for the release of all hostages held in the Middle East resulted in the release of Terry Anderson on December 4, 1991.[16]

Other important instances of citizen diplomacy occurred during the Vietnam War era (1954–1975), when the lack of consensus in U.S. society on U.S. involvement in Vietnam led to a strong and sustained antiwar movement.[17] In an effort to gain a clearer understanding of the war, the concerns of the Vietnamese and to assess the damage to Vietnam, numerous U.S. citizens travelled to Hanoi. The diplomacy of Straughton Lynd, a civil rights activist and Yale professor, and Tom Hayden, a community activist and key member of Students for a Democratic Society (SDS), are worthy of discussion. The overriding purpose of their mission was to learn more about the "other side's" negotiating position.[18] They also sought to personally view the affects of the war on Vietnam and bring back to the United States a portrayal of the Vietnamese as valued human beings. With those objectives in mind, they hoped to break the monopoly that the Lyndon B. Johnson administration had on the information disseminated about the war. They also wanted to convey to the Vietnamese that there were U.S. citizens who did not support the war. Among other activities, Lynd and Hayden met with Prime Minister Pham Van Dong and secured answers to the written questions that they had submitted a week earlier and asked the prime minister a series of questions about the war and his negotiating position. Although no change occurred from Lynd's and Hayden's efforts, upon their return to the United States Lynd spent several hours with officials at the State Department reviewing notes from the meetings.

In 1972, Ramsey Clark, a former U.S. attorney general, ventured to Hanoi on a fact-finding mission and to meet with foreign officials about the U.S./Vietnam conflict.[19] Before leaving the United States on July 28, Clark met with officials in the Department of State, who asked him to deliver 102 letters to men who had not been heard from, but were believed to be alive and held captive by the Vietcong, and 300 letters to those known to be in the hands of the North Vietnamese. While in Hanoi he met with several officials and held conversations with the head of State as well as with people in the villages, hospitals and prisoner of war camps. Ramsey also delivered the Department of State letters to the representatives of the Vietcong, and they in turn provided him with seventeen letters from prisoners held captive by them.[20]

On August 12, Clark arrived in Burma carrying letters and tape recordings from U.S. prisoners and letters from the deputy prime minister of Hanoi and Minister of Foreign Affairs Nguyen Duy Trinh. At a news conference and interview in San Francisco he repeatedly attacked U.S. bombing of the dikes in Vietnam on moral grounds and read from his notes the statements of Mr. Trinh which guaranteed a solution to the prisoner problem. He also discussed his visit with the prisoners and his observation that they were being treated humanely.

The diplomatic efforts of Ramsey Clark were repeatedly attacked by government officials. The Defense Department, on August 16, 1972, accused him of withholding information about the U.S. prisoners. Daniel Z. Henkin, assistant secretary for public affairs said that Mr. Clark had an obligation as a responsible citizen and as a former government official to notify in advance the families of the prisoners shown in a video he made during the press conference.[21] Others accused Clark of being used for propaganda purposes by the Vietnam government. However, when on September 2, 1972, Hanoi announced that three U.S. pilots who had been visited by Clark would be released, many of the critics were silenced.[22]

After Hanoi, Clark became a noted international figure and has continued to travel abroad to problem solve and to interject his views on international crises. For instance, in 1980 Clark infuriated President Jimmy Carter by flying to Tehran, demanding the release of U.S. hostages and criticizing U.S. support for the shah. In July 1986, three months after the U.S. invasion of Libya, Clark flew to Tripoli to meet with Colonel Moammar Khadafy, voicing outrage over the attack and calling it a violation of international law. Still, in December 1989, when the U.S. missionary, Jennifer Casolo, was imprisoned by Salvadoran officials for "stockpiling" weapons for rebel troops, Clark was instrumental in arranging her release.[23] Ramsey Clark was the first U.S. citizen permitted to visit Basra, Iraq's second largest city, after the beginning of the Persian Gulf war.[24]

An earlier instance of citizen diplomacy occurred with the case of John Reed, most noted for his essential role in the formation of the American Communist Labor party in 1919 and for his work *Ten Days That Shook the World*, a firsthand account of the Bolshevik revolution.[25] On several occasions Reed met with V. I. Lenin and

Leon Trotsky regarding the potential for communism in the United States and in the world. Reed assisted the Soviets as a spokesperson, organizer, propagandist, and diplomat. For example, he completed two works for the official organ of the Comintern,[26] aided in the organization of the Second Congress, and served on the National Minorities and Colonial Question Commission and the Trade Union Activities Commission. Overall, Reed's contributions were mainly in the realm of ideological development and mobilization. Although Reed was well respected by the Communists, in his own country he was charged with espionage and treason. Nevertheless, Reed's activities were valued so greatly by the Soviets that after his death he was buried beside ancient kings and martyrs of the revolution.

The diversity of citizen diplomacy is illustrated by the activities of Robert Owens, a private citizen who worked with Oliver North on confidential Contra assistance projects from early 1984 through 1986. During an investigation of illegal aid given to the Contras, Owens stated that "he met with North about one hundred times and carried so many messages from North to the Contras that the CIA in Central America dubbed him 'the Carrier.' Owens also admitted that along with participating in meetings held with prominent Contra officials, he even flew to Honduras at North's request to give Adolpho Colera, head of the Contra movement, plans to blow up Soviet-made helicopters.[27] The actions of Owens and others who assisted the Contras in their civil war against the Sandinista government of Nicaragua were influential in forcing a 1990 election and the ultimate defeat of the Sandinistas by the National Opposition Union, a fourteen-party coalition led by Violeta de Barrios de Chamorro.

The activities of Robert Owens and other private citizens who worked for the the Contras is a difficult case for those attempting to distinguish between track two and citizen diplomacy. If Robert Owens and other Contra fund raisers were acting solely as private citizens in support of government policy with official assistance, then the activity should be considered track two and similar to the activities of Armand Hammer, who often pursued U.S. interests when meeting with Soviet officials, but whose personal agenda may have been different. What makes the Owens case difficult is the fact that the U.S. government officials he worked with were violating the law.[28] Consequently, private citizens such as Owens, must be seen as violating official policy and bypassing the official system, although he worked with government officials.

As demonstrated by the examples of citizen diplomacy, citizens circumvented official processes and initiated their own diplomatic efforts after failing to satisfactorily affect policy using conventional measures. In many cases, however, communication with the U.S. government remained opened, thereby allowing the citizen diplomat the opportunity to communicate his or her findings to the U.S. government and possibly influence U.S. policy. Paradoxically, citizen diplomacy emerges out of a failure of democratic processes to address the particular concerns of individuals. However, it affirms the process by providing an additional point of access to the system. Citizen diplomacy increases democratic participation.

The previous examples also illustrate that attempts by citizens to resolve problems in the international arena encompass a wide range of strategies and are not constrained by ideological bounds. Some citizens engage in conflict resolution in order to negotiate agreements themselves with foreign officials. Other citizens traveled to foreign nations to gain firsthand insight into a conflict from the opposing side's point of view. These diplomats then use that information to gain the support of U.S. public opinion in order to pressure the U.S. government into sincere negotiations. In other cases, citizens travel abroad to supply information to "the other side" to offer suggestions on how they can convince the United States that they are serious about resolving the conflict. Upon return, many citizen diplomats hold meetings with government officials to report on the mission and to offer suggestions on how to resolve the conflict.

Although the resolution of conflict cannot solely be attributed to the activities of the citizen diplomats, one can conclude that their efforts bring attention to the area of conflict, push issues of morality into the discussion, and provide some impetus for government action. For example, in the case of Hayden and Lynd, their travels provided a different perspective of Vietnam, thereby radicalizing more U.S. citizens' positions on the war, and in turn mobilizing them to pressure their government for change. Hence, the information brought back by citizen diplomats assisted in turning a significant portion of the U.S. population against the war and was definitely a factor in Nixon's decision to withdraw troops from Vietnam.[29] Even Ramsey Clark's visit, which provided a catalyst for the return of hostages, stimulated government action.

## Historical Analysis of African American Internationalism— Prelude to African American Citizen Diplomacy

After the United States declared its independence from Great Britain in 1776—citing abuses of inalienable rights and emphasizing the necessity for life, liberty, and the pursuit of happiness for all of its citizens—there was strong optimism on the part of Africans in America that they would experience an amelioration of conditions in their "New World." However, the Constitution of 1787, which implicitly recognized slavery, and the subsequent passing of the first fugitive slave law by Congress to implement the constitutional clause on slavery, made the Africans more conscious of their separateness from the dominant society. Hence, they began to organize for defense, mutual aid, and survival.

During this period, strong emigrationist sentiments emerged. In 1789 the Free African Society of Newport sent a proposal to the Free African Society of Philadelphia arguing for a return to Africa as a means to escape their deplorable conditions in the United States. Actual emigration occurred in 1815 when Paul Cuffe, a New Bedford shipowner, took thirty-eight free Africans at his own expense to Sierra Leone.[30] Cuffe's first venture was so widely accepted that over two thousand people had signed up for his second; but he died before he could embark upon the venture.

Many other ventures were proposed by emigration supporters. Among them was Martin Delany's idea of calling for a confidential conference that would appoint commissioners to go to East Africa to locate a suitable site for the resettlement of Africans taken from their native homeland. Delany's efforts were also an attempt to counteract the activities of the American Colonization Society (ACS), an organization founded by a group of white Americans who had purchased land early in the nineteenth century to repatriate free blacks. The ACS' activities were regarded by Delany and many other African Americans, as attempts on behalf of paternalistic whites to evade rather than solve the race question.[31]

Notwithstanding the prominence of emigration schemes and activity throughout the nineteenth century, during that same time a more progressive interest in Africa and its diaspora emerged. For instance, in 1890 George Washington Williams, a leading African American historian, traveled to the Congo on behalf of the U.S. Congress to investigate charges of brutality against the native population. In a report addressed to the king of Belgium, Williams presented a bill that supported the allegation that the Belgian government was engaged in the slave trade. William's report persuaded Booker T. Washington to agitate for reform in the Congo. Washington became vice president of the Congo Reform Association and helped rally American public opinion against King Leopold's administration.[32]

At the beginning of the twentieth century, African Americans advocated for a more humane and moral policy toward Africa and the black world. The Du Boisian Pan-African movement was used as the structure to guide the discussions and address concerns. While promoting the idea that the problem of the twentieth century was a problem of the color line, W. E. B. Du Bois posited that pan-Africanism was the key to African liberation. Du Bois stressed the view that African Americans must recognize their "oneness" with all Africans and further postulated that the struggle for equality in the United States was tied directly to the fight for African independence. Considered the intellectual father of Pan-Africanism, Du Bois organized four meetings between 1919 and 1945.

Du Bois' activities were manifested in the establishment of the Mandates Commission under the League of Nations (LON) and later the UN Trusteeship Council, which kept Southwest Africa from being incorporated into South Africa. The Fifth Pan-African Congress, organized by Trinidadian George Padmore but chaired by Du Bois, was attended by such future African heads of states as Kwame Nkrumah and Jomo Kenyatta. Both leaders used the meeting as a springboard to galvanize support for their burgeoning independence movements.

Although the Du Boisian Pan-African movement united black leaders throughout the world intellectually, the masses of blacks on the African continent and in the diaspora were largely unaffected. It was Marcus Garvey's appeal to the masses using the slogan, "Africa for Africans at Home and Abroad," that ignited the masses in the African world. Through his organization, the Universal Negro Improvement Association (UNIA), founded in 1917, Garvey preached pride of self and heritage. He called for a return to Africa—of which he named himself the provisional president, and the unity of all Africans under one great single body. The UNIA also advocated economic nationalism and identified the problems of African Americans with the problems of colonialism in Africa.[33] The Garvey movement, as it became known, eventually became the largest mass movement of African Americans and perhaps more than any other movement or organization did more to educate African Americans about Africa. The decline of the UNIA and the Garvey movement began in the 1920s and continued until World War II.

The popularity and acceptance of Garvey's messages were demonstrated in 1935 when the Italian leader Benito Mussolini attempted to colonize Ethiopia. In response, African Americans boycotted Italian merchants, engaged in protests and lobbied government officials. Citizen organizations were also set up to aid Ethiopia, and a delegation of African Americans attended the International Peace Campaign in Brussels in 1936.[34]

In addition to the domestic battle for equality and justice they were engaged in, African Americans continued to acknowledge that the question of color pervaded the formulation and execution of U.S. foreign policy. Combining lobbying, advocacy, and diplomacy, African Americans fought to eliminate racial biases in U.S. foreign policy. For instance, in 1937, Paul Robeson and Max Yergen organized the Council on African Affairs (CAA), the first African American-led group dedicated to influencing U.S. policy toward Africa. The CAA established close working relationships with African nationalists and labor leaders and lobbied the U.S. government on their behalf. It was specifically interested in racial policies in South Africa and forged links with the African National Congress (ANC). An example of the CAA's concern for the well-being of the continent was demonstrated in 1945, toward the end of WWII, when it "unsuccessfully urged the State Department to convince the British, French, and Belgians to give up their African colonies, or at least to put them under some sort of international supervision as was previously done with the German colonies."[35] The politics of the Cold War and charges of Communist ties were responsible for curtailing the CAA efforts.

Anticolonial agitation in Africa spurred the formation of two important but shortlived groups: the American Society for African Culture (AMSAC) and the American Negro Leadership Conference on Africa (ANLCA). AMSAC was formed by American delegates to a conference of African American intellectuals in 1956. It brought African leaders to the United States, held regular conferences on issues related to Africa, published a journal, and helped African American colleges develop African programs and African studies courses. The ANLCA, on the other hand, lobbied the White House, Congress, and the State Department. The AMSAC and the ANLCA were unable to survive revelations that during the 1960s they had been infiltrated by the CIA.[36]

African independence movements, particularly in Kenya and in the Congo, also energized African Americans. For instance, in the Congo, the 1961 murder of African nationalist leader Patrice Lumumba led to a riot by African Americans in the visitor's gallery of the UN, the most serious disruption inside the headquarters of the world organization since its founding.[37] In addition, there were marches and demonstrations held within the United States to protest against Lumumba's death. In Kenya, the insurrection of the Mau Mau stimulated the formation of a group called the Harlem Mau Mau.

African American civil and human rights leaders and organizations also focused on African liberation. In 1969, the Congress of Racial Equality (CORE) announced its desire to assist African liberation movements and established a chapter of its organization in Kenya after a visit there by its leader Roy Innis.[38] Martin Luther King, leader of the Southern Christian Leadership Conference (SCLC) spoke out against the United States' and Great Britain's policies that led to economic benefits for South Africa and openly opposed the war in Vietnam.[39] Malcolm X, the former spokesman of the Nation of Islam, helped make the connection between the oppression of African Americans and the problems of Africa when he visited Africa in 1964. While there, Malcolm X participated in a summit of the Organization of African Unity (OAU), the organization of African heads of state. At the meeting, Malcolm X presented a memorandum that equated the racist practices of the United States with those of South Africa. Upon his return, he formed the Organization of African American Unity (OAAU) to champion the cause of Pan-Africanism throughout the world and to promote the worldwide liberation of African peoples.[40]

As the freedom struggle within the United States progressed, African Americans who held more radical views began to take over the leadership of civil rights organizations, such as the Student

Nonviolent Coordinating Committee (SNCC). Under the leadership of James Forman, a delegation of SNCC leaders visited Africa in 1964. When they returned home, they set in place programs to help forge closer relationships between Africans and African Americans. These same activists began using colonial metaphors to explain the conditions of African Americans and visited not only Africa but other nations of color and nations with an orientation toward socialism.

Around this same time, African American scholars began to place more emphasis on African studies. This pan-African spirit was evidenced in May 1970 at Howard University, where approximately two thousand people attended the Second Annual Conference of the African Heritage Studies Association. With the objective of uniting all African people, faculty and students from the United States and Africa worked toward realizing that goal under the theme, "Africanism—Toward a New Definition."[41] Many of these scholars took on a more activist role in the fall of 1970 when President Richard Nixon refused to schedule a meeting with President Kenneth Kaunda of Zambia, while he was in New York to speak to the General Assembly of the UN. African American scholars, under the leadership of Dr. Elliot Skinner, former ambassador to Upper Volta, formed an ad hoc committee of "Afro-Americans Concerned About U.S. Policy in Africa." They expressed displeasure with U.S. policy toward Africa, and requested that the U.S. president, among other things, revise the policy and develop one that was more meaningful.[42]

African Americans continued to demonstrate an interest in Africa through conferences. For instance, in September of 1970, 2,500 delegates convened at the Congress of African People, held to promote the unity of Africans throughout the world. Although most were African American, African people from various other parts of the world also attended, including Australian Aborigines and a member of the parliament of Bermuda.

By the 1970s African Americans began to focus more intently on the elimination of apartheid in South Africa. Pushing for sanctions against South Africa were student groups on college campuses, liberation support committees throughout the country, and African American members of Congress. Representative Charles Diggs of Detroit became the chair of the House Subcommittee on Africa and an important spokesperson on African issues.[43]

Randall Robinson, a former staff aide to Diggs and a leader of student demonstrations on behalf of sanctions, was instrumental in the founding of TransAfrica, the African American lobby for Africa and the Caribbean in 1978. TransAfrica mobilized the African American community to defeat efforts to lift sanctions against Rhodesia and persuaded African American leaders to support sanctions and rally voters in their districts. Through TransAfrica, and other organizations such as Africare, African Americans also contributed to relief efforts for Africans who were victims of drought and famine. African Americans solicited resources to help famine victims and ultimately shifted their focus from relief to long-term development.

In the 1980s, African American individuals and organizations continued relief efforts, provided leadership to the anti-apartheid movement, publicly denounced U.S. foreign policy toward Africa and its diaspora, and attempted to steer policy in the direction that would be more beneficial to those areas. During this period African American political influence toward Africa was exerted primarily through the legislative branch. The Free South Africa Movement (FSAM), which TransAfrica helped to establish soon after the 1984 elections, mobilized the public and lobbied Congress to pass the Comprehensive Anti-Apartheid Act of 1986. The FSAM also campaigned for the release of Nelson Mandela, a former political prisoner—who has become the first black African president of South African.

Although the primary international concerns of African Americans have been focused on Africa, African Americans are also involved in peace and humanitarian efforts throughout the world. For instance, the massive earthquakes in Mexico in 1985 and Armenia in 1990 received the attention of African Americans. Assuredly, as international communication technologies improve, African Americans will continue to respond in earnest to transcontinental calls.

This historical discussion of African American internationalism elucidates a central paradox in the history of African Americans. While they were battling for full participation in society, many African Americans were repudiating the very system they were struggling to penetrate. Frequently, these denunciations occurred abroad, and on occasion African Americans sought the assistance of other nations to help them accomplish specific objectives. In fact, those efforts led to African American involvement in the plight of foreign peoples, and eventually they began to speak out in opposition to perceived atrocities committed abroad by the United States, the home nations of foreign peoples, and third-party nations.

## African Americans and Citizen Diplomacy

As in the cases of other Americans, African Americans have ventured abroad and contacted foreign governments, often unfriendly ones, to promote their personal and group agendas. As demonstrated in the previous discussion, the most common international concerns of Americans relate to issues of peace, war, hostages, and business deals. However, when African Americans enter the international arena their concerns often are related to moral disagreements with U.S. policy, black nationalism, pan-Africanism, or ideological affinity. Hence, the cases of African Americans presented in this discussion are focused on nationalism/pan-Africanism and ideological affinity. It should be noted that by no means is this discussion exhaustive. It is only presented with the purpose of providing some insight into citizen diplomacy when it is conducted by African Americans.[44]

First, a few cautionary notes. Highlighting these instances of diplomacy does not imply that Reverend Jesse Jackson is in agreement with or supports the ideology or methodology of the citizen diplomat. These examples are used only to elucidate the various approaches to citizen diplomacy. Second, the instances of citizen diplomacy discussed here are most often ignored in the discussions on private citizen participation in the international arena and therefore may not be usually coined as citizen diplomacy.

### Ideological Affinity

Intense ideological agreement or disagreement with the political, economic, social, or religious system of the home or foreign nation is one inducement for citizen diplomacy. This approach is perhaps the most diverse and embodies many different strategies. Inherent in this mode of citizen diplomacy are two objectives. First, an attempt is made to gain firsthand knowledge of the principles and applications of a foreign ideology and social system, and second, the citizen diplomat usually endeavors to gain acceptance from the foreign power of his or her interpretation of the ideology or practice.

Most strategies are geared toward obtaining assistance from the foreign power in an effort to promote the foreign ideology in the home nation or toward assisting a foreign nation perceived as being persecuted unfairly for ideological reasons. Citizen diplomats may also attempt to persuade a nation to adopt a specific ideology or implement new programs that they consider conducive to the growth and development of that country. In the case of ideological disagreement, the efforts are aimed at changing or abolishing the ideology and the resultant offending practice.

One example of this approach can be demonstrated by the case of an African American socialist who traveled abroad in the early twentieth century to help foment revolution in the United States. The nature of engaging in citizen diplomacy based on ideological solidarity with a hostile, socialist nation inevitably places a U.S. citizen in a position that is counter to that of his or her government interests, and invariably the hope of working within existing societal structures to bring about change is virtually nil. Interest group activity is also limited because the activity, which centers on the replacement of U.S. capitalism with Soviet-style socialism usually requires that the citizen diplomat's strongest ally be the Soviet Union. In the past, this kind of activity required the citizen diplomat to break laws in order to accomplish goals and sometimes placed him or her in a position that warranted charges of treason.

## Harry Haywood: African American Bolshevik

Some of the earliest contacts between U.S. and Soviet citizens were initiated by U.S. Socialists who were developing strategies to promote the Soviet's political and economic system in the United States. The diplomatic forays of Harry Haywood were successful in influencing the Socialist movement both within the United States and abroad. Ironically, because of his intense work on behalf of socialism, this citizen gained much more respect from Soviet nationals than he received in the United States.

Although often discounted in the literature on citizen diplomacy and the activities of American Communists, many African American members of the Communist party were very active in shaping Communist policy at home and abroad. Communism appealed to these African Americans because of its emphasis on equality and social justice. During the 1920s and 1930s, for some African Americans, the Soviet Union was considered to be an egalitarian haven where racism and discrimination were virtually nonexistent. Pilgrimages to Russia were taken by African Americans for several reasons. Professionals traveled and sometimes settled there for employment and business opportunities, while African American artists traveled to embark upon cultural and creative projects. Still, many other African Americans traveled to the Soviet Union as an expression of ideological and political agreement. For example, Otto Huiswood, the first African American to attend a major Communist Congress hosted by the Soviet Union, was a delegate to the Fourth Congress of the Comintern in 1922. Huiswood was also the first African American to meet with V. I. Lenin and eventually serve as a member of the Executive Committee of the Communist International.[45]

During the 1920s several individuals of African descent were invited to attend schools established in the Soviet Union to train Communist leaders in various parts of the world. Harry Haywood was a prime candidate for Soviet influence considering that his brother Otto Hall was already a member of the Communist party, and the many hardships that he experienced as a result of racism in the United States.[46] Haywood joined several Communist-affiliated organizations. Among them were the Communist Youth League, the African Blood Brotherhood—an organization of African American Communists, and eventually the Communist party. Although several other African Americans had visited the Soviet Union previously, Haywood's case is significant because his activity on behalf of the Communist cause was directly related to questions not only about the role of African American communists, but also how African Americans perceived Soviet aspirations on what their relationship to the U.S. government should be.

Haywood first arrived in Leningrad in April 1926 to attend the Far East University and later transferred to the New Lenin School as the first African American student. He soon became a staunch supporter of the Josef Stalin regime and worked diligently on the Communist party's policy on nationalities.[47]

One of Haywood's first acts of citizen diplomacy took place at the Sixth Congress, where he participated in the adoption of the 1928 resolution on the Black Nation in the United States. The resolution defined African Americans as an oppressed nation and promoted the establishment of an African American republic in the South. The resolution also stated in part that African Americans had a right to self-determination and that the entire Communist

International would assist in their fight for an independent nation under the leadership of the Communist party.[48]

After completing his studies in June 1930, Haywood stayed in the Soviet Union to strengthen the 1928 resolution.[49] During that time he and six other African Americans attended a meeting of the Fifth Congress of the Red International Labor Union held in August. In November, he went back to New York to resume his work for the party.

Haywood was eventually selected by the Soviets as vice chair of the Negro Subcommittee and was one of three delegates to travel back to Moscow in 1932 to attend the Twelfth Plenum of the Executive Committee of the Communist International. The purpose was to review the work of the Comintern sections and its affiliates and analyze the international situation.[50]

The Spanish Civil War (1936–1939) sparked another occasion for Haywood to demonstrate his ideological differences with U.S. policy. The Western capitalist powers responded to General Francisco Franco's rebellion in mid-1936 with a noninterventionist pact. However, the Soviet Union viewed General Franco's actions as a front for German dictator Adolf Hitler and Italian leader Benito Mussolini's worldwide drive for fascism, and thus advocated collective action to stop the aggression. Communist parties throughout the world rallied to the defense of Spain and organized international brigades to fight against Fascist aggression. Haywood, holding the view that the Western power's noninterventionist pact allowed Hitler and Mussolini to flood men and ammunition into Spain also traveled to Spain to fight in 1936. As deputy brigade commissar for six months, Haywood was the highest member of the U.S. Communist party in Spain and sole member of the Politburo.[51]

Harry Haywood's commitment to Communism led him to the Soviet Union and other foreign nations to influence the international Communist agenda and to advocate for social change in the United States. Because of his support of Stalinism, his vehement opposition to U.S. foreign policy, and the tension between the United States and the Soviet Union, Haywood and like-minded individuals could not use conventional avenues to influence U.S. foreign policy. Haywood's exploits pushed to the limits the idea of citizen diplomacy because it seemed that his loyalty was to Communist governments and parties. However, Haywood refused to relinquish his citizenship and continued to hold a solid constituency in the United States.[52]

## Nationalism and Citizen Diplomacy:
## Focus on Pan-Africanism

Similar in nature to ideological affinity is the second approach to citizen diplomacy. Diplomacy rooted in ethnic, racial, or religious nationalism[53] is manifested in a devotion to the interests and culture of a particular people or "nation." This kind of diplomacy parallels ideological affinity in that private citizens travel abroad to offer assistance and protection to a foreign nation, seek to gain acceptance of their perceptions of the foreign nation's activities, attempt to participate in the decision-making process on important issues affecting the welfare of the nation, and demonstrate loyalty to the foreign nation. However, citizen diplomacy is unique in this sense because often the goal is to foster feelings of nationalism within a particular group and to influence the behavior and policies of a foreign government toward that group. Hence, the concerns of the citizen diplomat are usually focused on a certain group of people within a foreign nation, not the entire government.

Often citizen diplomacy as a consequence of nationalism is materialized in the form of worldwide conferences of high-ranking citizens in a particular government. These citizen diplomats are thought to have influence beyond their official position in society that extends to considerable influence within their own ethnic group.

Perhaps the group most recognized for traveling abroad to influence the behavior of foreign nations on behalf of its people are members of the American Jewish community. An illustrative example of citizen diplomacy can be found in the case of Israel Singer, the secretary general of the World Jewish Council (WJC) who has traveled to the Soviet Union on several occasions to initiate talks with high-level party officials to secure better treatment of the Jews living there.[54] Polish and Irish Americans have also been very active in citizen diplomacy on behalf of the people in their native homelands.[55]

The attempts of African Americans to influence policy toward Africa is often trivialized and perceived as futile—suggesting that the efforts of African Americans in the international arena cannot be taken seriously.[56] Due to the predominance of this perception, it is no wonder that the idea of African American citizen diplomacy has just begun to surface. If not for the diplomacy of Jesse Jackson, the efforts of African Americans would not be included in the discourse.[57] It is for this reason and the significance of African American missions abroad to influence the behavior of other nations toward Africa, to promote African unity, and to speak on behalf of African Americans and the African diaspora that the issue of pan-Africanism is being addressed.

## W. E. B. Du Bois:
## Pan-Africanism and Citizen Diplomacy

Pan-African thinking emerged out of a common history of oppression and discrimination that Africans in the "new world" experienced. This collective experience brought forth a realization that people of African descent not only share the same heritage but also similar oppression and therefore should unite in order to find a collective solution to common problems. Therefore, pan-Africanism should be viewed as a form of nationalism, aimed at unifying people of African descent throughout the world.

W. E. B. Du Bois, an African American intellectual and celebrated advocate of pan-Africanism, is most noted for his writings and for organizing four major pan-African congresses that were attended by some of the most prominent persons of African descent living during the time of each conference. However, Du Bois was not the originator of the pan-African idea. The birth of the movement can be traced to a West Indian barrister, Henry Sylvester Williams, who organized the first Pan-African Conference in 1900. About thirty delegates attended, mostly from the United States and the West Indies. Du Bois was designated chairperson of the committee on the Address to the Nations of the World. In his speech, he repudiated segregation and discrimination and asked England to yield responsibility of self-government to the African and West Indian nations. Other European powers were asked to be just and fair to the Africans in their colonies.[58]

Nineteen years later Du Bois convened what is known today as the first Pan-African Congress (PAC). At first, Du Bois aimed to interest President Woodrow Wilson and his staff in the PAC, but acting on the premise that the French viewed such a gathering as dangerous and ill-timed, the Department of State refused to issue passports to those African Americans who wanted to attend.[59] Du Bois therefore sought the assistance of Blaise Diagne, a Senegalese representative to the Chamber of Deputies in France. Eventually, the French granted permission to hold the meeting there.

The PAC was convened to consider the conditions of Africans throughout the world and to determine policy for African people. The "call" to participate went out to prominent personalities and was attended by fifty-seven delegates from fifteen countries—nine African and the rest from the United States, Europe, and the Caribbean. The success of the first PAC was based on its standing as one of the first international arenas in which Africans initiated their own discussions on questions of land, labor, education, and capital. The resolutions adopted hinted that the great powers should issue an international code for the protection of Africans and should ensure enforcement of that code by the League of Nations (LON). However, no concrete demands were issued.[60]

More in tune with the postwar agitation for freedom were the resolutions adopted at the second PAC, which met in London on August 28 and 29 and in Paris on September 5 and 6, 1921. With 113 official delegates present, appeals were made to the LON concerning African land, labor, and capital. However, this time, special reference was made to the barbaric nature of European behavior in the Congo. The resolutions at the second congress critiqued race relations and the colonial system, and called for respect of the sovereignty of noncolonized African nations.

Immediately following the second PAC, Du Bois traveled to Geneva in order to present the pan-African resolutions to the LON and to ask the International Labor Bureau to set up a division to investigate native labor conditions. At the hearing before the LON's Mandate Commission, Du Bois argued that Africans should be appointed to the commission since many lived in mandated areas. He also asked the LON to use its moral power to influence world public opinion on issues of racial equality. Albert Thomas, the head of the International Labor Bureau declared support for the PACs position, but stated that the bureau's budget could only employ one person.[61]

The issues at the third PAC, held in Lisbon in 1923, were similar to the ideas presented at the previous congresses, but the demands were set forth with more clarity. The participants insisted, among other things, that Africans be granted a voice in their own government and that the right to self-determination be respected.

After the third PAC, Du Bois journeyed to Africa, and upon his return began planning the fourth PAC. Du Bois intended to hold the fourth PAC on a series of islands in the Caribbean where large numbers of Africans lived in hopes of gaining their support for home rule. Despite Du Bois' efforts, the colonial powers "quickly thwarted this plan by making sea transportation unavailable."[62] The PAC, however, convened in New York with an agenda and resolutions analogous to that of the previous meetings.

George Padmore, a Trinidadian, was the major organizer of the fifth PAC, with Du Bois assisting in its preparation. This congress, held in Manchester, England, in 1945 was by far the most radical and included such future African heads of states as Kwame Nkrumah of Ghana and Jomo Kenyatta of Kenya.[63]

In addition to his diplomacy on behalf of Africans, Du Bois was intricately involved in promoting world peace. In 1949, Du Bois addressed an all-Soviet Peace Conference in Moscow where he declared that he represented the million citizens of the United States, who were opposed to World War II and viciously attacked the United States for its involvement in the oppression of Africans and other poor people and the war itself.[64] The purpose of that meeting was to call a second World Congress and make a new plea for disarmament.[65] In addition to the foregoing efforts for peace, in the early part of the 1950s Du Bois and sixty other U.S. citizens formed the Peace Information Center, an organization which grew out of their attendance at the Paris Defenders of Peace in Prague in August 1951.[66]

Du Bois' diplomacy also took him to the Soviet Union. He first traveled to the Soviet Union in 1926, then returned in 1936, 1949, 1958, and 1959. In 1959 he was awarded the International Lenin Peace Prize. In a long interview with Nikita Khrushchev, Du Bois suggested that the Soviet Academy of Sciences establish an institute for the study of pan-African history, sociology, and similar disciplines. He viewed the later creation of the Africa Institute under his friend Ivan Potekhin as the realization of his initial suggestion.[67]

To be sure, Du Bois' diplomacy led to conflict with the U.S. government. One such instance was in 1951 when Du Bois was refused a passport because he criticized the U.S. government's treatment of Africans during his travels abroad.[68] Later, Du Bois was informed that he would receive a passport if he declared in writing that he was not a member of the Communist party. Because of his refusal, Du Bois could not leave the country until 1958 when the Supreme Court held that Congress had never given the Department of State the authority to demand a political affidavit as a prerequisite to issue a passport.[69] Therefore, all those citizens that had been denied the right to travel were eventually granted passports. Du Bois was also indicted for not registering as a foreign agent, but was subsequently acquitted.

Although Du Bois promoted world peace and socialism, his diplomacy was rooted in pan-Africanism. His attempts to interfere with European colonialism in Africa, his efforts to enlighten the world about U.S. racism, and his aims at transforming African leaders throughout the world into diplomats on behalf of their individual ethnic group, illustrates a nation-within-a-nation construct for citizen diplomacy. Du Bois created an alternate system to accomplish his goals. His modis operandi included organizing international conferences and holding personal meetings with high-level officials of foreign governments and participating in international meetings. Outcomes of Du Bois' diplomacy were organizing and politicizing leaders and future leaders on behalf of Africa and Africans in the diaspora, promoting international peace, keeping the spirit of nationalism and pan-Africanism alive, and affecting the policy of nations and international organizations.

## Internationalism and Malcolm X

After Du Bois and before the Black Power era took hold, Malcolm X became one of the few African American leaders to independently travel to Africa. In his move from nationalism to internationalism, Malcolm X became an accepted spokesperson for African Americans and other exploited people in the world. However, unlike the efforts of other citizen diplomats mentioned here, Malcolm X's diplomacy was not focused on changing the economic and political structure of the United States. He was primarily concerned with ameliorating the conditions of African Americans, and thus a nation-within-a-nation construct guided his efforts.

As an African American Muslim minister, Malcolm X taught separation from white America and self-determination. However, after his break with the Nation of Islam, Malcolm X began to develop his own programs to establish closer relationships between Africans and African Americans and to achieve the liberation of Africans throughout the world. Part of his strategy was to unite all Africans under the framework of pan-Africanism and bring the case of African Americans before the UN. This strategy, he hoped, would place the type of international pressure on the United States that would force it to deal with African Americans in an equitable and just manner. Because at that time the UN primarily afforded recognition to independent nations, Malcolm X had to persuade an independent nation to represent African Americans before the international body. Therefore, during the spring and summer of 1964, Malcolm X traveled to Africa to seek assistance.

Malcolm X first went to Lagos, Nigeria, where he spoke at Ibadan University and urged independent African nations to charge the United States with violating the human rights of African Americans before the UN.[70] In turn, he told African Americans that they must join the world's pan-Africanists. Although African Americans would physically remain in the United States fighting for their constitutional rights, they should be aligned philosophically and culturally to all Africans under the framework of pan-Africanism.[71]

From Lagos, Malcolm X flew to Ghana for a stay of seven days. While there he was honored by dignitaries from Ghana, Algeria, and China and met with several black people from the United States who had given up their U.S. citizenship to become citizens of Ghana. At several press conferences, Malcolm X stressed the need for mutual communication and support between continental Africans and African Americans and warned of the unscrupulous nature of the U.S. State Department and the Central Intelligence Agency.[72]

Malcolm X was also given the opportunity to address the Ghanaian Parliament. His speech argued that U.S. racism against African Americans and U.S. colonialism must be condemned. In a meeting with President Kwame Nkrumah, the unity of Africans and peoples of African heritage was discussed. Malcolm X and Nkrumah both concluded that pan-Africanism was the key solution to the problems of African descendents.[73]

While still in Ghana, on June 29, 1964, Malcolm X formed the Organization of Afro-American Unity (OAAU). Modeled after the Organization of African Unity (OAU), the OAAU's purpose was to bring about the complete independence of people of African descent. On behalf of the OAAU, Malcolm X flew to Cairo in July 1964 to participate in a Head of States Summit Meeting of the OAU. Admitted as an observer to that meeting, his goal was to have the plight of African Americans treated as an African problem. As a result of Malcolm X's influence, a resolution was adopted which stated that the OAU deplored U.S. racism, and some delegates promised officially to assist the OAAU in its efforts.[74]

The impact of Malcolm X's diplomacy cannot be overstated. He initiated dialogue officially and unofficially between leaders of Africa and those in the diaspora, presented an alternate image of African Americans abroad, linked the problems of African Americans with the problems of Africans throughout the world, and opened doors for other African Americans to travel abroad to discuss their concerns with other African people.

It must be emphasized that Malcolm X's diplomacy on behalf of African Americans was not confined to Africa. He visited Europe on several occasions and made major public addresses to intellectuals, students, and other foreign nationals on racism, colonialism, and assistance for African Americans.[75]

## Summary

This chapter profiled various motives, methods, and outcomes of citizen diplomacy. It also highlighted its breadth and complexity. At the outset, it is clear that each approach to citizen diplomacy is the embodiment of purpose and strategy and that the concern of each citizen diplomat is generally the determinant of method. The most common methods for accomplishing objectives include negotiations, mediation, conciliation, personal and group meetings with foreign officials and\or rebel leaders, organizing international conferences, accepting official positions in foreign nations or international and regional bodies, and offering support to nations or foreign causes. The effectiveness of citizen diplomacy is dependent upon various factors, such as the prestige of the citizen diplomat, the willingness of nations to resolve disputes, goal congruence between the citizen diplomat and other negotiating parties, the political advantages and/ or vulnerability of the disputing parties involved, and timeliness.

As demonstrated by these various case studies, private citizens are interested in a wide range of international issues and are capable of involving themselves in foreign affairs using a variety of approaches. For instance, W. E. B. Du Bois and Malcolm X were primarily concerned with eliminating the exploitation of African people and thus used pan-Africanism as a guiding ideology. In contrast, Harry Haywood was interested in transforming the United States. from a capitalist-oriented society to a socialist society and therefore used his ideological affinity with Socialist nations as the primary tool for his diplomacy.

As was also illustrated, the motive for citizen diplomacy is a primary determinant of the method. Because Peggy Say was interested in securing the release of a hostage, she travelled abroad to meet with officials who she thought could influence the kidnappers. Ramsey Clark, whose concern was to discover ways to end a war, held meetings with leaders of adversarial nations and engaged in fact finding to bring attention to the devastating consequences of violent confrontation between nations.

What is clear about the activities of the citizen diplomats highlighted in this chapter is that their efforts and policy concerns were not analogous to U.S. official policy efforts, and hence can be distinguished from track two, which must be supportive of track one. These citizens also circumvented the conventional modes for participation in order to inject their viewpoints into international affairs.

In some instances, the system opened to include the activities of some citizen diplomats. For instance, Ramsey Clark, the former attorney general, had relationships with State Department and other government officials which provided him with some degree of access to policy-makers. Hence, Clark's activities demonstrate that citizen diplomacy can be used as a source of information for foreign policy elites. In other cases, such as John Reed's and Harry Haywood's, where the citizen diplomat accepted positions inside the agencies of a hostile government, the official system was not accessible. Many of the strategies employed by the citizen diplomats discussed in this chapter were used by Jesse Jackson during the 1984 presidential election campaign and during his 1986 trip to Southern Africa.

# Jesse Jackson: The Emergence of a Citizen Diplomat

Reverend Jesse Jackson's citizen diplomacy and international efforts before the 1984 presidential election campaign will be discussed in this chapter. The discussion will include a brief biographical sketch of Jesse Jackson, his ideological foundations and his political perspective. The purpose is to illuminate how and why Jackson became involved in citizen diplomacy and to explain how his personality and background influence his ideals and predilections on international questions. Also in this chapter, Jackson's pre-1984 international concerns and selected examples of his diplomatic endeavors will be discussed. The objective is to illuminate his foreign policy positions and activities before the influence of the campaign and to demonstrate the continuity of his citizen diplomacy.

## Jesse Louis Jackson

Jesse Louis Jackson was born in Greenville, South Carolina, on October 8, 1941, to Helen Burns and Noah Robinson. He was adopted at the age of two by his stepfather, Charles Jackson, a post office maintenance worker who later married his mother. Jackson, the eldest of five children, grew up under the laws of segregation. He graduated from Sterling High School, then an all-black school in Greenville, where he was elected president of student government, of the honor society, and of his school's chapter of the Future Teachers of America. He was also a star quarterback and starred on the baseball and basketball teams.[1]

Jackson's early hatred for Jim Crow marked the beginning of his political development. In an article he describes the humiliation he felt under the brutal system.

Humiliation: go to the back of the bus even though you pay the same fare. Humiliation: no public parks or libraries you can use even though you pay taxes. Humiliation: upstairs in movies. Back doors in hotels and cafe's . . . Humiliation: all white police with no police warrants who were absolute in their power until they were called "the law." Humiliation: a dual school system. Black teachers and white teachers working the same hours, only the Black teachers taught more students and taught double shifts and received less pay. . . We used books exactly three years after white students used them. We used desks exactly four years after white students used them. There were no Black schoolboard members. No Black members on the budget committee. No Black members on the Planning Committee. No Blacks building the schools that we were required to attend. We were rewarded for docility and punished for expressing personhood.[2]

Jackson accepted a football scholarship to attend the University of Illinois in Urbana-Champaign where, according to Jackson an assistant coach "informed him that, ability notwithstanding whites were quarterbacks and blacks played half backs or end."[3] He thus transferred to North Carolina Agricultural and Technical State University (A&T) in Greensboro, an all-black college where he would have a chance to play quarterback. At A&T Jackson became the star quarterback and was elected president of his student body. While at A&T, in 1962, Jesse married Jacqueline Lavina Davis.

It was in Greensboro where the sit-in movement exploded and where Jackson first participated in the struggle for civil rights. Jackson first became involved with the student sit-ins and subsequently became involved in CORE activities. On the basis of his leadership capabilities, he inevitably became field director of the group's southeastern operations. In 1963, Jackson graduated with a Bachelor of Arts degree in sociology. That same year he went to work briefly for the Democratic governor of North Carolina, Terry Sanford, organizing Young Democratic Clubs. Sanford sponsored Jackson as one of the first black delegates to the Young Democrats Convention, and Jackson has been active in the party since that time.

After college, Jackson enrolled in the Chicago Theological Seminary (CTS). While matriculating at CTS, Jackson led a large group of university students to Alabama to participate in the 1965 Selma, Alabama, demonstrations. At one point during the course of those demonstrations, Martin Luther King, Ralph Abernathy, and other leaders of the SCLC addressed the demonstrators from the steps of the city hall. During a lull, Jackson, virtually unknown and uninvited, climbed the steps and addressed the crowd. "The SCLC leaders were appalled at his audacity, but the crowd and media responded enthusiastically and King commended him personally."[4] Ralph Abernathy, King's second in command, was impressed with Jackson, and thus when Jackson asked for a job, Abernathy convinced King to hire him. In the spring of 1965, Jackson dropped out of school six months before his anticipated graduation in order to take a full-time role in the civil rights movement.

When King decided to initiate activities in Chicago to give SCLC a national platform, Jackson was conferred the job of organizing black ministers in Chicago. Although the local black ministers were afraid of offending Mayor Richard Daley and his strong political machine, Jackson still managed to gather support. After failing to reach agreements with Mayor Daley on issues such as open housing, King led demonstrations through various sections of Chicago where he and his followers were assaulted continuously. Jackson's boldness was demonstrated again when he announced a march on Cicero, regarded as one of the most racist suburbs in Illinois, without authorization from King to publicize the event. Fearing racial violence, Mayor Daley capitulated and signed an open housing agreement.

Impressed with Jackson's leadership capabilities, in 1967, King appointed him to serve as executive director of the economic arm of the SCLC in Chicago. Known as Operation Breadbasket, the purpose of the program was to locate jobs for African Americans in bakeries, milk companies, and other firms that were the beneficiaries of heavy minority patronage. Jackson's first significant victory occurred in 1966, when he obtained an agreement from four large Chicago grocery corporations to carry African American products and to deposit the income from their stores, located in the ghetto, into African American banks.[5] Moreover, within a year Jackson's program had obtained 2,200 jobs for African American Chicagoans in white-owned firms. His success was so great that King authorized a conference of 150 ministers from 42 cities, held at CTS on July 20, 1967, to expand Operation Breadbasket to a national level and charged Jackson with the task. The basic strategy connected African American economic needs with traditional civil rights protest activities. Ministers were charged with presenting proposals to businesses that would call for hiring and upgrading African Americans in proportion to their population in the city. If negotiations failed, SCLC affiliates would resort to boycotts, picketing, and other forms of nonviolent disruption. Jackson held the position of National Director of Operation Breadbasket from 1967 to 1971 and worked closely with Dr. King for the last three years of his life. Jackson was also with King in Memphis when he was slain. Ordained a Baptist minister on June 30, 1968, Jackson has remained an independent minister affiliated with the National Baptist Convention and the Progressive National Baptist Convention.

After King's assassination on April 4, 1968, Jackson's prominence as a leader elevated to a national level. *Playboy* magazine in November 1969 proclaimed Jackson as "King's heir apparent," and in April 1970, *Time* magazine featured Jackson in a cover story. As a result of Jackson's growing prestige, tension began mounting between SCLC members and Jackson: "There was bitterness that Jackson was trying to seize control but was not the rightful heir."[6] In December 1971, SCLC's board suspended Jackson temporarily for administrative impropriety and for violations of organizational discipline, primarily because he had not incorporated Black expo/trade fairs for African American businessmen under SCLC. Jackson resigned the same month, declaring he needed room to grow. He established his own organization, People United to Save Humanity (PUSH) which was later changed to People United to Serve Humanity.

PUSH, also referred to as Opertion Push, was launched on Christmas Day, 1971. It received the support of African American celebrities and other renowned persons in the country. PUSH board members included people such as Mayor Richard Hatcher, Aretha Franklin, Jim Brown, and Ossie Davis. Its goals were similar to Operation Breadbasket's—boosting minority employment and minority businesses and organizing those who were not making livable wages. Jackson also used the organization to negotiate with major corporations to hire and promote minority workers. Using threats of boycotts and persuasion, PUSH succeeded in negotiating covenants with firms such as Burger King Corporation, 7-Eleven Stores, the Coca-Cola Company, Southland Corporation, Adolph Coors, and so on.

An affiliate organization, Push for Excellence, or PUSH-Excel, was founded to improve inner-city schools and to promote educational advancement for minorities. As head of PUSH, Jackson inspired students nationally with themes of developing self-esteem and self-discipline. School chants that would later become a trademark of his presidential campaigns were similar to the following: "I am somebody . . . I may be poor . . . but I am somebody . . . Respect me . . . I am somebody . . . My mind . . . is a pearl . . . I can learn anything . . . in the world . . . Down with dope . . . Up with hope . . . Nobody will save us but us . . . I am somebody."

Jackson was president of PUSH from 1971 through 1983. Over the twelve years between the founding of PUSH and his first run for the presidency, PUSH and its affiliates succeeded in obtaining more than $17 million in federal grants as well as millions in private and corporate donations. However, questions about PUSH operations soon arose, and Jackson was questioned about his ability to manage the organization, both administratively and financially. Finally, after numerous audits by the U.S. government, in 1988 PUSH-Excel agreed to pay $550,000 to the federal government to settle longstanding civil claims of more than $ 1.1 million sought by the Justice Department.[7]

Despite his problems with PUSH, Jackson's popularity skyrocketed by virtue of his oratorical skills and ingenuity. During the 1970s, Jackson spoke before more than five hundred groups, including the United Negro College Fund, the National Conference of Mayors, and the National League of Cities. He became a syndicated columnist with the *Los Angeles Times* and accepted an appointment as visiting professor at the University of Southern California. By 1980, Jackson had been awarded more than twenty-five honorary doctorates from universities and theological schools.[8] Opinion polls in 1983 named Jackson the most important African American leader by 51 percent of African Americans questioned.[9]

Overall, Jackson's political activity has been varied and is exemplary of his tumultuous relationship with the Democratic party— sometimes actively working within the party to promote the interests of African Americans, and at other times distancing himself from the party and its ideas. For instance, Jackson was an Independent candidate for the mayor of Chicago in 1971, but failed to get enough signatures to appear on the ballot. After unseating the "regular" Cook County Delegation, Jackson became a George McGovern delegate to the Democratic National Convention in Miami and 1972 cochairman of the Illinois delegation. Around that same time, Jackson founded the Liberation party, which was an attempt to nominate an African American for U.S. President or an African American Democratic vice-presidential candidate in Chicago in 1972. Attesting to his long history of organizing around the issue of African American independent politics, Jackson was a major presenter at the Gary convention in 1972, which sought to set forth a black nationalist political agenda. However, Jackson has persistently organized and led national drives to register Democrats across the country to vote.

## Jackson's Ideological Perspective and Foundations

Understanding the philosophical and ideological convictions of Reverend Jackson can help discern his motivation for engaging in citizen diplomacy and the reasons why his endeavors took him to certain areas in the world. Examining the history of Jackson's international efforts can also shed some insight into the approach he used and the factors that contributed to the outcome of each mission.

It is acknowledged that a myriad of factors can explain the philosophical basis of political behavior, for example theories related to ontology, theology, and/or teleology. However, for the purposes of this discussion, four factors are viewed as relevant for understanding Jackson's internationalism: African American political culture, which embodies the African American Christian tradition and its central symbol the Afro-American "Jeremiad"; the activities of the African American church; a personal concern with issues of morality; and the tradition of African American internationalism.

As postulated earlier, in order to understand Jackson's political and international activity, some discussion of African American political culture must take place, for Jackson's political perspectives are rooted in the African American experience and therefore must be considered within that context. In *The Politics of the Black Nation*, Matthew Holden argues that what African American leaders do and how they do it is significantly influenced by African American culture. Holden also contends that the basic themes expressed by these leaders and the resulting political activity is rooted in and is a function of the African American Christian tradition. Consequently, African American churches are usually the strongest institutions in the African American community, and its ministers hold a position of great influence and status.[10]

Within that context, Holden identifies five politically significant attributes of African American culture that shape and condition the internal politics of the African American community. The hope for deliverance is the most common theme and is rooted in the African American church and its spirit of evangelical Protestantism. For example, African American leaders such as Martin Luther King, Jr., and Frederick Douglass believed that African American oppression would be overcome through the intervention of divine providence. The wish for defiance is the second theme and is premised on the idea that within the psyche of African Americans, there is the capacity to go against the odds and take risks to overcome their oppression. The third theme, Dionysian independence, is centered on maintaining one's honor even in the face of attack. Moralism, the fourth theme, expresses the notion that African American people seem to emphasize a greater humanness or sensitivity to suffering. African Americans demand from their leaders that they do right. Moral authority, like oratorical skill, thus becomes an important ingredient in African American leadership. The final theme which Holden views as having political significance is cynicism-and fear. Cynicism is related to the prospects for succeeding, while fear is based on a belief that trying means destruction for the individual. In the end, however, martyrdom is good. These five themes set forth by Holden are rooted in the African American Christian tradition. It is the contention here that African American political culture and the African American Christian tradition are embodied in Jackson's rhetoric and are key to understanding his philosophy.

Charles Henry also examines the cultural politics of the African American community in *Culture and African-American Politics*. However, Henry focuses on the oral traditions of the community, especially as they are manifested in music and in folklore. Because of their importance to the African American community, the church and its leadership are central subjects of Henry's analysis. His basic contention is that African American politics is distinguished by its unique style and worldview, which contains the possibility of a synthesis between selfish individualism and group responsibility, and an instructive moral vision for the entire society.[11] He also asserts that African American politics includes a variety of political expressions which is exemplified by its dependence on rhetoric and charisma, and by its roots in the African American church tradition which blends sacred and secular visions.

Henry suggests that the significance of the 1984 Jackson presidential election campaign is based on what it reveals about African American politics in the 1980s. Essentially, the campaign symbolized an attempt by African Americans to recapture the moral hegemony that was briefly enjoyed during the civil rights movement.

Holden and Henry's discussion of the significance of African American political culture provides a frame of reference for analyzing Jesse Jackson's political perspective. Hence, Jackson's theoretical and programmatic views come first and foremost from his role as an African American baptist preacher. Jackson's natural father, Noah Robinson, remembers that Jesse talked of being a preacher at the age of fourteen. "I remember the age that the dream started so well because I thought it was peculiar that it was the same age when Jesse's grandfather began preaching. Jesse told me he dreamed he would lead an army across the waters like Moses did. I remember telling him, I don't know if you could really lead an army, but you might be a good preacher like your granddaddy was."[12] The decision to enter the ministry instead of his earlier goal of going to law school, also grew out of Jackson's recognition that the church was the most important institution in the African American community. Indeed, the African American church has remained Jackson's main basis of popular support throughout his career. Jackson often refers to himself as a "country preacher," and an important source of his influence was Operation PUSH's Saturday morning church rally, held from 9:00 to 12:00 A.M. The service was carried over the radio to local and national audiences. Those political rallies with religious undercurrents frequently resembled church revivals.[13]

Jesse Jackson's activism fits into the context of what Howard-Pitney calls the "Afro-American jeremiad." In a study of several African American leaders, Howard-Pitney examines how Martin Luther King and other national African American leaders employed a rhetoric of social prophecy and criticism defined as the American jeremiad, to create a variant that is specifically Afro-American.[14] The term *jeremiad*, meaning a lamentation or doleful complaint, is derived from the Old Testament prophet Jeremiah, who warned of

Israel's fall and the destruction of the Jerusalem temple by Babylonia as punishment for the people's failure to keep the Mosaic covenant. Although Jeremiah denounced Israel's wickedness and foresaw tribulation in the near term, he also looked forward to the nation's repentance and restoration in a future golden age. The American jeremiad has been adapted by African American protest leaders since the abolitionist crusade against slavery. The African American jeremiad was symbolized by constant warnings issued by blacks to whites concerning the harsh judgement that would come from the sin of slavery.

Messianic themes of coming social liberation and redemption have deep roots in African American culture. Marcus Garvey's Universal Negro Improvement Association (UNIA) and the Nation of Islam posit a messianic destiny for African Americans. Malcolm X customarily addressed jeremiads to African American audiences, delivering attacks against social depravity, drug addiction, and family instability. Malcolm X called on African Americans to repent in order to fulfill their divine destiny, castigated whites for their wicked oppression of African Americans, and predicted Allah's vengeance against whites.

Howard-Pitney's commentary suggests that the Afro-American jeremiad, then, is paradoxically both radical and conservative. By affirming American social beliefs, the jeremiad maintains current order. "To the extent that major black figures have employed a rhetoric anchored in social consensus, they have had to keep their goals within its non-revolutionary bounds. On the other hand, the jeremiad of African American leaders consistently examines America's faults and advocates unconventional action."[15] Basically, the Afro-American jeremiad accepts cultural norms, the American creed, and the themes embodied in the Declaration of Independence and in the Bill of Rights.

Howard Pitney considers Jesse Jackson a "reformer-jeremiah," one who unceasingly criticizes present social immorality and urges repentance and reform, while promising that victory and salvation will follow as a result of Americans' right actions.[16] A constant theme in Jackson's rhetoric is that the United States has consistently declined into a state of spiritual decadence and despair. Jackson contended that during the 1970s the United States began to drift away from social progress and the gains of civil rights. This downward turn was accelerated by the election of Ronald Reagan to the presidency, who took from the poor and gave to the rich in a reverse Robin Hood process.[17] Internationally, Jackson stressed the idea that the U.S. government was aligned with forces of tyranny and oppression against popular democratic movements. "Americans, argued Jackson, must therefore reexamine every aspect of United States foreign and domestic policy that has favored . . . the few over the many."[18] Even before his 1984 presidential election campaign, Jackson frequently used biblical metaphors to describe the redemptive traits of African Americans and the poor.

With regard to the question of style, Charles Henry posits that the success of the Jackson campaign rests in part on Jackson's rhythmical oratory, which helped to attract the media. In his analyses of five speeches made by Jackson, Henry found that Jackson's style contains the traditional blending of sacred and secular elements of the African American sermon, with an emotional delivery that involves the audience. Jackson uses rhythm and rhyme, interplay with the audience, and music and prayer, which are all traditional. Themes of self-respect, hope, and redemptive suffering, which all have deep roots in the African American religious tradition, are also key points in Jackson's rhetoric.

Although Jackson's aggressive preaching style alienated some white voters who saw it as demagogic and threatening, his style attracted the media and African American audiences. By using his personality and style, Jackson was able to take progressive stands on issues and at the same time focus on family values without taking the socially conservative positions of the African American religious establishment. Ultimately, Jackson's style allowed him to blend sacred and secular values into pragmatic politics.

This discussion on the roots of Jackson's ideological perspective and activism also acknowledges the contribution of Martin Luther King's practice of the Social Gospel. King was interested in changing social structures in order to help ameliorate the conditions of African Americans. He therefore developed a theological rationale for the Christian church's role as a change agent in society. King argued that the church must be the voice of moral and spiritual authority on earth.[19]

King's goal was to help realize a "Beloved Community," which would transcend the barriers of race, religion, and national and social position. The essence of the community reflects the Judeo-

Christian understanding of the Kingdom of God. The dream of the Beloved Community was found in King's earliest writings, and his preoccupation with it continued through his final articles and addresses. As stated in *The Social Vision of Martin Luther King Jr.*, the Social Gospel provides the theological framework to articulate it, nonviolence provides the means by which to establish it, and personalism provides the philosophical base for supporting the personal nature of the community.[20]

Moralism as a key theme in African American political culture is also at the heart of Jackson's philosophical thinking and is evidenced by his reiterations that African Americans have a unique moral responsibility to save the human race. As argued by David Coolidge in "The Reverend Jesse Jackson and the Palestinian Question," while some of Jackson's beliefs can be attributed to his own personal experiences in the South and his ideological affinity with the oppressed, it is the moral factor with its roots in the African American Christian tradition and the African American church that is a more plausible explanation for Jackson's Middle East policy.[21] Essentially when one compares the general ethic of the African American Christian tradition with the specific ethic of Jackson's position on the Palestinian question, one finds structural similarities. Coolidge concludes that the moral factor is a key consideration in Jackson's ideas regarding U.S. foreign policy.

Throughout his public career, Jackson also has emphasized building African American self-esteem and promoting self-help, two ideas that are embodied in his slogan, "I Am Somebody." Racial pride, educational achievement and the idea that the struggle for equality involves functions of the market place and a social democratic agenda, are other key themes advanced by Jackson.

The nature of Jackson's diplomatic efforts is also rooted in the tradition of African American internationalism, with its emphasis on moralism and social justice in U.S. foreign policy. The writings and practice of the social gospel, especially as promulgated by Jackson's mentor, Dr. Martin Luther King, Jr., set the immediate example for Jackson to emulate. Personal attributes—an explicit audaciousness and training as an African American preacher, which provided leadership skills—helped shape Jackson's international efforts and foreign policy concerns.

## Citizen Diplomacy before the
## 1984 Presidential Election Campaigns

One of Jackson's earliest statements on international questions emphasized establishing closer ties between African Americans and Africa, and for stronger business opportunities for continental Africans in the United States. This concern was made public in October 1971 when Governor Richard B. Ogilvie of Illinois announced at Operation PUSH's Third Annual Black Expo that his office had helped to set up a trading venture between African American businessmen in his state and African businesses in Ghana and Nigeria. Jackson was a prime mover in setting up the African American/West African trade venture that was projected to have a value of nearly $50 million over a two year period.[22]

Another instance of Jackson's early international involvement was on November 20, 1972, when he led a delegation to Monrovia, Liberia, to develop a plan for African Americans to acquire U.S.-Liberian citizenship. The plan was to be similar to the one enjoyed by U.S. Jews in Israel and would have enabled African Americans to bypass the Liberian law that only its citizens could own property there. A statement issued by the Liberian Ministry of Information said that both sides agreed that the talks were perhaps the most significant ever in relations between an African government and African Americans. It added that several other far-reaching measures were discussed which "drew a warm reaction from President William Tolbert and members of his cabinet."[23]

In a press conference in Monrovia, Jackson said he would use his influence to open the U.S. market for goods made in Liberia. "It is high time for the nearly 30 million American blacks, who gave a gross national product of some $42 billion, to start moving from lip service to ship service with Africa, which means black Americans buying products made in Africa, in Liberia in this case, and exchanging a variety of skills with African countries."[24] This venture, however, did not come to fruition and no concrete results were produced.

One venture in Africa that did produce results took place when Jackson, as the leader of Operation PUSH, spearheaded a national drive to help six nations in Africa—namely Chad, Mali, Mauritania, Niger, Senegal, and Upper Volta—which were going through a five-year drought. Jackson believed that the United States had not given the same kind of attention to the disaster they had previously provided to Israel during the Middle East crisis and henceforth, embarked upon his own effort to assist the starving nations. Jackson approached many of the white businesses he had worked with in the past, such as Quaker Oats and General Foods. And in July 1973 he met with Mayor Daley, several African American aldermen, and Telefore Yaguibou, ambassador from Upper Volta, to discuss the plight of the six nations suffering from the drought. Daley agreed to introduce a resolution in city council which would call for Chicago's support of a food and fund drive for those nations. Similar resolutions were passed by Mayor Tom Bradley in Los Angeles and Mayor Richard Hatcher in Gary.[25]

Jackson's efforts eventually produced more than sixty-five tons of food and medical supplies from over thirty cities. In addition, Jackson's call for donations produced $92,000 which was turned over to the Niger ambassador, Abdoulaye Diallo, at the PUSH Expo in September 1973.[26] However, a problem occurred with shipping the food and supplies, and for some time the drought relief remained in a Southside warehouse as federal officials failed to respond to pleas for air transportation. Disheartened, Jackson sent a telegram to Secretary of State-Designate Henry Kissinger voicing his concerns and asking for assistance. Eventually, Stanley F. Scott, a special assistant to President Nixon, was authorized to help make the arrangements for transporting the food and medical supplies.[27]

South Africa has received long-standing attention from Jackson. One of his early pronouncements on South Africa occurred in April 1972, during a special program at the Apollo Theater in New York observing the fourth anniversary of the assassination of Dr. King. Jackson, after his eulogy of King and discussion on the plight of African Americans, ended the hour-and-a-half talk by calling for boycotts, rent strikes, and action against U.S. aid to South Africa and Portugal—two countries he described as having antiblack regimes.[28]

With regard to the Sixth Pan African Congress in Dar es Salaam, Tanzania, in June 1974, Jackson's comments again focused on establishing business ties between Africans and African Americans. He asserted that African Americans can offer African blacks a consumer base for African products, training, and education. He also criticized U.S. policy for being preoccupied with the crisis in the Middle East and demonstrating insufficient concern with the massive drought in Central Africa. Ultimately Jackson stated, "One important result of the Congress could be to stimulate American blacks to influence American foreign policy on Africa."[29]

The crisis in South Africa was responsible for increasing Jackson's international involvement. On August 23, 1976, Jackson led a delegation of African Americans to meet with Secretary of State Henry Kissinger to urge him to communicate to South Africa U.S. opposition to the racial policies that had led to several weeks of rioting and over 250 deaths. The eight-member group also pushed for a privately sponsored African American fact-finding team to visit South Africa, the granting of political refugee status for blacks fleeing South Africa, government pressure on U.S. corporations doing business there, and disclosure of the then recent talks held between the secretary of state and the prime minister, John Vorster, of South Africa. During his talks with reporters after the meeting, Jackson began to discuss the formation of an African American lobby for Africa—an idea that had been discussed among African American leadership, but had not yet come to fruition. Jackson said that blacks hoped to build the broadest possible base to lobby for an official American policy on Africa that would reflect their vital concerns for the continent. Jackson said, "Today's talks, as well as moves on the part of the Congressional Black Caucus (CBC) and other interested black groups would lead to the formation of such a lobby."[30]

Jackson initiated other efforts to put pressure on the South African regime from inside the United States. For instance, in early 1979, Jackson led a successful campaign to have one of South Africa's leading boxers, Kallie Knoetze, barred from fighting in the United States. The move against Knoetze, which the State Department successfully upheld in court, was part of a wider campaign by Jackson to penalize South Africa for its racial policies.[31]

Then, in July 1979, Jackson embarked upon a twelve-day tour of South Africa at the invitation of South African church groups. Earlier, the South African government had refused Jackson a visa, but with the assistance of Minister for Black Affairs Piet G. J. Koornhof, a liberal by his party's standards, Jackson was cleared for the visit. Although Jackson was not travelling to South Africa as an advocate of U.S. policy, it was reported that the Carter administration pressured the South Africans to accept him.[32] The Carter administration's support of Jackson is one example of how officials in government can help transform a closed system into one that is more inclusive of persons that are normally denied access to foreign nations and officials.

Jackson's itinerary included speaking engagements in many of the main black centers in the country, meetings with a number of dissident black leaders and possible interviews with Prime Minister P. W. Botha and other senior officials. While in South Africa, Jackson visited several black townships, held talks with U.S. businesspersons, and met with Piet G. J. Koornhof. Throughout his visit, Jackson extolled his political and religious messages of freedom and dignity for all races. He told the South African Council of Churches that apartheid was "worse than Hitler" because it stood in the way of economic growth. Jackson said he would appeal to President Carter to disallow U.S. participation in South Africa's SASOL (fuel program) or any other project until there were human rights for all people there. Jackson also called for a national convention at which rights in South Africa could be discussed and stated that clergy should adopt the tactics of Dr. King: "We must have economic and political confrontation, but not bloody confrontation between black and white." Ultimately, he considered the South African government a "terrorist dictatorship" and urged blacks in Soweto to engage in massive disobedience.[33] However, in most of his public appearances Jackson urged neither disinvestment nor violent revolution, two topics that were sensitive to the South African government. Although there were criticisms of Jackson's visit by black and white South African political leaders, the people in general responded positively to his message.[34]

Before his 1984 presidential election bid, Africa proved to be the central area of focus for Jackson. However, Jackson was involved with other global issues, especially those with potential to adversely affect African Americans and the poor. For instance, Jackson was concerned with the U.S. government's use of resources for war instead of for food, education, and other social programs for the poor. As a matter of fact, the earliest case of Jackson's citizen diplomacy was on behalf of another nation. In December 1977, Jackson, as a private citizen, traveled to Panama for a week-long visit to discuss the Panama Canal treaty. The tour included a two-hour meeting with General Omar Torrijos, the Panamanian president. Upon his return to the United States, Jackson met with several senators on the issue, and he testified before the Senate Foreign

Relations Committee in support of the treaties. Jackson's position was that the ratification of the treaties was a matter of human rights for Panamanians.[35]

Another example of Jackson's outspokenness on international questions occurred in May 1975, when Jackson called for the suspension of Vietnamese refugee settlement in the United States and a commitment to rehabilitating Vietnam. At a press conference Jackson said, "If we spent $150 billion in the destruction of Vietnam we certainly owe the Vietnamese an investment of larger and different proportions than we projected for the refuge reserve operations."[36] Jackson further stated that joblessness in America preempted any justification for the airlift, and emphasized that he was not opposed to assistance to the refugees, but he sincerely believed that the priorities of the United States should be redirected toward the reconstruction of Vietnam and the restructuring of U.S. cities. According to Jackson, if the military budget were cut, there would be enough money to rehabilitate Vietnam, help the nation's poor, and help those refugees who desired to stay in the United States.

Of all of his international endeavors, Jackson's involvement in the Middle East has by far been the most controversial. Jackson's contact with the Arab-American community occurred very early in his political career. In December 1974, Jackson arranged a meeting with leaders of Arab American groups as part of a series of meetings held with disenfranchised minorities to "open new areas of dialogue" and to develop a common domestic agenda.[37]

Jackson's perspective on the Middle East is partially influenced by the African American tradition of identifying with oppressed people, such as in the case of the Palestinians, and African American concerns about the Israeli alliance with the oppressive white regime in South Africa. For years African Americans had quietly discussed the alliance between racist South Africa and Israel and bemoaned the continuation of that relationship. However, it was not until the "Andrew Young incident" in 1979 that African Americans openly criticized U.S. Jews for their seemingly unwavering support of Israel, their overt opposition to self-determination for the Palestinians, and their indirect oppression of South African blacks.[38]

The Andrew Young incident began in June 1979 when Jack O'Dell, the international affairs director of Operation PUSH, organized a trip to the Middle East.[39] The delegation visited southern

Lebanon for ten days under the sponsorship of the Association of Arab-American University Graduates. Upon their return, delegation members conveyed their concerns about the Palestinian crisis to U.N. Ambassador Andrew Young. Young held the highest appointed office that any African American had ever held in a presidential administration. Several weeks later news reports began to appear about Young's alleged unauthorized conversations with Zehdi Labib Terzi, the PLO's observer at the UN.[40] When word leaked out about Young's discussion with Terzi, many people in the Jewish community demanded Young's ouster. Under pressure, Ambassador Young was forced to resign. This move in turn outraged the African American community who rallied to Young's support. In part of an effort to restore harmony with the African American community, President Carter appointed another African American, Donald McHenry, to replace Andrew Young.

The African American community and its leadership, still enraged, called for a reassessment of U.S. relations with Israel. In addition, Joseph Lowery, successor to Ralph Abernathy as president of the SCLC, invited the PLO's Observer at the UN, Zehdi Labib Terzi and Israeli representative Yehuda Blum to a conference to give them an opportunity to set forth their positions on the conflict. Also speaking at that conference, on the eve of his own departure to the Middle East, Reverend Jackson warned that the forced resignation of Young posed a serious threat to African American/Jewish relations and declared, "When there wasn't much decency in society Jews were willing to share decency. The conflict began when we started our quest for power. Jews were willing to share decency, but not power."[41] Jackson also urged President Carter to call a White House meeting between African Americans and Jews, saying that relations between the two groups were "more tense this night than they've been in 25 years."[42] Specifically, with regard to the controversy between the Israelis and the Palestinians, Jackson asserted that "the no talk policy toward the PLO is ridiculous . . . The most important link in civilization is communication; so we affirm communication."[43] Ultimately, Jackson argued that U.S. national interest rested on affirming Israeli security within internationally recognized borders and Palestinian justice, which includes an independent state on the West Bank and Gaza.

After weighing the evidence presented at the conference, Lowery and other prominent African American leaders decided to support the PLO.[44] Shortly thereafter, African American civil rights leaders announced to the *New York Times* that they would reassess their relationship with Israel, establish closer ties with the Palestinians, and try to force a change in American Middle East policy.[45]

In the fall of that same year, Lowery led a delegation of ten prominent African American leaders to the Middle East to meet with the PLO. While in Beirut, Lowery invited Arafat to open a series of meetings in ten cities to discuss Middle East and African problems and the relationship of both regions to African Americans. They ended the meetings linking arms with Arafat and singing "We Shall Overcome."[46]

Just after the Lowery mission, Jackson led a delegation to the Middle East, unleashing the most negative press he had received. Michael Shilch, an Israeli foreign minister, expressed to the State Department outrage over Jackson's visit, stating he "has appointed himself to a mission which he has prejudged before he even began." The message was that these "self-appointed African American envoys" were unwelcome in the Middle East.[47]

Despite the challenges, it is believed that Jackson's mission received some form of unofficial support from the Carter administration.[48] The purpose of Jackson's tour was to find the best possible solution to the problems in the Middle East and return to Washington and submit his findings to the president. Jackson met with the mayor of Jerusalem and Arab leaders such as King Hussein of Jordan, Anwar Sadat of Egypt, Syria's Hafez al-Assad, and PLO leader Yassar Arafat. Prime Minister Begin, acting on the advice of Moshe Dayan and several U.S. Jewish organizations, declined to meet with Jackson, asserting that he had made anti-Semitic remarks. Jackson counter-charged that Begin made "a racist decision based on skin color."[49] Jackson also visited a Palestinian refugee camp and a Jewish holocaust memorial, attempting to give equal audience to the hardships of both factions. During his meeting with Arafat, Jackson said that while he affirmed the right of the Palestinian people to self-determination, he also believed that the PLO should recognize Israel's equal right to exist. Jackson emerged from the meeting to announce that he would serve as a go-between to establish communications between Arafat and the United States. Arafat proclaimed Jackson as a friend and a friend of justice and humanity.

Jackson told reporters that he would return to Beirut to meet with the executive committee of the PLO to draft a statement for him to take back to Washington. "Terming the PLO leader 'flexible' he passed on the information that his friend "Mr. Arafat wants to talk to President Carter."[50] A photograph of Jackson and Arafat was taken during one of their meetings. This now very famous picture appeared in the papers on September 30, 1979, and has been consistently used by people on the left and right of the Middle East conflict in attempts to prove what side of an issue Jackson supports.[51]

By 1979, Anwar Sadat was considered by many U.S. citizens as one of the wisest and most benevolent of the Arab leaders after his peace initiative with Israel which resulted in the Camp David Accords. Jackson gave Sadat a message from Arafat, and Sadat gave Jackson a reply to take back to Beirut. There was also a message from Sadat to Israel, urging the Israelis to resist frustrating the peace process by building settlements in occupied territories and to stop threatening the territorial integrity of Lebanon. Jackson, at this stage, was involved in citizen diplomacy, acting as go-between for heads of state, attempting to solve complex problems, and functioning as minister without portfolio for African Americans.

Emerging from his second meeting with Sadat, Jackson announced that he would inform the PLO that Egypt would welcome its participation in Middle East discussions if it would affirm Israel's right to exist. After that meeting, Jackson became ill and ended up in a Beirut hospital where Arafat flew to meet him. Based upon that meeting and other information received, Jackson emerged from the hospital announcing that a cease fire had been agreed to in South Lebanon.

During his Middle East visit, Jackson made a commitment to support mutual recognition of Israel and the PLO and pledged that African Americans would challenge the official policy of the United States. Jackson told Palestinians that the African American civil rights movement in America should be their model for future action. During rallys hundreds of Palestinians cheered Jackson on, hoisting him to their shoulders, shouting "black pride" and "Jackson! Arafat!" On the other end, Israelis and U.S. Jews were very frustrated with Jackson's visit. A headline appeared in the Jerusalem *Post* that illustrated Israeli anger—"GOOD PREACHER, BAD LISTENER."[52]

The outcome of the mission was varied. Jackson's visit boosted the Palestinian cause and its leadership, who for the first time began to receive public support from a significant segment of the U.S. population. When Jackson returned to Washington, he was debriefed by Robert Strauss of the Department of State. In addition, Jackson made numerous media appearances where he criticized U.S. policy as being biased in favor of Israel.[53] A poll, conducted by the *Los Angeles Times* and Lou Harris for the U.S. Department of State, showed a marked increase of support for U.S. recognition of the PLO.[54]

The trip also created tremendous problems for one of Jackson's premier educational initiatives, PUSH for Excellence (PUSH/Excel). PUSH/Excel was designed to help students obtain the goal of academic excellence by increasing parental and community involvement in the school districts, stressing greater discipline and hard work from students and generating greater commitments from teachers. Unfortunately, Jackson's diplomacy in the Middle East stifled the enthusiasm of several school districts and former supporters for the program and strained relations between local initiatives and the PUSH/Excel national office. As a result, many PUSH/Excel programs suffered severe losses of financial and political support. For example, the Louisiana state legislature canceled its grant to PUSH operations in New Orleans. In addition, PUSH suffered a loss of support from the Jewish community. Ultimately, the backlash from the trip dealt PUSH/Excel a serious financial blow."[55]

The Middle East trip also exacerbated poor relations between African Americans and U.S. Jews, between Jackson and the Jewish community, and between Jackson and the Israelis. The Israelis began to see Jackson as a tool of foreign powers hostile to Israel and to the United States. Jackson also lost the support of many whites for PUSH programs and as with Dr. King and the Vietnam War issue, ultimately came to be regarded as dangerous.

Notwithstanding the foregoing problems, the mission did yield some positive results, although they were mainly symbolic in nature. Specifically, as a result of the venture, Jackson's stature was elevated to international prominence, which provided him with international recognition and credibility, especially among Arabs. Moreover, Jackson became accepted among the world's leaders on the basis that he had been officially received in Middle East capitals and had gained recognition from international leaders such as Assad, Sadat, and Arafat. Jackson was also treated with a respect and affection that he had not commanded in Washington.

Other results of the mission were that Jackson established closer ties to the Arab and African world which laid the groundwork for his 1984 trip to Syria to rescue U.S. Navy pilot Lieutenant Goodman. Moreover, one could speculate that Jackson raised the consciousness of African Americans on U.S. policies abroad and ultimately established a certain legitimacy for the idea of a separate African American foreign policy. He proved that African Americans possessed the right to set forth their views in the international arena, independent of government. Jackson's symbolic victory also opened doors for his future negotiations with the governments of Central and South America and other foreign leaders. This symbolism was thus converted into material benefits and ultimately was able to be used as a source of political power.[56] Jackson has continued to criticize what he perceives as a misguided U.S. position toward the Palestinian-Israeli conflict up to the present time.

## Summary

Jackson's citizen diplomacy evolved out of African American political culture, which is rooted in a religious ethos and a tradition of protest. Martin Luther King's practice of the Social Gospel, Jackson's personal sense of morality in foreign policy, and his training in the African American church provided the basis for his activism. Jackson's pan-African sentiments help to explain his concern for Africa, especially South Africa and his foremost objective of establishing closer ties between African Americans and continental Africans. Audaciousness, a characteristic that a citizen diplomat must possess, is evidenced in Jackson's activities during the civil rights movement. This audaciousness helps to explain his willingness to engage in citizen diplomacy.

All of these factors help to provide the context for Jackson's pre-1984 international concerns and endeavors. As demonstrated, Jackson emphasized the concerns of those considered oppressed and spoke out on issues of morality. Similar issues were embodied in his presidential election campaign's foreign policy agenda and international initiatives.

# 4

# The 1984 Jackson Campaign: Progressive Perceptions of U.S. Foreign Policy

E. E. Schattsneider describes a democracy in *The Semi-Sovereign People* as "a competitive political system in which competing leaders and organizations define the alternatives of public policy in such a way that the public can participate in the decision-making process."[1] Intrinsic to the workings of U.S. representative democracy is that groups fight for their ambitions by supporting leaders and policies that reflect their interests and then attempt to manage the scope of the conflict in a manner that maximizes their chances of accomplishing objectives. Schattsneider recognizes, however, that American democracy is far from neutral. He argues that the problem results from a pressure system, i.e. the arena of conflict where political alternatives are determined, that is highly restricted and limited mainly to "legitimate groups" that have already gained access to the political arena.[2] One result of this limited and biased pressure system is that benefits are mainly distributed to certain "acceptable" groups, while the concerns of other groups remain marginal at best. The primary impetus for the Jackson campaign for the presidency in 1984 and the formation of the Rainbow Coalition was to influence the political system and "legitimate agendas" on behalf of deprived and marginalized groups.

Understanding the nature of the Jackson campaign, which can be described as an independent political movement within the confines of the Democratic party, helps discern how citizen diplomacy naturally arose within the context of his presidential bid. Primarily consisting of a constituency whose political aspirations were considered left of center, Jackson supporters invariably believed that their policy positions were ignored and therefore frequently participated in unconventional means of political expression. Although a large section of this constituency was organized into interest groups, many of them had relinquished the idea of projecting measurable influence into the U.S. two-party system.

The foreign policy concerns of the Jackson constituency were most striking in their deviation from mainstream opinion, and as a consequence their perspective was often ignored or unfairly challenged. Accordingly, it became necessary to legitimize the Jackson approach to foreign policy by using unconventional strategies and tactics. Henceforth, the catalyst for Jackson's use of citizen diplomacy during the 1984 presidential election campaign was similar to the motivation for the campaign itself—the inability of the Jackson constituency to influence domestic and foreign policy within the narrow confines of American pluralism.

This chapter is focused on the 1984 Jackson campaign. One purpose is to underscore the rationale for the campaign and the establishment of the Rainbow Coalition. A second purpose is to outline the Jackson campaign's foreign policy agenda in order to provide the ideological basis for Jackson's citizen diplomacy. A discussion of the constituency is also required, because it was Jackson supporters who shaped the campaign agenda and stimulated his international interference.

## Impetus for the Jackson Campaign

Jesse Jackson's 1984 presidential election campaign emerged out of the incipient mobilization of African Americans against President Ronald Reagan's conservative agenda and thus served as a vehicle for the expression of their political aspirations.[3] The stated objective was to provide a "voice for the locked out" and to redirect U.S. policy on issues related to jobs, peace, and justice. The strategic purposes were

> to serve as a vehicle to express African American opposition to the Reagan issue agenda, to halt the rightward movement in the Democratic Party, to inject progressive perspectives on foreign and domestic issues into the campaign debates and party platform, to mobilize the African American

vote by increasing registration and turnout, to serve as the balance of power in determining the choice of the nominee and to lay the groundwork for the mobilization of a multi-ethnic, multi-class Rainbow Coalition that might become an electorial majority in presidential politics.[4]

Although the campaign was motivated by marginalized interest groups seeking to influence the national agenda, several distinctive factors were responsible for its emergence and for the development of the Rainbow Coalition. The main factor was the dissatisfaction of most African Americans with the policies and practices of the Democratic party. Another factor was a rising "misery index" in the country resulting from the attitudes and actions of the Reagan administration toward African Americans and other minorities, and finally, the campaign was motivated by what Sheila Collins calls the "new political paradigm": the linking of social movement activities and activists with progressive electoral politics in the 1970s. This political paradigm signified the move of progressive grassroots leaders such as Marion Barry, formerly of the Student Nonviolent Coordinating Committee (SNCC), to mayorship in the District of Columbia and Students for a Democratic Society (SDS) leader Tom Hayden to the California State Assembly.[5]

## The African American Base

African American participation in electoral politics commenced when "free" African Americans were given the right to vote in certain Northern and New England states and two Southern states.[6] Since then, the African American vote has been attached to the party that appeared to be the most sympathetic to its concerns but utilized predominately for the benefit of white politicians and their African American surrogates.

African Americans were linked first to the Federalist and Whig parties. Large-scale courting of their vote began during Reconstruction by the Republican party, to which African Americans were extremely loyal until 1876, when the Republican party's presidential candidate, Rutherford B. Hayes, lost to Democrat Samuel J. Tilden. As a result, a deal was struck in which Hayes was given the presidency and he in return promised to (1) obtain millions in federal subsidies through Congress to promote economic expansion; (2) withdraw military troops from the South that were used for African American protection and; (3) give white conservatives free control over state governments. The Democrats also were given control of the House of Representatives.[7]

However, it was not until the election of 1932 that the first noticeable shift of the African American vote from the Republican party to the Democratic party occurred. Because Democratic New Deal programs afforded African Americans access to greater employment and social opportunities and appointments under the Franklin D. Roosevelt administration and in local governments, by 1936 African Americans had begun to vote overwhelmingly for Democratic candidates. The African American vote was secure in the Democratic party by 1948.[8]

During the 1980s, the Democrats under President Jimmy Carter began moving toward the kind of economic conservatism that had previously been promoted by the Republicans. And while Republicans appeared openly hostile to African American interests, the Democrats, too, were becoming increasingly insensitive to their concerns. Inevitably, many African Americans became disenchanted with the Democrats, believing that they were not receiving the kinds of benefits and respect they believed their loyalty and support warranted.

Particularly disturbing to many African American leaders was the Democratic reaction to the Harold Washington mayoral campaign of 1983. Both former Vice President Mondale and Senator Edward Kennedy chose to endorse Washington's white opponents in the Democratic primary, with Mondale endorsing Jane Byrne and Kennedy choosing Richard M. Daley. And although party leaders eventually united to support Washington in the general election, Chicago's white Democrats did not similarly respond.[9] Unavoidably, the 1983 election came to symbolize the lack of respect and support shown by white party leaders and voters toward African American leaders and candidates and the interests of the African American community.

The Chicago experience rekindled the idea among African American leaders to chart an independent political strategy for the upcoming 1984 elections. Jesse Jackson and other African American leaders met to discuss the viability of running an African

American for the presidency. At the same time, the "Southern Crusade," launched by Operation PUSH in 1983 to focus on voter registration, voter education, and voting rights enforcement began to seriously promote the idea that an African American could and should run for president in 1984.[10] This campaign proved to be the compelling force for Jackson's presidential bid. The entrance of Jesse Jackson into the race for the presidency represented a new stage of development in the African American struggle for equality within the context of U.S. electoral politics.

As the 1984 presidential election primaries approached, African American leaders who had originally grouped around the Congressional Black Caucus initiated Black Leadership Family Plan for the Unity, Survival, and Progress of Black People held a series of hearings around the country to develop a comprehensive African American political agenda that could serve to articulate the African American community's criteria for evaluating the presidential candidates.[11] The People's Platform, published by the Black Coalition for 1984 and the National Black Leadership Roundtable, also sharply critiqued the values and policy orientation of the Reagan administration and demanded that the nation reorder its priorities and place human needs and investment in human capital over the development of weapons and mass destruction.[12] The ideas expressed in the platform became, in large part, the early issue agenda of the Jackson campaign.

The Jackson campaign helped to unify the African American community by including a wide range of its leaders and organizers. The campaign incorporated the ideas, services, and skills of people such as former Student Non-Violent Coordinating Committee (SNCC) activists, Southern Christian Leadership Conference (SCLC) members, nationalists, separatists, Marxists, Democratic Socialists both in and outside the Democratic party, and center-left Democrats. In addition to near absolute support of the African American Christian churches, a variety of Islamic and African cultural sects supported the campaign, and for the first time, the Nation of Islam involved itself in electoral politics. Moreover, many sororities and fraternities, masonic lodges, women's networks and clubs, and African American businesses endorsed the campaign.

It is likely that those African American leaders who did not support the campaign were conservatives who had benefitted from President Reagan's economic policies or those most heavily tied to white support, either as mayors of large cities—Wilson Goode of Philadelphia, Andrew Young of Atlanta, Tom Bradley of Los Angeles, Coleman Young of Detroit—or by virtue of their rank in the old civil rights establishment—Coretta Scott King and Benjamin Hooks.[13] However, because most African American support went to Jackson, many of those African American leaders were ostracized at the 1984 Democratic Convention. As the 1988 campaign approached, many of those leaders who refused to endorse the Jackson candidacy in 1984—cast their support for Jackson and the Rainbow Coalition in 1988. Thus, as Robert Smith stated in "From Insurgency toward Inclusion," the Jackson campaigns not only represented a challenge to the Democratic party and its leadership, but also forged a challenge to the African American leadership establishment of elected officials and traditional civil rights leadership.[14]

## Policies and Attitude of the Reagan Administration: The Misery Index

The contemptuous attitude and actions of the Reagan administration toward minorities, women, the poor, and the disabled provided an additional incentive for the Jackson presidential bid.[15] Budgetary cuts of allocations to necessary social programs and legal aid services, as well as the failure to enforce civil rights laws indicated clearly that these issues were not a priority to the Reagan administration.

In Jackson's view the Reagan administration had increased the misery index for the "boats stuck at the bottom." According to Jackson, the Reagan administration "made life for the poor miserable."[16] Jackson maintained that budget cuts to Social Security, major tax breaks for big businesses, cuts in funding for screening children for lead poisoning (which leads to serious learning and behavioral difficulties), cuts in funding health care and education, lack of desire to pass the Equal Rights Amendment (ERA), refusal to clean up toxic waste dumps, and lack of initiatives to help farmers in crisis were indicative of the Reagan administration's aversion to the poor and the disaffected. Not only was Reagan's poor record responsible for Jackson's decision to enter the race, but many of those groups and individuals affected adversely by Reagan's policies formed the basis of his Rainbow Coalition.

## The New Political Paradigm: Progressive Electoral Politics

The wedding of social movements to electoral politics, was exemplified by those movement activists of the 1960s who moved into electoral politics in the 1970s. Mainly African American led, but multiracial in character, these campaigns had a value orientation decidedly to the left of previous African American campaigns. The advocates of this new political paradigm concentrated on registering people to vote who had not participated in electoral activity before and educating them on important issues to enhance the power of their vote. The viability of progressive politics is illustrated by the success of Harold Washington's 1983 mayoral campaign in Chicago over machine politics. Following the lead of these kinds of campaigns, progressive electoral politics also formed the ideological and practical rationale for the Jackson campaigns.[17]

## Campaign Ideology and Constituency

According to Manning Marable, the fact that the Jackson campaign took the shape of a democratic, anticorporate, antiracist social movement initiated and led by African Americans is what distinguished it from other campaigns and is what proved crucial to the formation of its agenda and base of support. In addition, the absence of many members of the African American petty bourgeois from the leadership of the internal campaign apparatus made room for previously peripheral forces to fill the void.[18] Hence, a call went out for African, Hispanic, Asian, and native Americans to join with progressive white Americans, women, and the poor to work together politically and spiritually.[19]

In an early campaign position paper entitled "Jesse Jackson's Philosophy," the Jackson campaign objectives were set forth:

> My commitment as a presidential candidate is to focus on and lift those boats stuck on the bottom full of unpolished pearls. For if the boats on the bottom rise, all boats above will rise—my views in this regard are the exact opposite of the "trickle down" views of President Reagan. The way I propose to do this is to build a new functional "Rainbow Coalition of the Rejected" spanning lines of color, sex, age,

religion, race, region and national origin. The old minorities—blacks, Hispanics, women, peace activists, environmentalists, youth, the elderly, small farmers, small businesspersons, poor people, gays and lesbians—if we remain apart, will continue to be a minority. But, if we come together, the old minorities constitute a new majority. That is how I propose to be nominated and elected President.[20]

Sheila Collins defines the groups that made up the Rainbow Coalition in five broad categories, noting that most of those individuals fit into more than one. First, there were groups defined by their ethnic or national/cultural origin: African Americans, Hispanic-Americans, Asian Americans, native Americans, Arab Americans, and Jewish Americans. Second were the groups defined by gender or sexual orientation: women, lesbians, and gays. Third were the groups defined by their relationship to the processes of production: farmers and labor. Fourth were the conscience or ideological constituencies: generally white middle-class peace and environmental activists. Finally, there were the entitlement groups: disabled people and public housing tenants.[21]

Those supporters of the campaign from institutionalized religion also became a key component of the Rainbow Coalition and were significant to the development of campaign ideas. The African American church was important to the entire mobilization of the campaign and gave to it orientation, ritual, strategy, and spirit. Leading ministers from many diverse races and faiths helped formulate the campaign's humanistic vision and colored its approach to important political events.[22]

In 1984, the campaign staff was about 75 percent African American, reflecting both its base and its national priorities. The other racial groups were represented, but many of their major organizational leaders were noticeably absent or only erratically supportive.[23] The top positions in the campaign were held by people who had experience with electoral politics, and in 1984, the Rainbow Coalition departments were staffed chiefly by people who had come out of the social movements of the 1960s and 1970s. The core campaign staff and advisors were longtime associates of the Chicago-based PUSH operation and also included a range of prominent African American clergy, academicians, and politicians. A distinctive characteristic of the 1984 organization were the constituency desks, which were a part of the campaign's effort to build a multi-ethnic, multi-issue coalition. (See figure 4.1 for an illustration of the 1984 Jackson campaign organization).

In contrast, the 1988 Jackson campaign relied heavily on organizations formed and led by African American elected officials as well as the various state and local chapters of the Rainbow Coalition. The campaign efforts also consisted of Washington insiders and an increased number of professionals experienced in running traditional campaign operations. The constituency desks and the association with the Nation of Islam and its leader Minister Louis Farrakhan were eliminated from 1988 organizational efforts.

The campaign issues evolved out of a combination of Jackson's personal concerns and the interests of the Rainbow Coalition constituencies. The first informal group of "issues" advisors were drawn together in October 1983, as it became probable that Reverend Jackson would seek the Democratic nomination. Out of that effort, the rudiments of the campaign's foreign and domestic policy positions developed. However, the issue agenda was developed only as the Rainbow Coalition matured and as the complexity of the issues before Reverend Jackson demanded.[24]

In articulating the concerns of his ethnic communities, Jackson addressed immigration and anti-Arab sentiments, which resulted from foreign affairs questions. He also attempted to destroy the myth of Asians as the model minority in order to address race and class oppression experienced by many Asians.[25] As an advocate for his Hispanic constituency, Jackson called for bilingual education

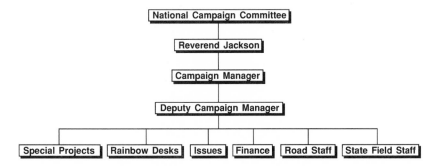

**Figure 4.1**  Jackson Campaign Organization (Taken from Ronald Walters, *Blacks Presidential Politics in America* (New York: State University of New York Press, 1988), 166.)

programs, focused on unemployment, opposed the Simpson-Mazzoli immigration bill, refused to use the term *illegal alien*—referring instead to undocumented workers—and spoke out against the abuse of farm workers.[26]

Jackson's white support primarily consisted of peace activists and environmentalists. On the environment Jackson supported federal initiatives such as the Clean Air Act, passage of the Safe Drinking Water Act and enforcement of the Toxic Waste Superfund program and the Acid Rain Superfund program.

Jackson made nuclear disarmament and a noninterventionary foreign policy keystones to his campaign and called for a 20 to 25 percent cut in the Pentagon budget, a bilateral nuclear freeze, and cancellation of all strategic defense initiatives, including the ballistic missile defense system and antisatellite weapons. Jackson was endorsed by organizations such as the Friends of the Earth—one of the largest environmental lobbies—and prominent peace organizations such as the Fellowship of Reconciliation, Mobilization for Survival, and the Coalition for Nuclear Disarmament.

The Jewish American community provided only modest support to Jackson's candidacy. The African American and Jewish community's disagreements over Affirmative Action and U.S. support for Israel, as well as African American perceptions of Jewish racism; and Jewish perceptions of African American anti-Semitism, were factors that suppressed coalition building between these two groups in 1984.[27] Jackson experienced even more resentment from American Jews after he began an open relationship with Louis Farrakhan, minister of the Nation of Islam and after the "Hymie controversy" in February 1984—Milton Coleman, a Washington Post journalist, reported that in an interview Jackson referred to Jews as "Hymies" and to New York as "Hymie Town." As a result, the plausible coalition between African Americans and American Jews to fight what both groups perceive as an oppressive system never materialized.

## The Rainbow Coalition and Foreign Policy

The formulation and implementation of U.S. foreign policy has primarily been dominated by those white males educated and employed in elite institutions and whose position in society frequently made them oblivious to the views of most minorities.[28] Hence, the attempts of African Americans and other ethnic groups to influence U.S. foreign relations has always been viewed by this select group as suspect and contrary to national interests. The Jackson campaign dismissed the idea that the views of African Americans and other ethnic groups were not germane in the discussion, formulation, and execution of American foreign policy. The campaign also recognized that the differences in ideology were partially a question of the differences in social class as well as race.

The foreign policy positions of the Rainbow Coalition were based on the humanistic and moral concerns of its members and Jackson's own international perspective. Essentially, the Jackson campaign advocated a "new direction" for U.S. foreign relations and raised serious questions about whether or not those decisions that exclude the concerns of most groups in society are really within the national interests. Basically, it was the issues surrounding foreign affairs and international relations that distinguished Jackson both from Republicans and from moderate Democrats and that proved to be the most contentious.

Jackson's controversial foreign policy views have often been attributed to his numerous left wing advisors.[29] Considered the strongest link between Jackson and the "radical left" was the Jackson campaign's chief foreign policy advisor, Jack O'Dell, the former international affairs director for Operation PUSH and a key staff member of the Rainbow Coalition. O'Dell, with a long history of involvement in the Civil Rights Movement, worked alongside Martin Luther King, Jr., on the staff of the Southern Christian Leadership Conference and is said to have a history of working on socialist causes.[30] O'Dell was eventually dropped as an aid to the SCLC because of the alleged Communist affiliations. In 1984 other advisors on international issues included Mary Tate of the World Peace Council and attorney Ramsey Clark, noted for speaking out against U.S. foreign policies. Others might be described as left of center academics or activists, such as Ronald Walters, a Ph.D. in International Relations and an intellectual who has a history of activism on issues related to U.S. foreign policy and the concerns of the African American community. Walters was also issues director of the 1984 Jackson campaign and platform consultant for the 1988 campaign. In addition, since 1984, Robert Borosage, former director of the progressive Institute for Policy Studies (IPS) and other IPS advisors have been prominent in the campaign.

With regard to Jackson's personal concerns and perspective, he lacked that "knee-jerk anticommunism" that pervaded the discourse on U.S. foreign policy in the 1980's.[31] Nor did Jackson consider the Soviet Union the only nation-state involved in creating international disorder. Jackson relied on the concerns and perspective of many third world leaders to help formulate his campaign's international agenda. The "third world" approach advocated by the Jackson campaign is a consensus view on foreign policy held by many African Americans and shared by its leadership establishment.[32] This view is based on the African American proclivity to identify with oppressed and poor nations. Jackson even stated that his views came from his understanding of the third world because he has "had a Third World experience right here in America."[33] Jackson described his approach to foreign policy on January 27, 1984, in a speech at the United Nations, where he was invited by ambassadors from African states.

> Early U.S. history was perverted by counting those of us who are African as three-fifths human and those of European descent as seven-fifths human. As a result, it imperiled our nation at its foundation and stunted its growth and global outlook. Peace requires justice and that we play the game by one set of rules. . . . My approach to foreign policy is to engage in negotiations, not confrontation.

> World leaders must initiate positive action, not just engage in negative reaction. Thus I urge an approach of presidential initiative. An American president ought to meet African leaders, visit the African continent, and learn and share. Our foreign policy ought to reflect diplomatic sharing, and agricultural, economic, technical, and cultural exchange. If we are to remain the hope of the free world, our challenge is not military escalation but a worldwide war on poverty, disease, and illiteracy. Domestic policy is foreign policy— they are interrelated.[34]

Throughout the campaign, Jackson made salient many issues considered important to the third world. Jackson charged that the United States employed a policy which viewed the third world only in relation to superpower conflict. He also argued that the United States had a history of backing repressive and regressive forces because of the cold war and racism. He demanded a new course in U.S. foreign policy that would be consistent with stated U.S. values. He advocated a new doctrine to guide U.S. relations, especially with third world nations. The Jackson Doctrine, highlighted in the 1988 campaign, was based on four principles: support for international law, self-determination, human rights, and the promotion of international economic justice and development.[35]

Jackson focused his framework for a new foreign policy in the regional areas of the Middle East, Central America, the Caribbean, Africa/Southern Africa and on issues of national security.

## Middle East

The Jackson campaign position on the Middle East was based on Jackson's own ideological perspectives and guided by his Arab and African American constituency. Jackson argued that U.S. foreign policy was often race-based and favored Europeans over other races. This explains why U.S. policy has been more pro-Israel and anti-Arab in the Middle East, while in Southern Africa, U.S. policy favored the repressive white minority leadership rather than the black majority seeking human rights and freedom.

Jackson considered Middle Eastern conflicts "costly, dangerous, and a detriment to achievement of our vital interests in the region."[36] He promoted solutions to problems in the Middle East that focused on U.S. national interests but would also promise political and economic strength to the people of the region. Jackson set forth four elements as essential for any Middle East settlement: (1) Israeli security within internationally recognized borders; (2) self-determination or the right to a Palestinian homeland; (3) respect for the territorial integrity of Lebanon; (4) normalization of relations between the United States and the Arab world.[37]

Specifically, with regard to the Israeli-Palestinian conflict, Jackson championed a mutual recognition policy on the part of Israel and the PLO, which contrasted sharply with the positions of his Democratic opponents. In the "New Directions platform" of Reverend Jackson's 1984 presidential campaign, a summary of his position on the Palestinian question is offered:

The Middle East conflict requires a balanced policy which supports the security of Israel within internationally recognized borders and an independent state for Palestinians with a commitment on the part of each country to live in peace with mutual respect for each other's rights. American policy will never be successful if it is founded on the militarization of a few nations at the expense of the interests of the majority of nations in the region.[38]

David Coolidge, Jr., in "The Reverend Jesse Jackson and the Palestinian Question" describes the Jackson approach to the Palestinian question as moral and ideological. He concludes that Jackson attempted to move U.S. foreign policy to a higher plane—a moral plane—so that U.S. action could be based on the pursuit of justice, equality, and meeting human needs.[39]

## Central America and the Caribbean

Jackson, like many members of the Rainbow Coalition, vehemently disagreed with President Reagan's Central American policy, theorizing that U.S. policy was founded on blind anticommunism, which caused it to support brutal and corrupt anti-Communist leaders rather than those seeking justice and democracy. Jackson argued for the type of economic, social, and cultural development that would meet the needs of the vast majority of Central Americans, not only the ruling business and political leadership. His campaign promoted ideas that would end the war waged on Nicaragua by engaging in negotiations with the Contras for a cease fire and with the Sandinista government to encourage their development of democratic institutions. The Jackson campaign also pushed the idea that the military complex under construction in Honduras should be dismantled. With regard to El Salvador, Jackson's plans were to cut off all U.S. military assistance to El Salvador, initiate negotiations to halt the violence, and help to develop an interim government involving all parties which could sponsor free elections. In addition, Jackson's strategy was to cut off military assistance to the Guatemalan government and provide aid to Guatemalan refugees in Mexico, support the thousands of Costa Ricans who marched in the streets against the militarization of their country by the Nicaraguan Contra forces, and normalize relations with Cuba. He also advocated support of the Contadora process and charged that the U.S. invasion of Grenada was wrong, immoral, and a case of an "elephant arrogantly and foolishly stepping on a gnat."[40]

Although the Rainbow Coalition's positions on Central America were anathema to many Cuban American immigrants, Jackson's campaign positions were praised by many Mexican Americans and Puerto Ricans, propelling the formation of "Latinos for Jackson" chapters throughout the country. In the New York state primary, Jackson won 34 percent of the Puerto Rican vote despite the nearly unanimous endorsement of Mondale by Puerto Rican officials. Mexican American organizations such as the Mexican American Political Association (MAPA) endorsed Jackson as did past presidents of the League of United Latin American Citizens (LULAC) Tony Bonilla and Mario Obledo. Several Latino local and state elected officials also endorsed the Jackson campaign.[41]

## Southern Africa

In Jackson's view, U.S. policies toward Africa essentially have been based on racism and ignorance. Because of that legacy Jackson maintained that some fundamental principles should be observed when developing future U.S. policy toward Africa. The first principle involved recognition that all U.S. citizens are not European descendants and that over 30 million U.S. citizens trace their ancestry to Africa. Henceforth, Africa should be considered as important to the United States and as much a part of U.S. foreign policy as are European nations, Israel, Japan, Canada, Russia, and Central America. Second, the U.S. government should recognize the similar struggles of African Americans and blacks in Africa, particularly in South Africa for economic emancipation, political and civil enfranchisement, basic opportunities, and human rights. Third, the United States should also recognize that its treatment of its African American citizens can either impact favorably on or impede the respect, trust, and confidence of African leaders. Finally, a true rainbow coalition could improve African confidence in and trust of the United States. Observing these principles could result in fair, just, and humane policies toward Africa.[42]

With the assistance of interest groups such as TransAfrica, the African American lobby for Africa and the Caribbean, and the

Washington Office on Africa, Jackson was successful in making the issue of South Africa one of his most vocal initiatives. Jackson's position on South Africa received overwhelming support from all segments of the African American population and those U.S. citizens who abhorred racism and colonialism. Other candidates, however, attempted to evade this issue, but Jackson constantly reiterated in debates that it was an important issue to a large segment of the U.S. population. An example of such an effort was in the New York City debates on April 1, 1984, where Jackson demanded "that both Hart and Mondale address the posture of American foreign policy. In response, they made positive but rather passive statements yielding little substantive discussion of what Americans could or should not do about apartheid."[43]

The measures advocated by the Jackson campaign regarding South Africa were in clear contrast to the Reagan administration's policy of "constructive engagement," which was based on the idea that through closer relations and better communications with the apartheid regime, change would occur. Specifically, Jackson sought to end all vestiges of the policy of constructive engagement; enforce sanctions; declare South Africa a terrorist state, which would allow the president to quickly implement comprehensive sanctions and create a climate for U.S. allies to join; hold a regional summit between South Africa's neighbors; compel the United States and the European community to coordinate a policy that would merge the political and economic forces of the region, to lessen their economic dependence on South Africa and to defend themselves militarily against South Africa's military aggression; and abolish the idea that the withdrawal of Cuban troops from Angola was a prerequisite for Namibian independence. In addition, Jackson promoted the idea of social and cultural exchanges between Africa and the United States; advocated addressing Africa's need for food, health, and education, addressed equity in trade, aid, reconstruction and development; and advocated massive increases in the amount of foreign aid to African countries.[44]

## Defense and National Security

Promoting nuclear disarmament and a nonmilitary-interventionist foreign policy were central objectives of the Jackson campaign. The leadership of many peace groups played an active role in formulating Jackson's defense policy and organizing rallies to gain support. Some of the peace leaders who endorsed the campaign were Reverend William Sloan Coffin of Riverside Church in New York City, Howard Morlan of the Coalition for a New Foreign and Military Policy, and Reverend Robert Moore who was executive director of the Coalition for Nuclear Disarmament.[45] The involvement of those activists assisted in moving Jackson's peace and environmental positions qualitatively to the left of the positions advocated by the Democratic party. The Jackson campaign called for a reduction in the military budget; pledged a "no first use" of nuclear weapons; developed a strong noninterventionist third world posture; advocated a bilateral nuclear freeze; called for a moratorium on the production, testing, and deployment of nuclear weapons; advocated U.S./Soviet negotiations to reduce both sides' nuclear arsenals; identified poverty and injustice as the root of war; and called for an end to cold war rhetoric and thinking. Jackson further proposed conventional force reductions between NATO and the Warsaw Pact and for European allies to pick up a greater share of the costs of their defense.[46] And finally Jackson argued that the United States should move beyond confrontation and containment of the Soviet Union to promoting common security arrangements.

## The Jackson Campaign's Foreign Policies and the Democratic Party

In contrast to the foreign policy positions of the Jackson campaign, the Democratic nominee, Walter Mondale, departed from his domestic liberal stance and "applauded the illegal invasion of Grenada, never criticized U.S. intervention in Central America, and was practically mute on Reagan's constructive engagement policies, which supported apartheid."[47] With regard to arms control, Mondale would not initiate defense cuts and if necessary would have provided military support to non-Communist regimes interested in overthrowing communism.

Because Jackson's foreign policy positions reflected the views of the Rainbow Coalition's center left positions, he inevitably encountered difficulty in procuring legitimacy for his views in the rightward-shifting Democratic party. However, Jackson's tenacity, oratorical skills, and style allowed him to effectively use campaign forums to gain public support. For instance, Jackson used the debates not only to put forth his own foreign policy objectives, but also to force other candidates to respond to them. Hence, despite the other candidate's preoccupation with the East-West conflict, and nuclear weapons, Jackson repeatedly questioned them about underdevelopment issues in the third world and apartheid in South Africa.[48]

The platform process gives each candidate an opportunity to legitimize his or her issue agenda within the party. Because "party platforms have a high incidence of influencing or becoming national plans," each candidate seeks to have the platform reflect his or her own interest. Some of Jackson's and Mondale's most obvious disagreements during the platform formulation process occurred around the objectives of U.S. foreign policy. For instance, in Jackson's platform draft he identified the purpose of U.S. foreign policy as establishing human rights and peace, while Mondale's platform stated: "The purpose of foreign policy is to attain a strong and secure United States and a world of peace, freedom and justice. On a planet threatened by dictatorships on the left and right, what is at stake may be freedom itself. On a planet shadowed by the threat of a nuclear holocaust, what is at stake may be nothing less than human survival."[49] Mondale's foreign policy conservatism was exemplied by his position on the Middle East. Mondale reiterated the need for strong support of Israel and called for a secure Israel with strong defensive borders. However, he did not mention a desire to communicate with the PLO, the Palestinian people's chosen representatives. Mondale's position was in contrast to Jackson's call for a readjustment of relations with Israel and a homeland for the Palestinians. Mondale felt so strongly about his stance on this issue that he objected to Jackson's Africa plank in retaliation.[50]

Despite Mondale's objection, Jackson's version of the African policy position section of the Democratic party platform was passed by the Platform Committee. The African plank included, among other things, pressure and sanctions against South Africa, release of political prisoners in South Africa, and economic strategies that would assist other nations in Africa. During the Platform Committee meetings, however, the Mondale forces attempted to inject "cold war" language into the Africa section reflecting the Reagan administration's concern with the status of Cuban troops in Angola. However, the attempt was successfully opposed.[51]

With regard to Central America, while Mondale would not pledge nonintervention, he promised that as president he would work for peace by pressing both for human rights and for the removal of all foreign forces from the region. However, Mondale and Jackson could not agree on the issue of Cuba. Jackson advocated normalizing relations with Cuba, while Mondale opposed such a policy.

Ultimately, the 1984 Jackson campaign was successful in projecting humanitarian approaches to foreign policies in the campaign debates. However, Jackson was unsuccessful in his attempts to incorporate most of his foreign policy positions in the Democratic party platform.

## Summary

The Jackson campaign's domestic and foreign policy positions, notably left of center, deviated from the more conservative positions of other Democratic contenders. The fact that the Jackson campaign could neither obtain legitimacy for its positions from incumbent politicians nor other important government institutions was a primary impetus for the Jackson candidacy in 1984. A similar rationale can be used to explain how and why citizen diplomacy was used within the context of Jackson's presidential election bid.

# 5

# Syria

Two contextual issues must be considered when examining Jackson's diplomatic initiative in Syria. First, the Syrian initiative requires an examination within the framework of the Jackson campaign for the presidency in 1984. The insurgent nature of the campaign not only was reflected in its dissident posturing relative to the conventional behavior of other election bids, but also in the international forays that Jackson initiated. The effort in Syria should also be viewed within the context of Jackson's ideological perspective. As discussed in chapter 3, Jackson's approach was to inject issues of morality into debates about American foreign policy. Hence, Jackson injected religious and moral tenets into discussions about the war-ravaged Middle East and used ethical ideas as the basis for his appeal to change the direction of U.S. foreign policy.

This chapter describes Jackson's citizen diplomacy in Syria. The objective is to explain the motivation for Jackson's efforts, the method utilized, and the effectiveness of the mission. An essential question is to what extent does engaging in citizen diplomacy allow one to influence foreign policy processes or international politics? Another closely related question is to what extent does citizen diplomacy expand the representation of views on key international issues? The contention here is that citizen diplomacy does provide an additional point of access into foreign policy processes and into international politics and thus increases participation and representation in U.S. foreign affairs. This chapter will also examine those factors that were instrumental in determining the outcome of the Syrian effort, how citizen diplomacy can affect political campaigns, and the Reagan administration response. The Syria case illustrates how the Reagan administration used citizen diplomacy to its own advantage.

## Precursor to the Syria Mission

By the time that Jackson announced his candidacy in November 1983, the New Hampshire primary was only four months away. As indicative of the nonconformist nature of the campaign, within days of his announcement Jackson publicly declared the delegate-selection rules of the Democratic party unfair. In a detailed letter to Democratic National Committee (DNC) Chairman Charles Manatt, Jackson charged that the rules of the Hunt Commission, named after Governor James Hunt of North Carolina who had chaired the body charged with formulating Democratic party rules, were part of an effort to lock out African Americans, Hispanics, women, and other nonestablished candidates like himself. His biggest complaint was that the "threshold rule" greatly reduced the delegate strength of candidates who were not able to collect at least 20 percent of the vote in presidential primaries or party caucuses. He also denounced the so-called winner-take-all rule, in use in seven important states, which disallowed splitting the delegates among the candidates in proportion to their share of votes. This rule made it possible for one candidate to claim all the delegates in a congressional district if delegates running under his/her name received a plurality of the vote. Jackson called for straight proportionate allocations of delegates for all candidates and an end to the rule.

Manatt agreed to meet with Jackson on December 20, and after a two-hour session they announced at a joint press conference that Jackson would be allowed to present his case before the party's executive committee at its next scheduled meeting in January 1984. While the Democratic party leaders were deliberating on how to handle the charges raised by Jackson, and while the Jackson campaign, still in its infancy, was immersed in formulating policy statements, the Reagan administration's Middle East policies were engendering a dangerous conflict between the United States and the Syrian government.

## U.S. Policy in the Middle East

The framework for U.S. policy in the Middle East was positioned in 1917 by President Woodrow Wilson, when he endorsed a letter from British Foreign Secretary Arthur Balfour to the leader of the

British Zionists Lord Lionel Rothschild, pledging that Britain would support the establishment in Palestine of a "national home" for the Jewish people.[1] As Jewish migration increased and after an independent Israeli state was established in 1948, the earlier hostilities between the Jews and Arabs intensified. When the British mandate came to an end on May 15, 1947, and their forces were departed, the Arab states of Egypt, Saudi Arabia, Jordan, Syria, Lebanon, and Iraq sent contingents of their armies into the area. Since that time, several wars and skirmishes have erupted between the Israelis and their Arab neighbors, leaving thousands dead, maimed, or homeless.

Since recognition of the Jewish nation, its security has been a fundamental principle in U.S. policy. However, before World War II there was little U.S. involvement in the Middle East, other than an interest in oil. Circumstances changed in early 1946 after the Soviets refused to withdraw troops from Iran as was agreed to in the Soviet-British wartime agreement designed to prevent Nazi influence in Iran. When Iran refused intricate Soviet involvement, the Soviets engineered a revolt and eventually established a Soviet-controlled regime in the northern province. Truman responded by threatening to move U.S. forces into the area. The Soviets avoided the confrontation by removing their troops.[2]

Since that time, U.S. policy in the Middle East has focused on four major objectives: (1) ensuring the security of Israel; (2) achieving an Arab-Israeli peace settlement; (3) maintaining U.S. access to Middle Eastern oil; and (4) blocking Soviet expansionism in the region.[3] Depending on the presidential administration, various aspects of those goals have been emphasized, and frequently those objectives have conflicted with each other. Throughout the cold war, when the threat of Soviet expansionism was the dominant theme in U.S. foreign policy, U.S. policy emphasized massive shipments of arms, economic assistance, political support, and manpower to assist Israel—the United States' number one ally in the war against communism in the region. However, support for Israel only fostered anti-American feelings among the Arabs and made them more receptive to Soviet assistance and influence. Inevitably, the Soviet Union and the United States became locked in a cyclical relationship where each superpower would support nations in the region based upon their friendliness to the opposing superpower.

On occasion American diplomacy was instrumental in bringing about cease-fire agreements and peace treaties. The most noted agreement was a peace treaty between Egypt and Israel known as the Camp David Accords, largely sponsored by the Carter administration.[4]

During the tenure of President Ronald Reagan, who brought to office a vigorous anti-Communist view of the world, the cold war approach toward diplomacy in the Middle East predominated. In the midst of his election campaign, Reagan charged that "earlier administrations were too accommodating to the Soviet Union and had allowed America's strength and reputation to decline."[5] In contrast to his immediate predecessor, President Carter, Reagan placed relatively little importance on the individual needs of nation-states; his preoccupation was globalist and hinged primarily on the strategic importance of nations with regard to combatting Soviet influence.

An example of the Reagan administration's unwavering support for Israel occurred in 1981, when fighting broke out between Syria and the Maronite Christian Phalange militia in the Lebanese city of Zahle. Israel, assisting the Phalanges, shot down two Syrian helicopters. Syria responded by moving air missiles into Lebanon's Bekaa Valley. The American public disapproved of Israeli use of American supplied F-16 aircraft in the attack because it was considered offensive and U.S. law restricted the use of U.S. arms for defensive purposes only. The Reagan administration justified its continued aid to Israel by arguing that abandoning the Middle East could lead to its consolidation into the Soviet bloc.

Reagan turned his attention to Lebanon almost as soon as his administration began. As the site where much of the tension in the Middle East is acted out, Lebanon suffered years of civil war and occupation by Syrian, Israeli, and PLO troops. Successive Arab-Israeli wars provided the primary impetus for Palestinian flight to Lebanon. Many more escaped to Lebanon after being driven out of Jordan after an unsuccessful attempt to seize power in that country. During the ten-year long civil war in Lebanon, the Palestinians usually sided with the Muslims against the Christians while at the same time used Lebanon's weakness for forays into northern Israel. The Israelis consistently supported the Christian Maronites of Lebanon.

Syria's involvement in Lebanon was a source of tension in the region for decades. Geography and the legacy of colonialism bound the fate of Syria to that of Lebanon. Syria shares a border with

Lebanon to the west and held the view that the French division of the former Mount Lebanon, which made Lebanon a separate state from Syria, was illegitimate. Given the close ties and the fragility of the Lebanese government, Syria aspired to maintain a strong and influential presence there. The Soviet Union was a prime supporter of the Syrian President Hafez Assad administration.

The events that led to Jackson's diplomacy in the Middle East involved an Israeli invasion of Lebanon on June 6, 1982, for the purpose of creating a twenty-five-mile buffer zone in southern Lebanon free of Palestinian guerrillas. Although the United States issued statements that indicated displeasure with the Israeli move, some Middle East experts suggested that U.S. officials gave Israel a "green light" for the invasion mainly on the grounds that the Israeli move supported its goal of seeking the withdrawal of all foreign forces from Lebanon.[6] Contrary to the positive effort sought, its consequences changed power relations in the region. The invasion enabled the Syrians to emerge from isolation to seize power, diminished Israel's standing in the area, provided an avenue for the re-emergence of the Soviet Union in the region, and brought U.S. troops in for peacekeeping.

In August of that same year, Israel began heavy shelling of the PLO camps in West Beirut. Tumult over Israeli actions led to a general public demand that Reagan dissociate the United States from Israeli actions. This controversy contributed to the resignation of Secretary of State Alexander Haig and the appointment of George Schultz in his place.[7]

The strife that resulted from Israeli actions led to intense international negotiations, and by September a compromise was reached where Israel agreed to lift the siege while a trilateral force of French, Italian, and American troops (marines) supervised the withdrawal of the PLO army from Beirut to Jordan and Tunisia. Reagan seized this opportunity and attempted to resume the Camp David process. He delivered a major foreign policy speech that committed the United States to a homeland and self-determination for the Palestinians on the West Bank and in Gaza in return for a guarantee from the Arab states of nonviolation of Israel's border and its right to exist. But soon after the PLO troop evacuation was complete and the trilateral force withdrew, Lebanon's President Elect, Bashir Gemayel, was assassinated. In retaliation, Israel's army returned to Beirut and assisted the Phalange militia in the massacre of hundreds of Palestinian civilians in the Shatila and Sabra refugee camps near Beirut.

The bloodbath horrified the world and forced a return of the international forces in an attempt to restore peace. Eventually, every faction with an interest in the conflict had its own militia in Lebanon. Syria occupied eastern Lebanon; Israel occupied southern Lebanon; what remained of the PLO occupied northern Lebanon; and the U.S. Marines and the other peacekeeping forces, with neither a clear objective nor the necessary force suffered casualties.[8]

It became increasingly difficult to see what point there was to keeping the marines in Lebanon, and President Reagan's actions were criticized severely by members of Congress who thought Reagan was evading the requirements of the 1973 War Powers Resolution in its refusal to seek congressional approval for the deployment of troops. Secretary Schultz, in response, restated the administration's position, which in essence was that although the marines in Lebanon "are involved in a situation where there is violence," they are not "in combat" and thus the War Powers Act did not apply. His statement confused more that it elucidated and satisfied almost no one.[9]

In September 1983, as fighting in Beirut escalated and the marines suffered even greater casualties, the U.S. Navy began bombing in Syria-controlled Lebanon. This indicated that the United States was using military force in the region where it professed to be neutral. Consequently, through its assistance to Amin Gemayel, the United States became more identified with the Phalange and more partisan. As this happened, Arab nations looked to the Soviets for more support and Assad's leadership strengthened.[10]

As the situation deteriorated, Reagan eventually sent in more troops. The violence against the United States reached its high point on October 23, 1983, when a suicide truck loaded with TNT drove into Marine headquarters and killed 241 marines. Reagan denounced the act but held his resolve to keep the marines in Lebanon.

The deaths of the marines erased any American support left for the commitment of U.S. troops in Lebanon. President Reagan placed most of the responsibility for the attack on Soviet-backed Syria, which he said had reneged on its promise to withdraw troops from the area of conflict.

In early December, in response to a concentrated Syrian anti-aircraft attack against U.S. reconnaissance jets over Lebanon, the United States launched its first air strikes and its first direct attack against Syrian forces. Twenty-eight carrier-based planes attacked Syrian gun positions in the mountains east of Beirut; two American jets were shot down. An A-8, two-man jet crashed into a mountainside near the village of Kfar Selouane in Syrian-held territory. The twenty-six-year-old pilot, Lt. Mark A. Lange of Fraser, Michigan, was killed, while Lt. Robert O. Goodman, Jr., of Portsmouth, New Hampshire, his twenty-seven-year-old bombardier-navigator, was ejected before the plane crashed.[11] Goodman, knocked unconscious when he parachuted to the ground, was quickly surrounded by Syrian soldiers and taken to a military prison in Damascus. Beaten by his captors the first day, he was eventually put in a large room, brought books, and fed three times a day.[12] The Syrians declared that he would not be released until the war in Lebanon was over and the United States was out of Lebanon.

## Impetus and Motivation for Diplomacy

Jackson had previously attempted to raise the level of debate about the problems in the Middle East, asserting that the Palestinian problem could not be ignored and that unwavering U.S. support for Israel was not in the best interest either of Israel or of the United States. The campaign's response to the crisis was to devote immediate attention to shaping a Middle East policy based on Reverend Jackson's approach, which claimed that these four elements were essential to any Middle East settlement: (1) Israeli security within internationally recognized borders; (2) self-determination and a right to a homeland for the Palestinians; (3) respect for the territorial integrity of Lebanon; and (4) normalization of relations between the United States and the Arab world.[13]

The Reagan administration responded to the crisis a few days later by holding a news conference and assuring the public, already distraught over the deaths of the marines stationed in Lebanon, that Lieutenant Goodman's release was high priority. Then Special U.S. Envoy to the Middle East Donald Rumsfeld was dispatched to Syria to pursue negotiations on the situation. Upon his return, however, Syrian officials publicly pronounced that Rumsfeld had not even inquired about Goodman. Embarrassed, the White House admitted that Rumsfeld had been under orders not to bring up the subject first, asserting that they did not want Goodman to become a bargaining chip in negotiations on Lebanon.

Described as irate that the Reagan administration had not even attempted to secure the release of Goodman, Jackson initiated his first act of intervention into the situation by sending a cable to President Assad asking for Goodman's release on humanitarian grounds. Jackson received a response from Assad through Rafic Jouejati, the Syrian ambassador to the United States, who extended an invitation to Jackson and a delegation of his choosing to visit Damascus.[14] Jouejati, a Christian Arab, had surmised that the United States had many friends in Syria and believed that such an effort might bring forth better relations between the two nations.

Jackson's first attempt at securing a delegation to go to Syria was on December 19, 1983, while in Memphis at a meeting with a group of activist African American clergy. Jackson proposed that a high-profile delegation of religious leaders go to Syria to attempt to gain Goodman's release.[15] Although Jackson had not intended to go himself, he began seriously to entertain the notion of interrupting his campaign and joining the delegation. It was clear to Jackson that the Reagan administration's record in the Middle East made efforts to secure Goodman's release difficult. As Ronald Walters points out in his discussion of the issue politics of Jackson's 1984 campaign, the Reagan administration had not established a positive diplomatic posture with Syria, nor had it established a personal rapport with President Assad. And because the presence of American troops in Lebanon appeared to be in support of Israel rather than in any mediating role, there was the question of whether or not the United States maintained influential channels to Syria which could, in fact, compel the Syrians to grant concessions to the United States.[16] Based upon those considerations, and in light of the personal invitation, Jackson believed that he should embark on the mission.

Immediately after Jackson announced his intentions to go to Syria, he was besieged with criticisms. Government officials hinted that the Jackson effort might scuttle delicate negotiations already underway. In a terse statement, spokesperson for President Reagan Mark Weinberg said, "At the President's direction diplomatic efforts are underway, as they have been since Lt. Goodman's capture, to secure his release ... History has proven that efforts of this type have a better chance for success when they are not politicized."[17]

Other critics of the mission questioned why Syrian President Assad, considered a brutal dictator capable of killing thousands of religious rivals, would release one airman as a humanitarian gesture, especially when keeping Goodman might discourage Washington from sending more reconnaissance flights over Syrian parts of Lebanon. Even Goodman's father, Robert Goodman, Sr., of York, Pennsylvania, suggested that Jackson stay home. "The Syrians have decided to treat Rob fairly well," he said. "These attempts by outside groups might cause a reversal of that situation." Goodman Sr. did, however, state that the family was not opposed to any effort to free his son but that he did not want him to become a political football.[18] As the Syrian initiative received more publicity, other antagonists publicly objected to Jackson's involvement. Among other concerns, they asserted that Jackson's involvement was selfishly motivated. Considering that the New Hampshire primary was just months away and Goodman was from New Hampshire, they hinted that Jackson's goal was to use Goodman's mishap to gain votes in New Hampshire. Critics also suggested that Jackson had no respect for the prerogatives of the chief executive and that going to Syria to seek the release of Goodman was a violation of the Logan Act. Moreover, criticizing the policies of his own government from a hostile forum was inexcusable. Some other criticisms rested upon the question of race. Many argued that because Goodman is African American, Jackson was only attempting to galvanize African American support in New Hampshire and around the nation.[19]

Jackson effectively countered these criticisms. First, he framed his mission as humanitarian. Second, he denied that his mission was politically motivated. Third, he reiterated that he was part of an interdenominational religious group.[20] In addition, Jackson justified his right to intervene by asserting that "(p)rivate citizens can either sit back and let this war expand and do nothing or make full use of the tools at their disposal, under the law, to help end the conflict."[21] At this point, Jackson was stressing that private citizens could utilize both conventional and unconventional methods to intervene in international affairs. With regard to the question of loyalty, Jackson had stated early on that he would abandon the trip if President Reagan requested he do so.[22] Jackson also considered it unfair to inject race into the proposed mission, asserting that he would attempt to win the release of a hostage regardless of race or ethnicity. In addition, he continued, the mission could bring the two governments closer together.

Politically, for Jackson the venture was a gamble because it did not appear that the chances were good for Goodman's release. Acknowledging that one problem was that the Syrians were holding out for an end to U.S. reconnaissance flights over Lebanon, Jackson understood that he did not have authority to discuss halting those flights. Even the Syrian defense minister was doubtful that there would be a release, stating that "a state of war exists between the U.S. and Syria" and that "military traditions are that prisoners of war are exchanged after the war ends."[23] If the mission did not prove successful, Jackson would look imprudent, and he would have exposed himself to charges of meddling in government business. However, the success of the mission would help him gain political support. Because of the risk of failure, several campaign advisors urged him not to go. But backing out after making the announcement would probably have been just as destructive. Hence, Jackson remained committed to the mission.

## The Delegation

A key element to the success of citizen diplomacy is the stature of the private citizen and his or her delegation. As discussed, citizen diplomats must wield some type of power—that is, there must be some reason why a foreign government would agree to meet with unofficial foreigners. Jackson thus considered several factors when he set about selecting his delegation. First, the individuals had to possess some expertise in the area and had to support his position on fundamental issues. Second, they had to enjoy some degree of standing in the local or national community. Third, Jackson determined that the delegation should be ecumenical, which would suggest unity on issues and cooperation among various sectors of the religious community in the United States. Fourth, considering that the race question had been raised, it was equally important to be interracial. Fifth, staff persons and assistants were also necessary to provide assistance with logistics, and a capable team of media persons were needed to document the trip. Finally, as with most of his international endeavors, Jackson included family members for support.

An ideal candidate was someone like Wyatt Tee Walker who had a history of participating in progressive politics. He was also a member of the clergy and had traveled extensively throughout the Middle East. Walker had made six trips to Egypt, four to Jordan, two to Lebanon, and eighteen to Israel and the occupied territories on the West Bank. In addition, his involvement in the World Peace movement had taken him to various other places in the world. There were attempts to enlist the aid of others such as William Sloan Coffin, an ex-CIA employee and controversial minister of the Riverside Church, who had been arrested with Walker during the freedom rides when he was Yale University Chaplain; Howard Moody, a Baptist pastor in Greenwich Village who had a long history of championing unpopular causes; and Bishop Paul Moore, a leader in the Episcopal church in New York City and in the nation on humanitarian issues. Unfortunately, for one reason or another, the aforementioned ministers were not able to accompany Jackson to Syria. Moore was committed to going to Nicaragua at the time, and neither was Moody and Coffin available.[24]

However, Jackson was able to secure commitments to go to Syria from other noted people that fit his criteria and vision. The party consisted of several ministers: Reverend Jesse Jackson; Reverend William Howard, former president of the National Council of Churches who held Christmas services for American hostages in Iran in 1979; Reverend Jack Mendelsohn, of First Parish, Unitarian Universalist, in Bedford, Massachusetts, who had accompanied Jackson to the Middle East in 1979; Reverend Wyatt Tee Walker, of New York City, a close associate of Reverend Martin Luther King, Jr.; Louis Farrakhan, leader of the Nation of Islam; Dr. Thelma Adair, a professor of education at Queens College in New York and president of Church Women United. Staff members and assistants who made the trip were Florence Tate, campaign press secretary; Minister Akbar Muhammed, Farrakhan's personal aide; Julia Jones, campaign photographer; Tom Porter, top policy adviser to Jackson and Jackson's road secretary; Eugene Wheeler, a Los Angeles businessman; Ed Theobald, Jackson's New Hampshire campaign chairman; Jackson's two sons, Jesse Jackson, Jr., and Jonathan Jackson; Dr. Andrew Thomas, Jackson's personal physician, who he hoped would be permitted to examine Goodman.[25]

Jackson appointed William Howard as the head of the delegation. Wyatt Walker was appointed to serve as chief of protocol and

Tom Porter and Dr. Thomas were to provide back-up when required. Delegation members were expected to pay for their own expenses.

## Diplomacy in Syria

The day before the delegation departed for Syria a prebriefing was held with the State Department. That same day, Walker met with Syrian Ambassador Jouejati to request three commitments from the Syrians required by the delegation: (1) a firm commitment to meet with the religious leaders of Syria; (2) a meeting with Goodman; and (3) a meeting with a high-ranking official in the Syrian government. Ambassador Jouejati agreed to all three requests.

Before Jackson left for Syria, the White House again disavowed any official connection with the mission. President Reagan even refused to accept phone calls from Jackson because he did not want to put any official imprint on the trip. White House spokesman Larry Speakes publicly declared that Jackson: would be "going as a private citizen and has no official standing with the U.S. government."[26] The administration's aim was to make clear their opinion that they considered Jackson's mission as politically motivated, counterproductive, and self-defeating.

Before the delegation left, another press briefing was held in New York. In the ambassador's lounge, Goodman's mother, Marilyn, gave Jackson a letter to deliver to her son. The delegation then boarded the plane to Frankfurt with only the three assurances from the Syrian ambassador to the United States.

From the origin of the mission to its completion, Jackson repeatedly would be forced to justify the focus of the trip as humanitarian, without political motivation. For instance, at the stopover in Frankfurt, after questioning, Jackson told reporters that neither race nor politics played a role in his decision to fly to Damascus and reiterated that his was a moral appeal above government-to-government relations. He recounted, "This is truly an American matter. I have been involved in humanitarian missions in the past."[27]

U.S. Ambassador Robert Paganelli met the Jackson delegation when they arrived at the Damascus airport on December 31, 1983. Paganelli said he welcomed Jackson's visit and "assistance in the job of gaining Lt. Goodman's release."[28] The delegation also was met by officials from the Assad government. One of them was Deputy Foreign Minister Issam Annayeb and his staff aide. In addition, one full Secret Service section was waiting for them in Damascus.

At the point of arrival the mission's chances for success seemed dismal. There were no guarantees that the delegation would be able to meet with Assad, and what made matters appear even more bleak was that a few weeks earlier, Assad had refused to meet with Rumsfeld. Jackson made a brief arrival statement for the press and told reporters, "We hope that somewhere in the course of these meetings, something can be done or said to allow us to break the deadlock and take a giant step toward peace, and that on high humanitarian grounds Lt. Goodman can be freed."[29]

That morning the Jackson delegation met with Abdel Khaddam, foreign secretary of the Republic of Syria at the Foreign Ministry. Jackson asked Farrakhan to begin this session in prayer. Farrakhan spoke in perfect Arabic from the Holy Qua'ran. Politically, Farrakhan's presence and prayers in Arabic were clever. They demonstrated, first, cultural respect and, second, that African America held ties with the Arabic world. Throughout the mission, Farrakhan would be asked to begin and close meetings with prayer.

After Farrakhan's prayer, Jackson made a passionate plea for Goodman's release, using phrases such as "break the cycle of pain" and "lower the temperature in the Mid-East." Khaddam responded to the appeal by saying, "You ask us to do what is difficult to do." He explained that the reality of the situation was that it would be a devastating blow to the morale of the Syrian troops who were the objects of Goodman's attack. There was no way he could as foreign minister recommend the release of the "enemy."[30] Khaddam also told Jackson that, in fact, many in the government were against releasing the prisoner. Still furious with the United States for its actions, they felt that keeping Goodman would both punish Washington and perhaps discourage other reconnaissance missions. After Khaddam's speech, which contained no hint of promise, Jackson responded that he appreciated all that was stated then said "We do not come seeking justice, we're asking for mercy." Jackson reiterated that the decision must rise above the government-to-government level. "The basis of the appeal is humanitarian and moral."[31]

Throughout that day and in subsequent days, Jackson held meetings with key individuals within and outside the Syrian government who had access to Assad, reasoning that those individuals close to Assad needed to have a clear focus of the mission. For example, he met with Khalid Fahoum, chairman of the Palestine National Council, which is considered a parliament in exile for Palestinians. Fahoum was regarded as an influential person with close ties to Syria. Fahoum endorsed Jackson's efforts to free Goodman.[32] On another occasion, a call came from Dr. Franklin, a Ph.D. in political science who was considered an expert on Middle East affairs. He arranged for a meeting between Jackson and Mahmoud Labadi, administratively, second in the PLO to Arafat. At that time, Labadi was living in Damascus. Jackson met with Labadi with an understanding of his great potential to influence Assad. This meeting was considered so important that *Time* magazine credits Labadi with turning the tide with Assad.[33]

The meeting with Goodman took place at four o'clock that afternoon, on the premises of the military compound in Damascus. Because Ambassador Paganelli was in bed with the flu his first deputy, William A. Rugh, represented the United States. Goodman expressed condolences to the family of pilot Mark Lange. When asked by the press what he thought about Jackson's efforts, he replied "I'm a naval flier, not a politician. I just hope that whoever's in charge of getting me released will do it as soon as possible."[34] Jackson delivered the letter from Goodman's mother. After the press was dismissed, the delegation was given some private time with Goodman. He shared his ordeal with the group and said he had been treated well.

After the meeting with Goodman the delegation headed for its six o'clock meeting with religious leaders at the office of the Ministry of Religion and Endowment. The Moslem cadre represented all shades of Islamic thought: Shiite, Alawite (Assad's sect), and Sunni. The Christian cadre included the Roman Catholic, Greek Catholic, Syrian Orthodox, Greek Orthodox, Armenian Orthodox, and a representative for the Protestant community in Syria. Howard, as chairman of the mission, in his previous posts as president of the National Council of Churches and Commissioner of the Program to Combat Racism of the World Council of Churches, already knew three of these prominent church figures. Jackson reiterated his appeal to the clergymen, who responded that they were supportive of his efforts to free Goodman in spite of the fact that they perceived the lieutenant as an agent of war and death. However, one of the clergymen said, "I ask you, who will wipe away the tears of the villagers on whom the bombs rained death and terror?"[35] After the lengthy discussion, the group attended a reception held in their honor hosted by the religious leaders.

This reception was the final official act on their first day in Damascus. It was held at the residence of the American ambassador to Syria at 8:40 P.M. The ambassador was still ill with the flu, but the full complement of embassy personnel was present. While there, the U.S. Marine detail invited the delegation to their Christmas party, which was less than two blocks away. The delegation accepted the invitation, and Jackson used the occasion to stress the importance of Goodman's release.

Jackson and his party had planned to leave Syria on January 2, but by the next morning—January 1, they still had not been able to arrange a meeting with Assad. The delegation was advised by the Syrians to keep its schedule open in case the Assad meeting was suddenly made possible. Meanwhile a proposed meeting with the Saudi ambassador and a visit to a Palestinian refugee camp were on the agenda for that day. Three years earlier, Jackson and Walker, on separate missions, had visited the Shatila and Sabra camps in Lebanon (the refugee camps of the 1982 massacres in Lebanon) and were eager to continue their tradition of meeting with Palestinian refugees. Syrian Chief of Protocol Khalil Abu Hadad, suggesting that the present division in the PLO made it too dangerous, offered as an alternative a visit to a camp on the outskirts of Damascus whose principal inhabitants were the displaced Syrians from the Golan Heights.

After the visit to the refugee camp, news arrived that the Saudi ambassador had canceled their meeting, but that a member of the Syrian Parliament was in place and that Inaan Raad, a member of the Lebanese Democratic Front, was waiting to meet with Jackson. Raad had been the key contact in Jackson's initial meeting with Assad two years earlier.[36] Raad also had access to Assad.

As it turned out, the meeting with President Assad had been arranged for 1:30 P.M. the following day. Although the meeting with Assad had been set for only two or three members of the Jackson delegation, Walker persuaded the Syrians to allow at least four.

On January 2, 1984, Jackson requested an early morning meeting with Paganelli in hopes of receiving some additional assistance. The ambassador informed Jackson that he was not in the position to provide any further aid, and hence, the ultimate release of Goodman was done without a significant contribution from Paganelli.

The meeting with the members of the Jackson delegation and Assad took place on January 2. Fortunately for Jackson, this was not his first visit to the Middle East nor his first meeting with Assad. During Jackson's previous encounters with Assad he had proven that he possessed some understanding of the problems in the region and had further shown that he was willing to listen to the Arab view of the conflict.

Due to concerns about Assad's health, his aides stressed that the meeting would be thirty minutes at most. The discussion team consisted of Jackson, Porter, Mendelsohn, and Howard.[37] Assad talked about his regret that U.S./Syrian relations had fallen to such a bad state, and he stated that Syria had nothing to gain by having poor relations with the United States. He also applauded some of the steps which the Carter administration had taken to help ease tension in the Middle East. He spoke favorably about a visit which Carter had paid him as a private citizen following his term in the White House. Assad's harshest words were reserved for the Israel-Lebanon peace treaty, which, among other items, called for the withdrawal of all troops, including Syria's, from the territory and placed limits on the Lebanese military presence near the Israeli border. Assad considered the treaty a fundamental compromise of Lebanese sovereignty.[38] Jackson, then appealing to Assad as a "simple country preacher," said that if Assad released Goodman he could "break the cycle of pain" that binds the United States and Syria. Jackson argued that keeping Goodman only made him "warbait" and was "an incentive to escalation of the conflict."[39]

What was notable about the meeting was the high regard Assad held for Jackson. After each interruption to mark the established time of the meeting, Assad directed his aides to allow them to continue. After ninety minutes, they concluded the discussion with Assad informing Jackson that he would appeal to his Council of Ministers to reconsider its policy regarding the release of Goodman. Jackson remained behind for a few extra minutes for a private discussion with Assad. During that conversation, Jackson said, "If I go back home empty-handed, people are able to see clearly that a humanitarian appeal does not work with you, but I think it does. It is important that you take a leap of faith and break the cycle of pain and return that boy to his parents and leave a good taste in the mouths of the American people."[40]

Even though there were no assurances as to what the outcome would be, the Jackson delegation was encouraged by the discussion.

After the meeting Jackson hurriedly issued a press statement. In part it said,

> Today, as you know, we met for one and one half hours with President Assad. It was a warm and meaningful meeting. He has heard our moral appeal to release Lt. Robert Goodman on humanitarian grounds as a way to relieve tension and break the cycle of pain. There is obviously great concern about the combat posture and reconnaissance flights . . . [41]

That same evening, after several hours of waiting for an answer from Assad, Jackson received an official request to delay the delegation's departure to the United States. A promise was made that a Syrian official would deliver the president's decision by 10:00 A.M. the following day.

About 10:11 A.M., the next morning, the official interpreter began: "Mr. Jackson, the meeting this morning will be a brief one . . . President Assad has asked me to inform you that on the basis of your moral appeal we shall release Lt. Goodman to you."[42] The secretary informed the group that because Goodman was military personnel, the U.S. government had to be involved. Ambassador Paganelli handled the paperwork, and at 11:30 Goodman was released into American custody. Although the relationship between the Jackson delegation and U.S. officials had been cordial, the delegation held fears that after the release it would be denied access to Goodman. Walker expressed those fears to Paganelli, whose response was, "Lt. Goodman is being released to Mr. Jackson and the U.S. Ambassador." He further stated that the U.S. government had no intention whatsoever of making Goodman unavailable to Jackson or to anyone else.[43]

The announcement of Goodman's release was made jointly by Jackson and Paganelli. The latter maintained that many hands were responsible for the release. Goodman, who was grateful for Jackson's efforts, but not profuse, stated that he was anxious to see his family and hoped he could return to his squadron as soon as possible. He said nothing that would reflect on his military branch of service. A victory luncheon was then held which included the Jackson delegation, Goodman, Syrian officials, Secret Service officers, Syrian security officers, American media, and leaders from most religious denominations.

Jackson had managed to persuade the Syrian government to allow a U.S. military transport plane to land on Syrian soil. The journey back to the United States in an air force jet provided by the White House ended at Andrews Air Force Base in Maryland, just as the next day's morning news programs were going on the air. After brief arrival statements from those who took part in the venture, they and supporters convened in the District of Columbia Congressional Delegate Walter Fauntroy's New Bethel Baptist Church for an eight o'clock service. Goodman was taken from Andrews Air Force base to Walter Reed Hospital for a medical examination and a private reunion with his family.

## Effectiveness of the Diplomatic Mission

The accomplishments of the mission were varied. Personally, Jackson demonstrated that he was capable of effective diplomacy and that he could handle a delicate diplomatic issue in a volatile area of the world. The mission also proved that Jackson was bold and wise enough to thrust himself in the center of Reagan's foreign policy "calamity," and it demonstrated his willingness to approach adversaries despite their past actions. The venture also granted Jackson the opportunity to restate his views on the Middle East and demonstrated that his approach to foreign affairs could be successful. With regard to Jackson's push for peace and advocacy for morality in U.S. foreign policy, the attention focused on Goodman would be an impetus for troop withdrawal.

Concerning the U.S.-Syrian relationship, the release of Goodman eased tensions between the two countries. Before the rescue, the United States and Syria had been locked into a barely communicative, non-negotiable position on various questions of Syria's role in the Lebanese conflict, such as its intentions in the Golan Heights and its relationship with the PLO. The Jackson initiative opened a small but critical line of communication between them. Reagan, still opposed to an immediate pull-out, sent a thank-you message to Assad saying, "This is an opportune moment to put all the issues on the table."[44] In response to Reagan's letter, Assad promised to see Middle East Special Envoy Donald Rumsfeld who had been denied entree to Assad during his last visit. This opened up the possibility of negotiations. As a result, Rumsfeld flew to the Middle East with a new plan to settle the conflict which acknowledged the Syrian's position and also included Assad as a principal negotiator in future attempts to end the conflict.[45]

With regard to the presidential election campaign, Jackson was taken more seriously after the rescue. While other candidates were debating about what might be done, Jackson had taken the risk and was successful. Though not totally as a result of the Goodman rescue, Jackson's ratings in New Hampshire doubled by mid-January, going from 7 percent to 15 percent.[46] More money came into his campaign, and his standing in the polls began to climb. In addition, the release brought forth public praises from party leaders. In a speech critical of Reagan's foreign policies to the National Press Club on January 3, Walter Mondale praised Reverend Jackson, saying "All of us are proud of Reverend Jackson's success," and adding that Jackson "conducted his negotiations with sensitivity and deserves our thanks."[47] Senator Edward Kennedy said, "This personal initiative by Reverend Jackson will rank as one of the finest achievements by a private citizen in the history of international relations."[48] And finally, the campaign received nationwide media attention and increased respect. This broadened Jackson's base and gave him more access to support from white liberals concerned about foreign policy issues. It also gave him and the other Democratic candidates an opportunity to intensify criticisms of Reagan's policies in the region, particularly sending Americans into Lebanon. However, the Damascus success was not translated into votes on the fairness issues raised by Jackson. At the January 20 meeting of the DNC in Washington, D.C., southern party chairpersons balked at the compromise worked out by Mondale's forces to lower the burdensome 20 percent "threshold" needed to win convention delegates in a district.

The success of the Damascus venture brought increased respect for Jackson in the African American community, especially considering that he had become the first African American private citizen to secure the release of a prisoner of war. It is likely that Reagan's negative image among African Americans increased because many people in the community believed that although it was in contact with Assad, the Reagan administration had made less effort to free a downed African American pilot than it was doing to secure the release of the "refuseniks" (dissident Jewish Soviet citizens).[49] And finally, Jackson was articulating the concerns and issue positions of many African Americans on U.S. policy in the Middle East, illuminating that they were not analogous to the official policies of the government.

The success of the Syria mission can be attributed to several factors. First, it behooved Assad to release Goodman, considering that the navy flier's detention had not produced any tangible results and that if Goodman was harmed, problems for the Assad regime may have increased. The Syrian president may have deduced that by responding to the humanitarian appeal, he improved his own image as a world leader. Moreover, the release of Goodman brought pressure on the Reagan administration to amend its policies in Lebanon.[50]

Second, the numerous conversations Jackson held with other influential leaders in the region who had access to Assad may have also contributed to the success of the mission. As noted previously, Jackson met with Syrian religious figures and members of the PLO before talking with Assad. He also persuaded Mahmoud Labadi, the PLO spokesman, to present his case to PLO faction leaders in Damascus. It was they who subsequently urged the Syrians to release the airman. The pressure exerted on the Assad regime by other influential leaders in the region most likely played a role in Jackson's success as well.

Cynical foreign affairs experts and journalists suggested with contempt that Assad used the capture of Goodman and his release to embarrass the White House; especially since Jackson was a contender for Reagan's job. An example of such an opinion appeared in an editorial printed in the *Yonkers' Herald Statement*, January 3, 1984, entitled "Opportunism in Damascus:" It said, "The release of Lt. O. Goodman Jr. shows what can happen when an improbable couple like the Rev. Jesse Jackson, Democratic presidential aspirant, and Syria's President Hafez Assad find common ground: a desire to confound and embarrass the Reagan administration."[51]

## U.S. Official Involvement and Citizen Diplomacy

In discussing the relationship between citizen diplomacy and U.S. democratic processes, it is important to take note of the State

Department's official and unofficial meetings with Jackson and overall U.S. assistance to the endeavor. After receiving the invitation from the Syrians, Jackson immediately contacted Senator Charles Percy (R-Ill.), chairman of the Senate Foreign Relations Committee to discuss the proposed visit. Senator Percy later arranged for a State Department briefing for Jackson and his delegation.[52] The briefing session was a key indication that the Reagan administration would not stop the group from traveling to Syria.

The first primary briefing session consisted of Richard Murphy, assistant secretary of state and head of the Mid-East section of the U.S. State Department; Bruce Earman; and Undersecretary Lawrence Eagleburger, Reagan's Foreign Policy Adviser. During the session, important geographic information was pointed out by Dick Murphy. Eagleburger shared with them as much as he could or would about the details of Goodman's capture and where he might be. Murphy made it clear that Ambassador Paganelli was the U.S. point man and that all actions must support him. They presented the State Department view, which was that Goodman should not be used as a bargaining chip and that under no circumstances could Jackson negotiate for the United States.[53] They also informed the delegation that the International Red Cross had privately made an attempt to secure Goodman's release.

U.S. official involvement was demonstrated again when Jackson arrived in Damascus on December 31, 1983, when he received an official greeting by Ambassador Paganelli. Throughout the mission, U.S. officials would be on hand to assist the delegation. As discussed earlier, U.S. officials held a reception in Damascus in honor of the delegation and there was U.S. presence at the Goodman meeting. Overall, although Jackson went as a private citizen, the U.S. government did supply logistical support, including the plane that the delegation used to return home.

Just as important as the official briefings was the administration's response after the release. Through Paganelli, the U.S. government took credit for assisting Jackson in his efforts. At the press conference, Ambassador Paganelli interjected that the release had been achieved "in response to and associated with the appeals the U.S. government made to the government of Syria . . . on humanitarian grounds."[54] Even though the Syrian foreign ministry affirmed that Assad's decision had been influenced by both factors—Jackson and U.S. officials—it was widely believed that the Syrians offered this statement to create circumstances that would facilitate the withdrawal of American troops in Lebanon. In addition, President Reagan treated Goodman's homecoming as a special celebration. He dispatched the airplane that flew the group back to the United States and presided over an official reception and "hero's welcome home" at the White House. During the Rose Garden ceremony, Reagan personally thanked the Reverend Jackson for his personal mission of mercy. [55] In turn, Jackson thanked the president for not impeding his efforts.

For Reagan, appearing to rejoice was good politics. By being generous with accolades he lost the appearance of being unreasonably hard-lined.[56] The diplomatic coup also raised hopes for a settlement in Lebanon that would allow the Reagan administration to gracefully withdraw the 1,800 U.S. Marines from Beirut. Moreover, Reagan had the opportunity to use his new line of communication with Assad to ease him away from his demand for total abrogation of the May 17 Israeli-troop withdrawal agreement with Lebanon. He further took the edge off of any future attacks by Jackson on the administration's handling of the Goodman case.

Meetings between Jackson and government officials took place after the release. On January 5, the day after his return, Jackson held a thirty-minute meeting with Defense Secretary Casper Weinburger. Jackson told Weinburger that the administration should not shun direct talks with Syria.[57]

Not all government officials were publicly pleased with the diplomatic coup. An example of their annoyance was demonstrated when Jackson campaign aides planned to feature Jackson with Goodman at a homecoming celebration for Goodman at his old high school in Portsmouth, New Hampshire. Navy officials were quick to point out that navy regulations forbade servicemen from participating in political events and thus prohibited Goodman from attending the rally with Jackson. Jackson's response was that the navy's announcement was a "political decision" made by a "political appointee," but that he would not let that stain his moral mission, nor would he try to transform that service into a political one. Jackson attended the Lt. Robert Goodman Day celebration at Goodman's high school without Goodman at his side.[58] There were also instances when the State Department publicly suggested that Goodman's release would have little diplomatic effect.[59]

Based on the fact that the troops were still stationed in Lebanon, on February 5 Jackson called for marches and other demonstrations throughout the nation to increase pressure on President Reagan to remove U.S. troops from Lebanon and Honduras.[60] Eventually, the pressure from Congress and the disapproval of the public forced Reagan to announce on February 7, that the remaining troops in Lebanon would be moved in stages to ships offshore.[61] Overall, after the Goodman-Jackson scenario, the departure of the marines and the near collapse of the Gemayel government, Syria emerged once again as the dominant force in Lebanon.

## Summary

The motivation for Jackson's mission to Syria was primarily humanitarian, although the opportunity for increased attention to his presidential bid provided added incentive. The objective was to secure the release of a U.S. POW. The primary method used was negotiations couched in moral appeals. Jackson's previous assertions, encounters, and activities surrounding conflicts in the Middle East, the motivations of Syrian officials, and those with access to President Assad all contributed to the success of the mission.

The accomplishments of the endeavor were many. First, Jackson's efforts bestowed increased legitimacy to citizen diplomacy as an approach for private citizens interested in influencing international affairs. The fact that the U.S. government provided assistance and other resources to the endeavor proved that although Jackson bypassed official foreign processes in order to rescue Goodman, legitimacy was ultimately attained for the effort, and his right to intervene into the international event was recognized. Hence, citizen diplomacy provided an additional point of access into U.S. policy processes. Other significant accomplishments of the mission were that Jackson's successful rescue of Goodman conferred increased legitimacy to the Jackson campaign for the presidency and as evidenced by his international diplomacy following the Goodman rescue, enhanced Jackson's personal standing internationally.

In addition, Jackson's positive intervention in Middle Eastern affairs during the Goodman crisis set forth the possibility of serious discussions on the Middle East that could have led to U.S. recognition of the PLO and the interests of Arab nations. Although the Reagan administration used the release to its advantage, the release squelched Reagan's ability to use further threats of force against Syria without great cause and gave a substantial push to the demands of many members of Congress to remove U.S. troops from the area.

# Central America and Cuba

One consistent determinant of political and economic progress in Central America has been U.S. foreign policy in each autonomous nation-state there. Essentially because Central America is important to the transit of U.S. trade and military arsenal, and is part of Latin America, an area that accounts for a significant portion of U.S. direct and financial investment, the United States has repeatedly interceded with force in specific countries in order to protect its perceived interests.[1] The cold war made Central America's geopolitical strategic location even more important to U.S. security and, accordingly, is one primary reason why the idea that the Unites States holds license to intervene in its affairs has been sustained.

U.S. policy in Central America was particularly aggressive during the early to mid-1980s. President Ronald Reagan refused to consider the internal roots of unrest in each locality and focused instead on the idea that the Soviets and Communist supporters were responsible for all of the political turmoil in the region.[2] Reagan thus adopted a strategy of confrontation and provided huge amounts of military and economic aid to those countries and organizations considered anti-Communist.

Jesse Jackson, whose perspective was antithetical to Reagan's, directed a diplomatic mission toward those countries that were most threatened with the possibility of U.S military intervention. Jackson was also determined to venture into those areas which had the most significant chance of assisting with peace efforts.

In this chapter, Jackson's diplomacy in Central America and Cuba during the 1984 presidential election campaign will be examined. The specific countries involved were Panama, Nicaragua, El Salvador, and Cuba. As in the previous chapter, the objective is to underscore the motivation for Jackson's diplomacy, the mode of operation used, and the outcome. An additional aim is to understand the interrelationship between citizen diplomacy and democratic participation in U.S. foreign policy. Key to this discussion will be the role of Hispanics in the United States and abroad in assisting with formulating the direction of Jackson's policy in Central America and in sustaining his diplomatic objectives. As in the Syria mission, material benefits resulted from this endeavor, and hence a discussion of the role of foreign governments in citizen diplomacy will follow. Also, in certain instances, objectives were not accomplished, and thus an attempt will be made to discern why citizen diplomats may not accomplish certain goals and what types of goals are most difficult for the citizen diplomat to attain. This examination will also include an appraisal of how the home government can ignore the accomplishments of the citizen diplomat. In addition to the foregoing, a brief discussion of the effects Jackson's diplomacy in Central American had on the campaign will follow.

Before discussing the precursor to the Central American mission, an analysis of U.S. foreign policy in the countries that Jackson visited is required. Understanding the history and nature of U.S. policy in those countries will highlight the reasons why, during a presidential election campaign, Jackson was compelled to embark upon the mission and why Jackson's attempt to persuade the Reagan administration to modify its policies toward Central America proved very difficult.

## Historical Discussion of U.S. Foreign Policy in the Sphere of Jackson's Diplomacy

Intrinsic U.S. involvement in Central America occurred soon after the Mexican-American War in the mid-1800s, when politicians and investors began to view the area as the next frontier. Soon thereafter, the United States began using force to maintain political order and to protect its interests. As early as 1903 President Theodore Roosevelt forcibly separated Panama from Columbia by sending in the U.S. Navy and Marines. In 1904 Roosevelt announced, as a corollary to the Monroe Doctrine, a right to intervene in neighboring republics to prevent chronic wrongdoing and declared that the Western hemisphere should not be considered for future colonization by any European powers.[3]

Roosevelt's corollary governed U.S. behavior in Central America until it was renounced by Secretary of State Henry Stimson in 1930. Nonintervention became the superseding doctrine after President Franklin Roosevelt announced his Good Neighbor policy and after signing the 1947 Inter-American (Rio) Treaty of Reciprocal Assistance and the 1948 charter of the Organization of American States (OAS). The onset of the cold war, however, justified U.S. reversion to its earlier policy—most notably in 1954, when the United States engineered the overthrow of the elected president of Guatemala, Jacob Arbenz; led a campaign against Castro in Cuba; and invaded the Dominican Republic in 1965 to extinguish a left-wing military rebellion.[4]

## Cuba

The United States was instrumental in freeing Cuba from Spain during the Spanish-American War at the turn of the century. Subsequently, the Platt Amendment (1901) was enacted, which granted to the United States the right to intervene in Cuba for the preservation of Cuban independence, for the discharge of Cuba's treaty obligations, and for the protection of life, property, and individual liberty. By 1934, when the amendment was repealed, the United States had intervened in Cuba militarily three times, and it had established a naval base at Guantanamo Bay. American influence in Cuba remained steadfast until Fidel Castro and his opposition forces overthrew the American-backed tyrannical dictatorship of Fulgencio Batista on January 1, 1959.

Castro had gained widespread popularity among the Cuban people by identifying himself with democratic government and social and economic justice. Before long, however, the regime centralized the economy, abolished all political parties except for the Communist party, and maintained control over all of the country's activities.[5] Castro also linked Cuba closely to other communist countries. Not only did he maintain diplomatic relations with the Communist bloc, but Cuba's economy became integrated into theirs. In addition, the Soviet Union supplied Cuba with vast amounts of arms and military advisers.

As the Cuban/Soviet relationship strengthened, successive U.S. administrations planned its demise. U.S. diplomatic ties to Cuba were severed, and an economic embargo was set in place. In 1961, the Kennedy administration engineered the "Bay of Pigs" coup-attempt by sending a small military force of Cuban exiles into Cuba. The operation failed largely because it was dependent on the mobilization of the Cuban masses in support of the exiles.

The conflict between the United States and the Castro governments became even more volatile when the Soviets attempted to establish a missile base in Cuba in the fall of 1962. After discovering soviet missiles, Kennedy placed a blockade around Cuba to prevent any further missile shipments and demanded the removal of those already in place. Khrushchev recognized that if he refused to remove the missiles, the hostilities had the potential to escalate into nuclear conflict. Therefore, he backed down and dislodged the arsenal.[6]

Kennedy also used economic persuasion to ferret out communism from the Western Hemisphere. He implemented the Alliance for Progress program, which was based on the belief that U.S. aid and military counterinsurgency programs could promote reform and halt communist influence. Therefore, the United States poured money into Central American nations—even into nations that did not follow the social and economic changes that would promote democracy.

Despite U.S. economic and military tactics, the Castro government continued to survive. Not only had the military invasion failed, but it also served to strengthen nationalism inside the country. Moreover, the U.S. economic embargo was counterbalanced by Soviet financial assistance. Recognizing that the Castro government would survive the Gerald Ford administration took steps to improve relation with Cuba. However, cold war considerations quickly halted such efforts especially after Cuban troops were sent into Angola in order to protect the Marxist government from South African aggression.

The Carter administration in 1977 also initiated programs to improve relations with Cuba. Carter allowed U.S. tourists to visit Cuba, canceled intelligence overflights, arrived at a fishing agreement, and in October 1977 exchanged diplomatic interest sections with Cuba. Nonetheless, cold war considerations reverberated. When Cuban troops were sent to assist the Ethiopian government which was at war with the American-backed Somalians, the attempts to reconcile were stalled once again.[7]

Internally, the Castro government was not without its problems. Evidence of discontent occurred in 1980, when 129,000 dis-

# PHOTOGRAPHS
by
D. Michael Cheers
and
Courtesy Jesse Jackson Archives

U.S. Navy pilot Lt. Robert Goodman and Jackson at a press conference after Jackson negotiated his release from a military prison in Damascus, Syria, 1984.

Cuban President Fidel Castro and Jackson in Cuba, 1984. During that
visit Castro released nearly fifty political prisoners to Jackson.

Reverend Jackson meeting with El Salvadoran President José Napoleón
Duarte, 1984.

A meeting between Angolan President Jose Eduardo Dos Santos and Jackson in Angola, 1986.

Reverend Jackson and *Washington Post* reporter Dorothy Gillian consoling victims of the Armenian earthquake, 1989.

Reverend Jackson on a humanitarian mission in Armenia, after the devastating earthquake in 1989.

New York businessman and civil rights leader Percy Sutton, Zambian President Kenneth Kaunda and Jackson at the African American Summit in Lusaka, Zambia, 1989.

Reverend Jackson in the Soviet Union meeting with Soviet dissident Andre Sakarov in 1989.

Reverend Jackson leading released hostages out of Kuwait, August 1990.

A picture shown throughout the world of Jackson and a former American hostage of Iraq upon their return to the United States, 1990.

Reverend Jackson and South African President Nelson Mandela in New York during Mandela's first stop in the United States after he was released from a South African prison, June 1990.

Reverend Jackson and former United Nations Secretary General Boutros Boutros-Ghali at the Organization of African Unity Summit in Senegal, 1992.

South African President Nelson Mandela, Mashood Abiola, and Jackson at the Organization of African Unity Summit in Dakar, Senegal, June 1992. Abiola was the projected winner of Nigeria's 1993 presidential election, which was later nullified by the Nigerian military government.

Nigerian military President Ibrahim Babangida and Jackson at the Organization for African Unity Summit in Senegal, 1992.

Reverend Jackson meeting with General Raoul Cedras, leader of the military coup that ousted Haitian President Aristide from power, 1993.

Exiled Haitian President Jean Bertrand Aristide, TransAfrica President Randall Robinson, and Jackson at TransAfrica Headquarters in Washington, D.C., 1993.

Congressman Charles Rangel (D-NY) and Jackson in Guantanomo Bay, Cuba, to protest U.S. treatment of HIV-positive Haitian refugees, March 1993.

PLO Chairman Yasser Arafat and Jackson in an embrace in front of Jackson's Washington, D.C., residence, 1993.

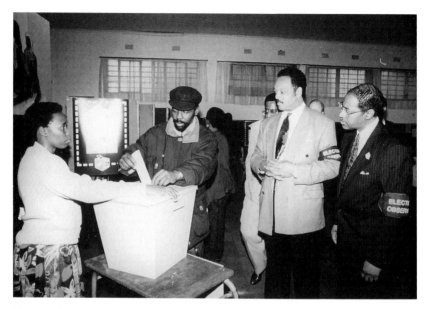

Reverend Jackson and Howard University Political Science Professor Ronald W. Walters as election observers for the first non-racial elections in South Africa. Jackson led the U.S. official observer team, April 1994.

Donald Payne (D-NJ), Namibian President Sam Nujoma, and Jackson at the Cradle of Civilization Symposium sponsored by the National Council of Negro Women in Cairo, Egypt, 1989. Payne was elected chairman of the Congressional Black Caucus in 1995.

gruntled Cubans immigrated to the United States on a boatlift to flee the Castro government. Approximately 2,700 of those who came were considered ineligible to remain in the United States because they admitted to having committed serious crimes in Cuba and in the United States or had suffered from severe mental disorders. Thus, along with the issues of democracy and Communist influence in the region, the U.S. aim of returning those undesirable Cubans became an additional source of tension between the two nations.[8]

## Nicaragua

Contemporary strife in Central America commenced during the 1960s when most nations in the region were attempting to modernize and laborers and peasants began to challenge the fact that their country's economic growth was beneficial to only a small elite of landowners, businessmen, and generals. In addition, the majority of the urban population and the peasantry remained poor while military regimes, or militarily supported regimes prevented social reform and political change. After continued attempts at peaceful change failed, the authoritarian governments in the region increasingly faced the opposition of armed, leftist forces.

The first of the revolutions came in 1979 when the Sandinistas of Nicaragua overthrew the Anastasio Somoza dictatorship. Initially, the Carter administration, which supported the overthrow of the Somoza regime,[9] attempted to promote good relations with Nicaragua through an aid program. But, as the revolution became more radical and because the Sandinistas accepted aid from Cuba and the Soviets, relations between the United States and Nicaragua deteriorated. The Reagan administration, convinced that the Sandinistas had ambitions beyond their frontiers, adopted a tougher policy. Among the punitive measures were limiting Nicaraguan access to international loans and the imposition of U.S. economic sanctions against the Sandinista regime. The Reagan administration's key instrument for challenging the Sandinista revolution was the Contras, a counterrevolutionary group founded, organized, and sponsored by the Central Intelligence Agency (CIA) in 1981 and based primarily in Honduras. The sponsorship of the Contras was a clear sign that the Reagan policy was moving far beyond the limited idea of containment and was aimed at overthrowing the Sandinista government.[10]

U.S. support for the Contras was problematic for several reasons. As expressed by Viron Vaky in "Positive Containment in Nicaragua," by establishing a "pole of opposition outside Nicaragua, it automatically weakened and delegitimated the opposition forces inside the country" and "much of the disaffection and opposition was drawn outward rather than allowed to ferment domestically." In addition, U.S. policies guaranteed that Nicaragua's domestic political system would become a matter of international conflict, thus enabling the Sandinista regime to rally nationalism on its behalf and to justify antidemocratic measures. Finally, it created an insurgency that logically ran counter to—and therefore preempted—alternatives for containing the Sandinista revolution.[11]

An impasse between the two nations was inevitable. The United States would not accept a plan that did not promise a change in regime, and the Sandinistas would not accept one that would. The Sandinistas would not agree to a settlement that did not require the United States to end support of the Contras and to cease in its efforts to overthrow them, and the United States would not accept one that did. Reagan's policies became so controversial in the United States and internationally that congressional action was used to thwart his plans. In one instance, Congress passed a bill, known as the Boland Amendment, to prohibit the use of U.S. funds to furnish support to any group or individual not part of a country's armed forces, for the purpose of overthrowing the government of Nicaragua or provoking a military exchange between Nicaragua and Honduras.[12]

Relations between the two nations continued to decline when, in June 1983, Nicaragua expelled three U.S. diplomats, claiming that they had been involved in a plot to assassinate a foreign minister and were instigating actions against their regime. In retaliation, the United States ordered the expulsion of twenty-one Nicaraguan diplomats attached to consular offices outside of Washington. Around that time, the Nicaraguans issued a six-point plan which stated, among other things, that they were prepared to negotiate under the auspices of the Contadora group, but, to no avail. The Reagan administration ignored the offer and intensified its pressure on Nicaragua by announcing that U.S. Navy warships were instructed to show themselves to Soviet vessels entering Central American waters who were suspected of carrying military equipment to the Sandinistas.[13] By the time Jackson had announced his intentions to travel to Nicaragua, relations between the two nations were at a stalemate.

## El Salvador

Between 1961 and 1975 the number of peasants in El Salvador increased from 11% to 40% of the rural population. "And while the manufacturing sector expanded 24% in the 1960s, manufacturing jobs only increased 6%."[14] Poverty and oppressive political conditions persuaded many El Salvadorans to join opposition groups to fight against the government and ruling class for change.

El Salvador's leftist guerrilla organizations began forming in 1969 but did not become a major force until the late 1970s when increased government repression under President Carlos Humbert Romero Mena drove the activists underground. The Sandinista victory in Nicaragua gave encouragement to the popular organizations in El Salvador, and by March 1980, four separate and, until then frequently antagonistic, guerrilla organizations formed the Unified Revolutionary Directorate (DRU) to coordinate their operations. In October 1980 the DRU became known as the Farabundo Marti Liberation Front (FMLN), and during the early 1980s its forces had doubled to an estimated 8,000 regular troops.[15]

The FMLN components identified themselves variously as Marxist, Marxist-Leninist, and of Marxist influence and were supported by Communists and pro-leftist regimes. From its inception, the FMLN called for a negotiated settlement to the conflict. Working alongside the FMLN was the Democratic Revolutionary Front (FDR), which was formed in April 1980 and represented the disenfranchised left-center political parties, trade unions, and several civic organizations.

A reformist military coup in 1979 led to a series of government changes and growing political unrest, which erupted into open war in 1980, pitting leftist guerilla groups against the army. The center-right Christian Democratic Party (PDC) leader José Napoleón Duarte formed the third junta government which lasted until March 28, 1982, when Major Roberto D'Aubuisson, leader of the country's most right-wing party, gained political power. U.S.-sponsored elections held in 1984, considered at that time the most expensive in Central American history, brought Duarte back into power. Asserting that the government of Duarte was moderate, the United States decided that Duarte had the best chance of carrying out domestic social reforms while preventing a radical left-wing assumption of power. The United States therefore backed him with military equipment and advisers. The Duarte government was also supported by the El Salvadoran military, the private sector, and key members of the right wing who all believed that they could control Duarte.[16]

Virtually as soon as the Reagan administration took office, it placed El Salvador in the midst of the superpower conflict. Ascribing to the "domino theory," Reagan was convinced that if El Salvador, as in the case of Nicaragua, fell to the left wing, the whole region would follow. Hence, any possibility of Soviet influence in El Salvador had to be frustrated.

For the U.S. public, Reagan's policies in Nicaragua and El Salvador brought back memories of Vietnam, and serious controversy developed over U.S. policy there. Congress refused to provide Reagan with the necessary funds to carry out the war against the Central American revolutionaries successfully by limiting military assistance to El Salvador and by regularly cutting the president's request for military aid. Congress also required the president to certify that progress was being made in reducing human rights abuses and strongly encouraged a negotiated settlement to the conflict.[17] Despite those actions, many congressional members believed that Reagan had some legitimate concerns and therefore, he was not forced to withdraw from the area altogether.

## Panama

At the beginning of the twentieth century, U.S. military leaders lobbied for the construction of an interoceanic canal across Panama. However, when the Columbian senate, which controlled Panama at that time, rejected a U.S. petition in 1903 to build a canal through Panama, the United States began to work toward achieving Panama's independence. Immediately thereafter, the first canal treaty between the United States and Panama was signed.

The 1903 treaty between the two countries granted to the U.S. control of a ten-mile-wide zone to build, run, and protect the canal.[18] Although the sovereignty of the territory remained vested with the Panamanian government, the result was a virtual colonial situation. The Canal Zone cut Panama in two and was run by the U.S. Army, and Panamanians in the zone were subject to U.S. law administered by U.S. courts. All business enterprises were operated by the United States, which also controlled large tracts of land and water needed by native Panamanians. The Panamanians, concluding that they had received rather scanty economic benefits from the canal, criticized U.S. control. Eventually, in 1936 the General Treaty of Friendship and Cooperation abrogated the U.S. right to unilateral intervention in Panama's political affairs.

Sincere negotiations for a change in treaty obligations began in the 1960s and continued throughout the Nixon-Ford administrations. Brigadier General Omar Torrijos became the country's supreme commander in a 1968 coup by the National Guard that ousted from office Dr. Arnulfo Arias Madrid, a member of the Panamanian oligarchy. Torrijos initiated a populist program that involved increased government services, support for agrarian cooperatives, and better government relations with the labor movement. Torrijos also pursued negotiations on the Panama Canal Treaty.

By the 1970s the canal's economic benefits to the United States declined, and due to the design of new U.S. military equipment that did not need to go through it, the canal's military value was reduced. Therefore, negotiations between Torrijos and Carter resulted in an agreement over the ownership and operation of the Panama Canal.[19] In April 1978 the Senate voted to turn the canal over to Panama by the year 2,000. In 1981, Torrijos was killed in a plane crash. Many suspected CIA involvement because of Torrijos' nationalist politics and his friendly relations with Cuba.[20]

At the time of Jackson's visit, Panama was the only Central American member of the Contadora group of four Latin American countries which sought a negotiated settlement to conflicts in the region.

## Contadora

By the end of 1982, several Latin American countries concerned about the prospect of a regional war and of direct U.S. intervention began to organize.[21] A regional peace effort was made by Mexico, Venezuela, Colombia, and Panama in 1981 and 1982. At the instigation of Mexico in 1983 these four countries formed the Contadora group, named after the Panamanian Island where each country's foreign minister met in early January. The official purpose of the meeting was to discuss the obstacles and dangers to regional peace and the Central American crisis. Contradicting the view of the Reagan administration, the document issued by the ministers who attended that meeting stated that the root causes of the region's instability lay not in East-West tensions but in specific problems endemic to each country. The group also reaffirmed the validity of the principles of nonintervention, self-determination, dialogue, and negotiations.[22]

The first summit meeting of the four presidents of the Contadora nations took place in Cancun, Mexico, in July 1983. The resulting Declaration of Cancun formalized the basic concerns of Contadora: control of the arms race; elimination of foreign advisors; creation of demilitarized zones; prohibition of political or military activities intended to destabilize another country; elimination of arms traffic; and prohibition of aggressive or political intervention in the internal affairs of another country.[23]

The Reagan administration believed that the Contadora group ignored U.S. security concerns and therefore did not provide any concrete support for the peace effort. Its disregard for the peace initiative was demonstrated blatantly when the United States invaded Grenada on October 25, 1983, while Contadora nations were meeting in Panama. Also during that time the United States continued sending military support to the area, financing the Contras, mining Nicaraguan harbors, and pursuing other destabilization activities.[24]

In addition to the foregoing, the administration put forth efforts to neutralize Contadora by convening other forums and devising alternative mechanisms to promote multilateral action. One act was the initiation of the National Bipartisan Commission on Central America (Kissinger Commission) created by Reagan in 1984. The Kissinger Report acknowledged the need for development to alleviate poverty, but also underlined the necessity for military aid to confront the Soviet-Cuban threat. Its recommendations were incorporated into Reagan's Central America Democracy, Peace, and Development Initiative Act, which called for over $8 billion in economic assistance to the region by the end of the decade. The act was never passed as a unit, but most of its main features were approved as part of foreign assistance appropriations. By the time Jackson left for his mission, the Reagan administration appeared to be encouraging increased military involvement in the region.


## Precursor to the Central American Mission—Mexico

At the initial stages of the 1984 Jackson presidential bid, a desk that was focused on the concerns of each major ethnic group in the United States was set up in the national Rainbow Coalition office. The "Hispanic desk" pinpointed issues and concerns germane to the Hispanic population and targeted organizations and actors in the Hispanic community who might be beneficial to the campaign. Initially "concentrating on Puerto Rican issues for the New York primary, the desk later expanded to focus on Mexican Americans and on issues related to South and Central America and the Caribbean."[25]

Approximately "9 million Hispanics—60 percent of the national total—live in the five southwestern states of Arizona, California, Colorado, New Mexico and Texas." Sixty-five percent of Hispanic registered voters are found in those states. At that time, Central Americans, people indigenous to the Caribbean Islands, and Mexicans constituted the largest and fastest growing source of immigration to the United States.[26]

As the 1984 presidential election campaign entered those states with large Hispanic populations, the need to address issues of relevance to them became critical. Notwithstanding issues such as unemployment, healthcare, and education, in order to ignite the Hispanic electorate, two major issues endemic to their community had to be addressed. These issues would eventually compel Jackson to embark upon a mission to Central America. The first issue was that of immigration and undocumented workers; the second was U.S. policy in Latin America.

The issues surrounding immigration and undocumented workers were very salient during that election year. At that time, there was intense debate in Congress on the Simpson-Mazzoli Bill, which had passed the House and Senate in June 1984 in slightly different forms. The bill sought to control illegal immigration by imposing sanctions on employers who hired undocumented workers. It also offered amnesty to most illegals already in the country, and expanded the agricultural guest-worker program, which allowed a specified number of foreigners to work with American agricultural producers, mainly as perishable crop laborers. A particular problem that Hispanics and others envisaged was that the bill had the potential to discriminate against anyone "Hispanic looking" or with Spanish-sounding surnames.

Beyond domestic concerns, the second issue was U.S. involvement in crisis areas in Central America. At that time, there was a military build-up throughout the region and less talk between rival or rebel groups. In addition, the United States was taking sides instead of pushing parties to compromise and negotiate. Alarmed peace activists believed that a regional war was imminent and that the Reagan administration appeared to be gearing up for a major armed confrontation in the region.[27] For those reasons it was essential for Jackson to address Central America.

However, there had been previous contact between Jackson and important actors in the region. For instance, Jacqueline Jackson, Jesse Jackson's wife, had visited Nicaragua with a women's peace group when Reverend Jackson was in Syria. In addition, the FMLN/FDR sent letters to Jackson requesting his intervention. Despite this previous contact, the first real thrust for a mission to Central America and Cuba did not occur until May 14 when Jackson ventured into Tijuana, Mexico.

The idea of a trip to Mexico was presented to Jackson by Armando Gutierrez, a University of Houston political science professor and senior policy advisor for the Jackson campaign, as an avenue for Jackson to fully appreciate the question of immigration. Gutierrez had surmised that it would be helpful to the campaign if Jackson gained an understanding of the Mexican perspective and the push-pull factors that caused Mexicans to immigrate to the United States. Jackson agreed to the idea, and thus a meeting was set up between Jackson and Jorge Bustamante, a professor at the University of Texas at Austin, who writes on the Mexican perspective of immigration. At that time, Bustamante was also conducting a large "border study" in Tijuana, Mexico, that was being funded by the Mexican government.

The day before the scheduled trip, Jackson was informed that the U.S. Secret Service agents assigned to him were not authorized to go across the border. Understanding that there was a security risk involved, Jackson was determined to enter into Mexico anyway. Before leaving, Jackson addressed the Mexican American Political Association in San Jose, California, and set forth his position on the question of immigration and the problems of Central America and Cuba. In Tijuana, Jackson gained insight into the immigration issue and expressed his views on the Mexican situation. On May 14, 1984, when Jackson addressed a group of students and scholars at the invitation of Bustamante, his message was that the Reagan administration's economic policies added to the flow of immigration by impeding economic recovery in Mexico and that the United States should look to internal factors, such as high corporate profits, for the underlying causes of the unemployment problems in the United States instead of blaming undocumented workers.[28] Since Mexico was a key player in Contadora and considering that Jackson had been well received in Tijuana, a larger trip to Mexico City was planned.

On May 28 Jackson traveled to Mexico City to discuss the issue of immigration, the international debt crisis and its effects on the Mexican economy, the peace efforts coming out of the region, and his campaign's position on Central America. During that endeavor, Jackson met with high level Mexican officials, including Mexico's most influential senators; Foreign Minister Bernardo Sepulveda, who was playing a critical role in the Contadora process; and various leading Latin American students and intellectuals. He also met with members of the Revolutionary Institutional party (PRI), who had governed the nation for six decades.

In a meeting set up by the president of the senate, Jackson held discussions with representatives of the Foreign Ministry and Senate Committees on Hemispheric Issues, where he called for a dialogue on normalizing of relations between the United States and Nicaragua and the United States and Cuba, and an end to the militarization of the region's problems. In addition, he stressed that U.S. foreign policy should be redirected toward promoting the Contadora nations' proposals for a negotiated solution to disputes.[29]

Overall, Jackson was briefed by approximately fifteen Mexican representatives on different policy issues. Because the president of Mexico did not want to appear to be meddling in a U.S. election, Jackson was not able to arrange a meeting with him. However, Jackson did meet with representatives of the FMLN to discuss their plight and their views on issues such as drugs, Cuba, and communism.

What emerged from the trip was first the realization that many people in Latin America were following the Jackson campaign with great interest. Second, Mexico and other Contadora nations saw the Reagan administration's policy in Central America as ill-conceived and dangerous. Third, Jackson was perceived as someone with the political clout and the will to curb Reagan's policies.[30] Upon his return Jackson declared,

> Everywhere we went we heard the same message. The United States must stop pouring military aid and troops into Central America—We must stop the arms race. We must put our resources into human development, into economic development that meets the needs of all our people. The war in Central America is not between the Soviet Union and the United States, but a struggle between the very wealthy and the desperately poor, a struggle for food and jobs and dignity against dictator and death squads. We must end the militarization of Central America.[31]

As a result of the discussions that ensued in Mexico, not only had Jackson gained a better understanding of the problems in the region, but the idea was developed of a full-scale trip into Central America.

## Impetus and Motivation for Diplomacy

The idea of a regional foray into Central America and the trip to Cuba was not fully supported by many of Jackson's advisers. In fact, there was intense pressure inside the campaign for Jackson to abandon the mission so that he could continue to compete for delegates and press for internal party justice by going to as many state party conventions as possible. There was also concern about the costs of such an excursion, both financial and political. Although the venture legally could not be paid for with campaign monies, the time spent in raising the money from private sources was seen as much too valuable to spend on such a nebulous proposition. However, Armando Gutierrez pointed to the potential benefits of such a trip, especially with regards to attracting Hispanic voters. Moreover, Gutierrez argued, Jackson would be handed an opportunity to distance himself from the other candidates and force their hand on Hispanic and Central American questions. In the end, as the problems in Central America escalated daily, Jackson became convinced of the necessity of the trip. He concluded that an effort to avoid war in Central America far outweighed winning a handful of delegates for his candidacy and that the trip would underscore what he said was a major difference between his politics and those of Walter Mondale and Senator Hart. Therefore, he was willing to meet and negotiate in settings that might not be politically popular. The decision was made to go to Central America during the latter half of June.

The mission was coined a "fact-finding venture." The primary goal was to examine regional instability and ways of alleviating the possibility of regional war. Other fact-finding objectives of the trip were to study peace options and war consequences; find ways to deal with the debt crisis and promote economic development throughout the region; discover ways to bring about a cease fire in the region; and investigate avenues that could lead to normal relations between the United States and Cuba.

The policy goals for the mission included persuading the United States to agree to diplomatic exchanges with all nations in the hemisphere; convincing the United States to recognize the FDR/FMLN as a legitimate political force, as Mexico and France had; procuring U.S. respect for the sovereignty of Nicaragua, by putting an end to financing the Contras; and influencing the United States to provide concrete evidence of its support for Contadora. Ultimately, Jackson hoped to promote dialogue and understanding between Central America and the United States, take the information resulting from the trip home to the U.S. citizenry, and solidify a clearly progressive policy stance on the issues.

Considering the critical problems in virtually every corner of the region, the question of which countries to visit was difficult to answer. Two major issues were at hand. First, there was concern that a broad section of countries be visited so that Jackson would not be perceived as biased toward those countries identified as leftist. Second, Jackson was adamant about stopping in those countries that would help achieve his objectives of halting a regional war and normalizing relations. Since Jackson had already visited one Contadora country, Mexico, he decided to visit another in hopes of convening all of the foreign ministers of the Contadora nations.

Although Jackson's first choice was Columbia, the issue of drugs and other security concerns connected with a visit to such a perilous area of the world were deterrents. In addition, since the Columbian officials were at a summit meeting elsewhere, it would have been difficult, if not impossible, for Jackson to meet with high-level officials. Consequently, Panama appeared to be a much better choice.

Panama was considered a viable option for several reasons. First, since Panama was friendly to the United States, a trip there would help thwart claims of bias. Panama was also playing a significant peacekeeping role behind the scenes in trying to negotiate a settlement in El Salvador, which could help solve regional conflicts. Jackson also had a good friend in Panama who could assist with logistics and help gain access to key people. In addition, geographically, Panama made more sense. However, because the country was controlled by military forces, left-wing groups in the United States criticized its selection.

El Salvador was selected because it was at the center of conflict in the region and the scene of the most intense fighting. Moreover, the FMLN/FDR had been in continual contact with Jackson and had sent several letters requesting a meeting. In those letters the group had expressed a willingness to consider new proposals for resolving the conflict, using Jackson as the conduit for such proposals. In addition, despite Jackson's outspoken criticism of U.S. military aid to the government, he was determined to meet with President Duarte. Jackson's intention was to get President Duarte's personal assessment of the conflict in his country, believing that U.S. aid only served to prolong the war. Despite the concerns regarding his safety from the right wing in El Salvador, Jackson believed that the possibility of bringing about a break in the conflict was vital, and he was therefore committed to stopping there.[32] Another issue was the imprisonment of Salvadoran labor leader Hector Bernabe Recinos who had been held without any formal charges for four years. During campaign stops in California, Jackson had invited Recinos' three sons to march with him against the Simpson-Mazzoli Bill in Los Angeles. He was thus committed to attempt to win their father's release.

At that time Nicaragua was viewed as the country most vulnerable to destabilization and intervention. Jackson was convinced that U.S. military intervention was possible if the conflict continued. In addition, since Nicaragua was at a critical crossroad in its development, Jackson argued that it needed time to concentrate on consolidating its revolution. For those reasons, a stop in Nicaragua was considered essential.

Equally, Jackson was committed to the idea of stopping in Cuba. His primary objective was to persuade the United States to establish diplomatic relations with the island nation. The issue of prisoners also factored into his decision to go to Cuba. Most likely, resulting from his successful mission in Damascus, after Jackson announced that he would be visiting that country, he began receiving numerous phone calls and letters from people who had relatives in Cuban prisons and from others wishing to secure the release of Cuban political prisoners.

Ultimately, Jackson sought to meet with the key players in the region. In order to appear that he was not involved in a propaganda ploy that would serve only to promote the ideas of leftist forces, Jackson thought it necessary to meet both with the government and with opposition forces.

The assignment of organizing the trip and managing logistics was conferred on Gutierrez, who negotiated Jackson's itinerary with the countries involved. He met with the Cuba Interest Section, the Nicaraguan Embassy, the ambassador from El Salvador, officials from the Panamanian Embassy, and others to work out the details of the trip. El Salvador was the only country that resisted the request for Jackson to meet with leftist forces. This perhaps was related to the fact that the government of El Salvador was being funded by the Reagan administration.

For logistical purposes, Gutierrez visited each country ahead of Jackson and then went back to escort Jackson on the trip. In the meantime, Cirillio McSween, a delegation member in charge of the committee to raise funds for the trip, was securing resources. The agenda called for a five-day tour, which included meetings with representatives of the Contadora group in Panama City and meetings with government officials and opposition forces from each targeted country.

The U.S. State Department was kept apprised of Jackson's plans both before he left and throughout the mission. On June 12, 1984, a meeting was held between members of Jackson's delegation and Undersecretary Michael Armacost. "While Armacost and his Central American experts were cordial and informative, they offered little hope that significant movement could be made in the general atmosphere and events in the Central American region."[33]

Before leaving for Panama City Jackson stopped in El Paso, Texas, to address a convention of the League of United Latin American Citizens (LULAC). He was the only candidate to accept the invitation. The LULAC endorsed the effort along with other prominent members of the Hispanic community.[34]

## The Delegation

As in the case of Syria, it was important for the delegation to be comprised of individuals who were supportive of the mission, had expertise in the area, and had either local or national standing. The delegation members consisted of individuals such as Armando Gutierrez; Gloria Gutierrez, an advisor who had worked with Jackson through Operation PUSH; Mervyn M. Dymally of California and member of the House of Representatives; Rev. Willie Barrow—Acting Director of Operation PUSH; John Bustamante, Jackson's attorney from Cleveland; Ed Coaxum, also an attorney who handled certain legal issues for the trip; Frank Watkins of the Jackson campaign; Jackson's sons, Jonathan, Jesse, Jr., and Yusef. A key delegation member was native Panamanian Cirillio McSween, PUSH Boardmember, businessperson, and fundraiser for the trip. McSween, also an olympic track hero, had guided Jackson on his first trip to Panama. He was also the treasurer of the SCLC under Martin Luther King, Jr., and an advocate of human rights. Media, security, Rainbow Coalition members and staff, and other supporters of the Jackson campaign also went on the mission.

## Diplomacy in Central America

Jackson's diplomatic mission in Central American began in Panama. He was already familiar with the sociopolitical and economic conditions in Panama because he had previously visited the country when there was concern that the United States and Panama would not come to an agreement on a Panama Canal Treaty. The purpose of that mission was to study the issues involved in a potential treaty. During that weeklong trip, Jackson visited Panamanian schools, churches, and other organizations of interest and met with General Omar Torrijos. Upon returning to the United States, Jackson testified before the appropriate congressional committees in support of U.S. ratification of the treaty.

The 1984 venture in Panama centered on the peacemaking role Panama was playing in El Salvador and in Central America. Jackson restated the purpose of the visit in a statement on June 23, 1984:

> We have returned to Panama for the first part of our four nation journey to Central America to urge that we stand together again for peace and justice. We have come to Panama because as one of the four Contadora nations, you are integral to peace in the region. We come to Panama to say that we support the Contadora process not just in work but in deed. We look forward to the meeting with your Mayor, with government officials, and with the people of Panama.[35]

Jackson met with Panamanian President Jorge Illueca, Foreign Minister Oyden Ortega Duran, and other influential and noted leaders. On June 24 he met with insurgents from El Salvador who set forth their position on the conflict and the basis for their participation in negotiations. Jackson's discussions with the FDR/FMLN resulted in an agreement made by the insurgents to enter into a dialogue without any preconditions for a political rather than a military solution; to discuss implementation of a cease fire; to meet in San Salvador to engage in talks; and to show a willingness to begin the process immediately.[36]

After two days in Panama, the delegation went to El Salvador where Jackson attempted to initiate a dialogue with the government that would lead to peace. He set forth the proposal that was given to him by the El Salvadoran insurgents in Panama. President Duarte, who had taken office only earlier that month, hosted a luncheon in honor of the Jackson delegation, and afterwards Jackson and Duarte held a private and detailed discussion on removing obstacles to negotiations and reconciling the warring parties. In the discussions, described as very "up-front" and open, Duarte's tone was conciliatory. He stated that one problem was his lack of control over all of the military, which was of major concern to peace activists in the United States. Eventually, the discussions deadlocked around the terms that would lead to a meeting between the government and dissidents. Duarte's position was that he would meet with the FMLN if they would lay down their arms, while the FMLN told Jackson that they would not lay down their arms unless the United States agreed to preserve the peace. The problem was that the United States would not agree to intervene. Hence, Jackson's efforts in El Salvador did not result in the desired peace discussions between the two parties, and by the time he left the country, there was no end to the conflict in sight. Although opposition forces and government officials held discussions late in 1984 partly as a result of Jackson's urging, the peace agreement between the parties did not occur until January 1992.

Regarding the issue of Hector Bernabe Recinos, Jackson was given the opportunity to meet with him and other prisoners. Understanding that there would be no release of prisoners from El Salvador, Jackson's aim was to verify that the political prisoners were being properly treated and to focus some attention on the fact that political prisoners did exist in El Salvador. A dialogue surrounding the issue of prisoners did ensue, but no particular policy change occurred.[37]

The diplomatic effort in Nicaragua centered on three major issues: the Contras, elections and U.S. policy toward Nicaragua. Meetings took place between Jackson and the executive members of the Sandinista government. The Sandinista position was that as long as the United States was funding the Contras, they considered themselves a government under siege and therefore could not hold elections. The United States, on the other hand, demanded free and open elections.

Jackson tried to persuade the Sandinistas to agree to certain conditions in order to induce the United States to halt its funding of the Contras. Ultimately, twelve points were worked out which the Sandinistas said they would support. The most important were

1. an agreement on behalf of the Sandinistas to call for a major summit between themselves and the leadership of the Catholic and Protestant churches;
2. an agreement to proceed with the November 4, 1984, elections;

3. affirmation of their commitment to the "no first strike" pledge regarding border conflicts;
4. affirmation of their position to dialogue with the United States;
5. affirmation of their support for the Contadora process;
6. an agreement to attend a summit meeting among the governments and legitimate political forces of Central American and the Caribbean;
7. and an agreement to extend the December 1, 1983, deadline to Amnesty for counter-revolutionaries.[38]

Within Nicaragua, the leadership of the Catholic church and the private business sector presented the most serious opposition to the Sandinista government. As time moved on, the private sector and the government eventually moved toward accommodation and understanding, but the Catholic church hierarchy moved into the forefront of domestic opposition and lent considerable moral support to the idea of overthrowing the Sandinista government.[39] Jackson surmised that if he could gain the support of the Catholic church, important discussions could ensue. However, when the Jackson delegation met with members of the Catholic clergy, who were very antagonistic toward the Sandinista government, they received criticisms of their own position and efforts.[40]

In order to facilitate any meaningful dialogue that could lead to a peace agreement, the opposition forces in Nicaragua had to be involved, and the most important force was the Contras. The Contras, however, refused to meet with Jackson, and it was impossible to communicate with them. Nonetheless, the Jackson delegation talked with other opposition forces, including members of the current government whose aim was to hold free and fair elections.

Before leaving for Nicaragua, the Jackson campaign had been contacted by Armstrong Wiggins, coordinator of the Central America and South American project, on the concerns of the Indians. The Miskito, Suma, and Ramo peoples had charged the Sandinista government with human rights violations. They asked Jackson to discuss their concerns with the Sandinistas. The latter's position was that the Indians were being used to oppose their government, however, they still affirmed their rights and were attempting to incorporate them into mainstream society.

While the Jackson delegation was engaged in difficult negotiations in Nicaragua, a controversy was developing in the United States that involved alleged inflammatory statements made by Minister Louis Farrakhan. According to news reports, Minister Farrakhan called Judaism a "gutter religion" and the creation of Israel an "outlaw act."[41] Hence, the U.S. press in Nicaragua diverted attention from Central American issues and interrogated Jackson about Farrakhan's statements. Jackson at first said he felt no obligation to respond. Finally, some of his advisers convinced him that he had to act for his own sake as well as for that of the Rainbow Coalition.

Jackson was troubled that the problems with Farrakhan were taking attention away from the serious issue of peace in Central America. Therefore, while in Havana, Jackson's Washington campaign office issued a statement in his name denouncing the Farrakhan remarks as "reprehensible and morally indefensible."[42]

The attempts to bring about change in the relationship between Cuba and the United States were even more difficult, considering that the U.S. government had broken off relations with Castro years before. In advance of the trip to Cuba, Jackson met with personnel in charge of Latin American affairs at the State Department to discuss U.S. policy and the response they anticipated from the Cubans. He also met with a counselor from the Cuban Interests Section in Washington. Jackson was informed by the State Department that the more immediate problem with Cuba involved the desire by the United States to repatriate undesirable Mariel boat people who had illegally come into the United States and who were then being detained in Atlanta. Previously, Castro had refused to discuss the issue, not wanting to give President Reagan any foreign policy successes before the election in November. Hence, the issue of immigration was again on the Jackson agenda.

As alluded to previously, after the public became aware of Jackson's intended mission to Cuba, the Rainbow Coalition office was inundated with calls from people asking Jackson to help their family members leave. The Rainbow Coalition's practice was to ask the family to send as much information as possible on the relative in Cuba, and that data was subsequently put on a list that would be taken to Havana and presented to Castro. Before the delegation left, there were an estimated one hundred names on the list.[43]

Jackson's rapport with President Castro and Castro's own ambition to normalize relations with the United States manifested in a congenial environment for negotiations. Castro personally greeted Jackson at the Havana airport and afforded him red-carpet treatment. Castro also showed Jackson the ultimate courtesy by going to church with him. Castro had not attended church in decades. In addition, the president and his senior staff devoted some eight hours of formal talks to Jackson and his aides. The Jackson delegation also met with clergy members and were allowed to visit prisons and the university.

During his talks with Jackson, Castro backed away from his stated intentions of waiting until after the November elections to begin talking about immigration matters with the United States. Castro also talked with Jackson about visas for Cubans and U.S. citizens who wanted to visit family members and about the possible repatriation of Cubans detained in the United States after the 1980 boatlift. Eventually, Jackson and Castro announced their agreement in ten areas at a news conference held in Cuba's Palace of the Revolution shortly after midnight. At their joint news conference, Jackson said Castro agreed to an immediate exchange of ambassadors with the United States if that was acceptable to the Reagan administration. That would, of course, require re-establishment of formal diplomatic relations that had been broken in 1961. Castro was noncommittal about Jackson's invitation to visit the United States, commenting, "Naturally, in the present situation of the U.S. and Cuba, this matter must be examined and mediated in a careful manner." Castro also made a public commitment to other proposals, such as working to reunify Cuban families in the United States and pursuing the Contadora process.[44]

With regard to the issue of prisoners, the list was presented by Jackson to Castro, who asked his foreign minister to give him a briefing on each one. An investigation was conducted on each prisoner and the circumstances surrounding his/her incarceration. As a result of the investigation, it was discovered that most of the U.S. citizens were incarcerated for drug-related crimes and had been in custody for approximately two years. Castro said that twenty-two prisoners accounted for all U.S. citizens in Cuban jails except those arrested and sentenced for hijacking airliners. He contended that eighteen had been tried and sentenced, and four were awaiting trial. Less than half of the twenty-two U.S. citizens faced charges in the United States.[45]

The Jackson delegation discovered that most of the alleged political prisoners, were considered terrorists in Cuba. For instance, the Rainbow office was contacted by the daughter of political prisoner Patricio M. Gutierrez. After investigation, it was found that Gutierrez was a leader of Alpha 66, located in Miami, Florida, considered by the Castro regime to be a terrorist organization. When Jackson learned of the background of such people, he did not pursue their release.

In a most dramatic gesture, Castro released to Jackson twenty-two U.S. prisoners and twenty-six Cuban political prisoners. Upon his return to the United States, Jackson tried to impress upon the U.S. people and government the significance of the prisoner release, saying, "Our concern is that given the cold war behavior and the hot war rhetoric, creating so much pain, loss of trade and loss of life, that the release of American citizens was a good faith gesture and should be responded to in kind."[46]

Jackson set forth the results of the Cuba mission in a statement on July 5, 1984. He asserted that while in Cuba he had challenged Castro to be precise and direct in sending positive signals to the United States to assist the effort toward normalizing ties. According to Jackson they achieved the release of nearly fifty prisoners; a public commitment to negotiate with the United States the return of the Mariel detainees imprisoned in the Atlanta Federal Penitentiary; a public commitment from Castro to reunify Cuban and Cuban American families; an expressed willingness by Castro to pursue the Contadora process of negotiations as opposed to further militarization of the region; and an expressed willingness to exchange ambassadors without preconditions.[47]

## Effectiveness of the Diplomatic Mission

The outcome of the diplomatic mission to Central America and Cuba and the causes of the successes and failures were varied and endemic to the political situation in each country and its relationship to the United States. And, unlike the Syria mission, which had an easily identifiable goal of rescuing Lt. Robert Goodman, measuring effectiveness is more difficult. The fact-finding goals, which were to examine regional instability, required having access to the leadership in each country visited. That goal was easily accomplished considering that Armando Gutierrez and other Rainbow Coalition supporters made the necessary arrangements before the mission.

The policy goals, in contrast, were more difficult to achieve. The determination of policy effectiveness considers two issues: having input into the process and persuading the United States to alter its policies. The fact-finding mission in Panama resulted in a clearer understanding of the problems in the region and the role that Central American nations were attempting to play in their resolution. With regard to El Salvador, Jackson's delivering of messages from the FMLN/FDR and other opposition forces assisted in laying the groundwork for negotiations and was also critical in establishing communication between the government and opposition forces. However, Jackson was not able to persuade the United States to recognize FDR/FMLN as a legitimate political force. Concerning Nicaragua, Jackson was able to persuade Ortega to moderate his views toward his country's religious establishment[48] and was able to set forth the Sandinista view on elections. Moreover, the discussions Jackson had upon his return from El Salvador and Nicaragua played a role in educating the U.S. public, so the United States could not just give blanket support to the El Salvadoran government and the Contras.[49] In Cuba, forty-eight prisoners were released, and Castro moderated his views on the issues surrounding immigration. He also expressed a willingness to exchange ambassadors and actively work toward peace in the region. In contrast the United States reiterated its refusal to recognize the legitimacy of the Castro government.

As a matter of fact, the Reagan administration was very upset by Jackson's diplomatic foray into Central America and thus refused seriously to consider any change in policy. For instance, in the case of Nicaragua and El Salvador, Jackson was not able to break the deadlock on negotiations, considering that both the Sandinistas and FMLN requested U.S. action. The Sandinistas asked that the United States cease providing aid to the Contras, which the United States would not agree to, and the FDR/FMLN required U.S. peacekeeping in order to lay down their arms. Nevertheless, Jackson did succeed in opening another door for diplomatic negotiations which the Reagan administration could have utilized.

With regard to Cuba, Secretary of State George Schultz rebutted Jackson's remarks that were critical of U.S. policy, and instead of congratulating him for a job well done, denounced Castro's release of the prisoners as a "propaganda ploy." Moreover, despite the important signals that came from the Cubans, U.S. government officials suggested that there would be no significant changes in U.S. policy.[50] Asked about Jackson's proposal for normal diplomatic relations and about his invitation to Castro to visit the United States, White House spokesman Larry Speakes said, "We'd like to see some concrete examples of a change in behavior on the part of the Cubans before entertaining such proposals."[51] In addition, Speakes suggested that Castro "stop exporting revolution" and added that Cuba "has served as a surrogate for the Soviet Union and Central America, Africa and other places."[52]

Notwithstanding its negative response to the mission, the Reagan administration sent a communique to Cuba, and an agreement was reached at the end of the year on the return of the 2,700 Cubans who came to the United States on the Mariel boatlift. For the United States, this meant removing impediments to the normal processing of visas for Cuban applicants as had been the case in Havana prior to 1980. Despite this concession by Castro, the White House still maintained that the agreements on the boatlift issue would not lend itself to any change in U.S. policy toward Cuba.[53]

Other efforts were made to follow up on Jackson's mission. Responding to national and international pressure, President Duarte announced the first peace talks with the FDR/FMLN in late 1984. The Duarte government offered a general amnesty, guaranteed political participation, and supported measures to guarantee the return of guerrillas and other displaced people to their homes and jobs. The problem for the opposition forces was that Duarte refused to make any constitutional changes, and considering the FDR/FMLN agenda, the talks were doomed for failure. The FDR/FMLN demanded, among other things, a direct sharing of power in a transitional government that would include other political parties, representative political groups, and the private-enterprise sectors not tied to the oligarchy; the "purification" of the army to include soldiers from the rebel army and the present army; a mixed economy with reforms; full rights of trade-union organization and assembly, a respect for human rights, and freedom of expression and movement.[54] Many of these requisites required constitutional changes and government restructuring. Despite the fact that the first round of talks which ensued after Jackson's mission did not lead to any concrete success, this scenario demonstrates that if the political will is present, a citizen diplomat can assist in persuading parties to engage in dialogue and can assist in the resolution of dangerous conflicts.

The motive for the governments and opposition forces to meet with and grant concessions to Jackson were varied, but similar. The governments and opposition forces were interested in finding solutions to the problems that plagued the region. Panama was intricately involved in the Contadora process and was keenly interested in finding an avenue for peace. The key players in the Nicaraguan, El Salvadoran, and Cuban conflicts were interested in normalizing relations with the United States and considered the Jackson campaign, as a progressive force, their voice in the United States. Religion also gave Jackson an additional resource with which to "blunt the edge of both the political objectives of the U.S. State Department and those of the leaders of some countries he visited."[55]

As in the case of Syria, Jackson's efforts in Central America were severely criticized. It was argued that he had presumed to negotiate a settlement in the region which was a clear violation of the Logan Act. He was also criticized for "acting" as president and therefore interfering with the constitutional rights of the president and Congress to conduct foreign policy. Other denunciations centered on the fact that Jackson had condemned President Reagan's policies abroad. Many of those critics charged that Jackson had collaborated with enemies of the United States and flattered their interests, which jeopardized those of his own government's. Still others chastised Jackson's trip to Cuba as a propaganda ploy for Castro. They charged that Jackson had been used by the Cuban leader and further accused him of collaborating with the enemies of democracy.

Notwithstanding those criticisms, Jackson's trip won him considerable public acclaim from many sectors of U.S. society. African Americans saw Jackson's success as indicative of what they could and would do if they held important foreign policy-making positions. Many white Americans, who had no desire to see Jackson achieve his political objectives, "began to flood the campaign with requests for his assistance in releasing prisoners involved in every conceivable situation, including Sakharov in the Soviet Union, Americans held captive in Lebanon, other Latin American prisoners, and, of course, some prisoners in the U.S."[56] The trip had been watched closely by U.S. Hispanics, and upon their return, the Jackson delegation received an enthusiastic reaction from the Hispanic community. Jackson was praised for his boldness of vision, his peace stance, and his sensitivity to Hispanic concerns. In particular, his willingness to meet with Latin American leaders on their own terms struck a resonant chord.[57] It is estimated that Jackson received 30 percent of the Hispanic vote, excluding that of the Cuban American community who maintained its anti-Castro position.[58]

As with the Syria mission, the Democratic candidates were forced to respond. Walter Mondale said he would oppose exchanging ambassadors with Cuba "until Cuba changes some of its policies." However, he embraced the prisoner release saying, "As we well know, the prisons in Cuba are reportedly often very inhumane and if Reverend Jackson has been able to gain the release of prisoners on purely humanitarian grounds, well then, that's good."[59]

Unlike the accolades Jackson received at his homecoming after the Syria trip, President Reagan suggested that this trip might have violated the Logan Act. Jackson responded to the administration's criticisms in a statement July 5, 1984:

> Monday, President Reagan suggested that we violated the Logan Act during our recent trip to Cuba. There was the implication that our pursuit of a higher moral law was a violation of statutory law. This, we believe, is a political ploy by the White House to divert attention from its no-talk policy . . . a policy which has led to foreign policy failures and the tragic loss of lives in Grenada, Lebanon, and Central America. We are not attempting to usurp the authority of the President but we want to point out the danger of not negotiating with an adversary 90 miles from our border— the danger of not talking to Syria, of waiting until an election year to attempt to talk to the Russians.[60]

In the end, the Reagan administration could not ignore Jackson's efforts in Cuba and followed up by sending the aforementioned communique to Cuba, sending back the Mariel boatlift Cubans and processing the released prisoners.

## U.S. Official Involvement and Citizen Diplomacy

The Jackson campaign sought to influence U.S. foreign policy in Central America by embarking upon its own mission of peace. With the understanding that the Reagan administration disapproved of the mission, Jackson ventured into Central America and Cuba anyway. Although in this instance, the outcome of Jackson's diplomatic mission was very different from that of Syria, it held similar implications for citizen participation in U.S foreign policy processes. The U.S. government provided logistical support to the delegation before, during, and after the mission. It also aided in Jackson's accomplishments by processing the prisoners whose release was a direct result of the mission.

Specifically regarding U.S. official participation in the mission, at every country stop the delegation was met by U.S. officials and embassy personnel. The standard procedure was for embassy personnel to meet the Jackson group at the airport and then take them to meet the ambassador at the U.S. compound. This protocol was requested and received by Jackson. In addition, despite the fact that travel to Cuba was prohibited (with the exception of journalists, government officials, and emigre Cubans who were attempting to see their families), the U.S. Treasury Department briefed the Jackson delegation on protocol and the illegality of certain acts.[61]

Upon his return to the United States, Jackson debriefed with the State Department. He gave a report on his experiences and the Hispanic community's perspective on the conflict in the region. He also discussed the conditions under which the relationship between the United States and Central American countries could be changed. The release of Cuban prisoners was the focal point of the discussions.

Overall, Jackson's diplomacy in Central America and Cuba emerged out of a desire of his constituency to influence U.S. decisions there. The belief that their policy positions were being ignored was the primary impetus for the venture. U.S. assistance to the endeavor demonstrated a recognition of the legitimacy of private citizen activity in the international arena and citizen diplomacy.

## Summary

The purpose of Jackson's mission to Central America and Cuba was to reduce the chances for a regional war. The objectives were to reduce tensions between the warring parties in the region and to change U.S. policy toward specific nations and insurgents. Hispanic-Americans who supported the Jackson campaign played a vital role in the diplomatic effort. They assisted in the formulation of its goals and objectives and provided logistical support and access to Hispanic leadership. Notwithstanding the Cuban American community, one outcome of the mission was that Jackson made significant inroads into the Hispanic American community. In addition to the electoral benefit, Jackson assisted in releasing the gridlock on communications between parties and was able to persuade the leaders of governments and insurgency groups to agree to some of his proposals. The lack of success in several cases was predicated on the fact that to resolve policy conflicts, the U.S. government had to support Jackson's position and also had to make some concessions to move toward peace. But the Reagan administration refused to support Jackson's recommendations, and therefore little was done by the U.S. government to follow up on the unlocked doors. However, despite the Reagan administration's refusal to concede to Jackson's proposals the venture into Central America and Cuba was logistically supported by U.S. and foreign officials. Hence, increased validity was bestowed to citizen diplomacy as an alternate approach for private citizen participation in the international arena.

# 7

# Southern Africa

Of the various foreign policy issues, Africa and particularly Southern Africa were of foremost concern to the Jackson campaign in 1984. Accordingly, with the assistance of interest groups such as TransAfrica and the Congressional Black Caucus, Jackson was successful in making it his most vocal initiative. As a matter of fact, for most Americans, the essence of Jackson's foreign policies was illuminated by his efforts surrounding Southern Africa and accentuated the reality that his ideas were fundamentally antithetical to the positions set forth by the Reagan administration.

The mission to Southern Africa was conceived not only to underscore the fallacies of Reagan's policies and interest others in the issue of the Republic of South Africa's regional aggression, but it was also undertaken to highlight the necessity of passing the then upcoming comprehensive sanctions bill, introduced in the House by Congressman Ronald Dellums (D-CA). Another objective of the mission was to forge closer ties between Africans and African Americans politically, socially, and economically. And finally, the mission was undertaken to grant Jackson the opportunity to preserve in the minds of U.S. voters his prowess on international issues for the impending 1988 presidential election campaign.

Jesse Jackson's diplomatic initiative in Southern Africa in 1986 is the focus of this chapter. This case is similar to his efforts in Central America and Cuba on the basis that the effort was regional and involved negotiations with several leaders on various issues. However, unlike the Central America and Cuba excursions, a consensus existed among key actors on the nature of the problems in the southern region of Africa and the necessary changes that would lead to a cessation of strife and war. In addition, unlike Central America, where the nations not only were wracked with civil war, but also were at war with each other, the Frontline States were in agreement about who the aggressors and their benefactors were. Hence, in terms of brokering agreements, there were only two major powers to contend with; South Africa and the United States.

In order to adequately access Jackson's mission to Southern Africa it is necessary to provide background information on South Africa, its apartheid system, and its destabilization policy and activity. In addition, a brief historical discussion of the Frontline States and U.S. policy toward South Africa will be provided in order to highlight the issues that compelled Jackson to visit the region, and why he chose to at that particular time. An examination of the U.S. Congress' role is also relevant considering that one of Jackson's aims was to influence its actions on the Dellums Bill. And, as in the earlier chapters, the outcome of the mission and its relationship to democratic participation in U.S. foreign policy will be discussed.

## South Africa, Apartheid, and Destabilization

In 1948, apartheid, an Afrikaans word meaning "separateness," was introduced as government policy. Prior to that time, the country's racial segregation practices were generally based on custom and tradition rather than on any explicit ideological notions. However, in 1948, after the Afrikaner–National Party came to power on a platform promising to systemize and solidify existing segregation into a policy of separate development along ethnic and racial lines, the country was divided into separate homelands for each legally designated black ethnic group. "Under this policy, all black Africans (representing over 74 percent of the population) were permanently denied political and residential rights in 'white' areas comprising some 87% of the land area, including some of the areas richest in natural resources and developed infrastructure."[1] The system of apartheid, commonly regarded as forced racial separation, formed the basis for the political, economic, and social dominance of South Africa by the white minority until 1990.

The greatest opponent of apartheid and the most widely respected organization of blacks within South Africa is the African National Congress (ANC). Formed in 1912, the ANC had pursued majority rule non-violently for almost half a century. Their nonviolent posture changed, however, after the 1960 police shooting of protesters in the black township of Sharpville who were demonstrating against laws that required black South Africans to carry passbooks. In 1961, after the government banned the ANC, the organization took up sabotage and guerrilla warfare as its response. Soon thereafter, the ANC moved its base of operations to Lusaka, Zambia.

The Afrikaner regime was not the only white minority government to control the fate of the majority black population in the region. The Germans controlled southwest Africa, later to be called Namibia, while the British held claim to Botswana, Lesotho, Rhodesia, and Swaziland. In addition, the Portuguese controlled Angola, Guinea Bissau, and Mozambique. Eventually the British and the Germans transferred their territory to the local whites in the region. Thus the Afrikaners gained control of Botswana, Lesotho, and Swaziland while Rhodesia and southwest Africa came under the jurisdiction of the local whites in those territories. Inevitably, the Portuguese, white Rhodesians, and Afrikaners formed a triple alliance in their quest to maintain dominance over the region.

However, in April 1974 a military coup d' etat in Portugal toppled not only the Marcello Caetano dictatorship in Lisbon, but also the political status quo in Southern Africa. The coup signaled the collapse of the triple alliance of Rhodesia, Portugal, and South Africa to oppress blacks and therefore made South Africa vulnerable to attack. For blacks in the region, the coup d' etat provided the best opportunity to prevail in their national liberation struggles. The following year, Mozambique and Angola won their independence, while Zimbabwe (formally Rhodesia) was victorious in 1980.

During the liberation wars, the Portuguese and the Rhodesians co-opted many desperate people of the region to use as surrogates against the black nationalist parties. In Angola, there were three such groups, including: the National Union for the Total Independence of Angola (UNITA). In Mozambique, the Mozambique National Resistance (MNR or RENAMO) was created by the Rhodesian Central Intelligence Organization (CIO) in 1976 to fight against the black government. After the fall of the Portuguese empire and then Rhodesia, both the MNR and UNITA were inherited by South Africa and used as proxies.[2]

After the former colonies gained independence, the South Africa government considered itself under siege, and in order to maintain its regional hegemony it initiated a campaign to destabilize its neighboring states. Introduced first by Prime Minister B. J. Vorster, a scheme was outlined in a 1977 "Defence White Paper" to foster Pretoria's hegemony. The "Total Strategy" argued that white South Africa was threatened by a total onslaught from beyond its borders, and that in order to survive it had to respond with a total national strategy.[3] After P. W. Botha became Prime Minister in 1978, he adopted Total Strategy as official policy. The foremost objectives were to reassert economic and political hegemony over the region and to create so much chaos in the neighboring states that they would not have the opportunity to focus on apartheid inside South Africa. Other objectives of this policy were to prevent the neighboring states from harboring ANC members and members of the South West African People's Organization (SWAPO), the major opponent to South African occupation of Namibia; use the Frontline States as hostages to head off international sanctions; maintain the neighboring states as export markets for South African goods; and maintain poverty in those states to prove that black majority rule does not work.[4]

Through tactical programs, assassination, economic leverage, military invasion, and economic and military support for its proxies, South Africa desolated the infrastructure and economies of its neighbors. Moreover until March 1990, South Africa defied the United Nations, the International Court of Justice, the Organization of African Unity, and world opinion in its continued illegal occupation of Namibia. As outlined by Joseph Hanlon, between 1980 and 1986, in the eight black-ruled states of the region, South Africa:

- invaded three capitols (Lesotho, Botswana, Mozambique) and four other countries (Angola, Swaziland, Zimbabwe, and Zambia);
- tried to assassinate two prime ministers (Lesotho and Zimbabwe);
- backed dissident groups that brought chaos to two counties (Angola and Mozambique) and less serious disorder to two others (Lesotho and Zimbabwe);
- disrupted oil supplies of six countries (Angola, Botswana, Lesotho, Malawi, Mozambique, and Zimbabwe); and
- attacked the railways providing normal import and export routes of seven countries.[5]

By 1984, more than 100,000 people had been killed, most of them starved to death in Mozambique because South Africa-backed rebel activity prevented drought relief. More than 1 million were displaced—the largest group was Angolans fleeing various invasions. From 1980 through 1985 South Africa's destabilization policies cost their neighboring states at least 10 billion dollars.[6] (A breakdown of the cost of destabilization for five years after the founding of SADCC can be found in table 7.1).

South Africa's economic might and close proximity to the Frontline States helped to make its destabilization program effective. For instance, South Africa dominated the economies of three of the smallest states: Botswana, Lesotho, and Swaziland. It was the main trading partner for Zimbabwe and Malawi and the main source of imports for Zambia. It also provided an additional source of income to several Frontline States by employing migrant workers to work in South African mines.

**Table 7.1**   Cost of Destabilization for 5 years (Since the Founding of SADCC in 1980)*

| | |
|---|---|
| Direct war damage | 1,610† |
| Extra defence expenditure | 3,060 |
| Higher transport and energy costs | 970 |
| Lost exports and tourism | 230 |
| Smuggling | 190 |
| Refugees | 660 |
| Reduced production | 800 |
| Lost economic growth | 2,000 |
| Boycotts and embargos | 260 |
| Trading arrangements | 340 |
| TOTAL | 10,120 |

†Millions of U.S. dollars

*Memorandum presented by SADCC to the 1985 Summit of the Organization of African Unity. Taken from Joseph Hanlon, *Beggar Your Neighbors: Apartheid Power in Southern Africa,* Appendix 1 (Bloomington: Indiana University Press, 1986).

## Frontline States and the Southern Africa Development Coordinating Conference (SADCC)

Beginning in the 1960s, regular meetings were held among the eastern and central African states of Botswana, Tanzania, Uganda, Zambia, and Zaire. These meetings gave birth to what later became known as the Frontline States—Botswana, Tanzania, and Zambia in 1974, and joined later by Mozambique in 1975 and Angola in 1976. These states acted as a caucus on southern African affairs.[7] Because their major objective was to liberate the black nations in Southern Africa, the Frontline States provided assistance to guerrilla armies in the colonies of the region. The association and activities of the Frontline States during the liberation wars led to the formation of SADCC.

SADCC was constituted formally in Lusaka, Zambia, at the April 1, 1980, summit meeting of its nine members. The Frontline States of Angola, Botswana, Mozambique, Tanzania, Zambia, and Zimbabwe all joined SADCC along with Lesotho, Malawi, and Swaziland. Its four goals were: (1) a reduction of external dependence, especially dependence on the Republic of South Africa; (2) the creation of operational and equitable regional integration; (3) mobilization of domestic and regional resources to carry out national, interstate, and regional policies to reduce dependence and to build regional coordination; and (4) joint action to secure international understanding and practical support for the SADCC strategy.[8] SADCC took the lead in fighting the apartheid regime's destabilization policies and articulating the concerns of blacks in the region. SADCC continues to be the organization around which many of the Frontline States' activities are structured.

## U.S. Policy toward South Africa and the Region

Robert Price suggests that between 1960 and the election of Ronald Reagan to the presidency, the United States had adopted at least four distinct policy postures toward South Africa.[9] The first, existing from the end of World War II until 1975, was a policy of benign neglect. During this period, each presidential administration, while expressing general abhorrence of apartheid and colonialism, maintained good relations with the minority-controlled regimes in Southern Africa. Their disapproval was demonstrated in main by supporting various limited actions of the UN. However, the increased salience of access to minerals, the collapse of the old political order in the region, and the direct involvement of Cubans and the Soviet Union in Angola negated the policy of benign neglect and led to the containment policies under Nixon and Kissinger from 1973 through 1976. As part of its efforts to deal with the changing situation in Southern Africa, the United States advocated replacing the white regimes with moderate black ones and attempted to negotiate settlements that would end armed confrontation and achieve independence for Zimbabwe and Namibia.

The Carter administration which broke with the role of sympathizing with Pretoria, focused on human rights issues and sought to identify the United States more strongly with the forces for change. In particular, the United States began to play a role in defining the terms of an acceptable settlement in Rhodesia and Namibia; repeated calls for full participation of all of South Africa's citizens; invited the Frontline States to play a more active and initiating role with respect to the settlement of regional conflicts; and expanded U.S. contacts with black leaders inside South Africa. Carter also advocated a tightening up on "gray-area" exports to the South African police and military, especially after the death of Black Consciousness leader Steve Biko, who died while in police detention. However, cold war considerations caused Carter to moderate many of his policies, and ultimately very little substantial change occurred.

In November 1980 when Ronald Reagan was elected president, anticommunism was the principle theme in formulating U.S. foreign policy. And, because the Reagan administration defined Southern Africa as a region in which the activity of the Soviet Union threatened vital interests, it responded to South African internal and regional aggression with a policy of "Constructive Engagement." Hence, the Reagan administration toned down its criticisms of South Africa, relaxed export restrictions, received South African military officials, moved toward normalizing nuclear cooperative relations, facilitated the delay of Namibia's independence, allowed the opening of new South African consulates in the United States, and publicly claimed South Africa to be a reliable friend and ally.[10] Chester Crocker was named Assistant Secretary of State for African Affairs, and he largely determined U.S. policy in the region.

Critics of constructive engagement asserted that as a result of the United States' relaxed dealings with Pretoria, it had become overconfident and had no incentive to change. This assessment appeared to be correct, considering that during Reagan's first term, Pretoria strengthened apartheid at home and stepped up its destabilization activities. For instance, the South African military raided buildings in Mozambique and Lesotho which housed members of the ANC; increased economic and military pressure on Zimbabwe; and escalated the guerilla war against the Mozambican government by South African-backed RENAMO.[11]

Two critical issues can be used to exemplify the differences between the Jackson and Reagan approaches to Southern Africa. The first was Pretoria's continued illegal occupation of Namibia and second, the U.S. refusal to recognize Angola. Namibia was important to South Africa because of its location; it borders South Africa from the north, and the South African government, fearful of a government that it could not control that close to its borders, prevented its independence. In addition the most popular black liberation organization, SWAPO, was backed militarily and financially by the Soviet Union. With regard to the second issue, the stated obstacle to the establishment of U.S.-Angolan diplomatic ties was the presence of 30,000 Cuban troops in Angola and Angola's close ties with the Soviet Union. The Cuban troops entered Angola in 1975 to assist the Popular Movement for the Liberation of Angola (MPLA) in its struggle for victory against two western-supported armies. Angolan authorities contended that the Cubans were needed because of frequent South African attacks and equally needed to help combat UNITA rebels. The South African government's aim was the removal of the Cuban troops in order to enhance its sense of security, to weaken the MPLA, and to strengthen UNITA—the organization they wanted to take over Angola's government.

Whereas Jackson called for the immediate independence of Namibia and U.S. recognition of Angola, the Reagan administration introduced the concept of 'linkage'—that South Africa should withdraw from Namibia only when the Cuban troops withdrew from Angola. Moreover, in 1981 Reagan put forth a failed attempt to repeal the Clark Amendment, which barred U.S. support of UNITA. The measure was blocked by the House Foreign Affairs Committee and by the successful lobbying of U.S. companies doing business in Angola and Africa-related groups in Washington.

Because Reagan faced re-election in 1984, he aimed to show some foreign policy successes in the region. Thus in 1983, the Reagan administration began to put pressure on the apartheid regime. Suddenly, South Africa was at the negotiating table, and on February 16, 1984, signed the Lusaka agreement with Angola under which it promised to withdraw its troops. On March 16, South African President P. W. Botha and Mozambique President Samora Machel signed the Nkomati Accord on Nonaggression and Good Neighborliness. Certain measures in the Accord resulted in serious political costs to the Mozambique government, such as restricting the ANC to a small diplomatic office in Maputo. As a consequence, several hundred ANC members left Mozambique. These signings followed a referendum in which white voters in Pretoria agreed to establish Colored and Indian parliaments, hold talks with SWAPO in Lusaka, and improve relations with Zimbabwe. This period of detente was shortlived, however. Soon thereafter, Pretoria resumed its funding of UNITA and RENAMO in violation of the Lusaka agreement and the Nkomati Accords. Renewed pressures were also placed on Zimbabwe.[12]

As Reagan's second term began, it became increasingly difficult to pretend that U.S. engagement was constructive. Sustained rebellion in the black townships, beginning in late 1984 and continuing through 1986, mobilized anti-apartheid activists abroad. In November 1984, Randall Robinson of TransAfrica, Dr. Mary Francis Berry of the U.S. Civil Rights Commission, and Delegate Walter Fauntroy of the District of Columbia set out to influence public opinion on South Africa by staging a sit-in at the South African Embassy in Washington, D.C. Their arrests marked the beginning of daily demonstrations at the embassy by the Free South Africa Movement (FSAM). The symbolic action, with arrests day after day for an entire year, sparked and sustained an upsurge of anti-apartheid demonstrations in dozens of cities and universities around the United States. These demonstrations symbolized the commitment of African American leadership to play a role in U.S. policy toward South Africa.[13] In addition to the foregoing, Jesse Jackson made South Africa a prominent issue during the 1984 presidential election campaign.

The sustained controversy compelled members of Congress to act. In 1983 sanctions, including a ban on new investments in South Africa, were attached to the Export Administration Act and passed in the House of Representatives. However, the Senate rejected the sanctions, which infuriated members of the Congressional Blacks Caucus (CBC) and Jesse Jackson.

Soon thereafter, Congressmen William Gray (D-PA) and Howard Wolpe (D-MI) introduced the Anti-Apartheid Act of 1985. The draft bill, among other things, barred new U.S. investment in South Africa. The Reagan administration waged a formidable battle against sanctions, and, despite the fact that African leaders endorsed the measures, argued that not only could South Africa withstand sanctions, but some of its negative effects could be passed on to black neighboring states. Moreover, the Reagan administration contended that the economic suffering of the Frontline States might increase as a result of South Africa's potential retaliatory countersanctions.[14] To head off Senate approval of the modified bill that had won overwhelming approval in the House of Representatives, Reagan issued an executive order which imposed limited sanctions. Although it incorporated items, such as a ban on the import of Krugerrands and on new loans to the South African government, it was subject to discretionary reversal by the U.S. president. In addition, it omitted the threat of future sanctions in case of South African intransigence.[15] Reagan's true perspective came forward in November 1985 when the United States and Britain vetoed the mandatory UN sanctions proposed against South Africa for its continued occupation of Namibia.

Repression in South Africa continued, and in 1985 South African attacks on Botswana, Zimbabwe, and Zambia led to increased pressure for change. In February 1985, Congressman Ronald Dellums of California introduced the bill that mandated comprehensive sanctions. On June 18, 1986 the Dellums measure passed by an overwhelming voice vote in the United States House of Representatives.

## Precursor to the Southern Africa Mission

From its outset, Jackson strongly opposed Reagan's policy of constructive engagement toward South Africa, a position which he believed made the United States an active collaborator in maintaining the immoral apartheid system. He had previously met with Oliver Tambo of the ANC, not only to learn firsthand about apartheid, but also to pledge his support and that of African Americans to the struggle to end it. Jackson was also a supporter of Reverend Leon

Sullivan's 'principles' which were designed to force U.S. corporations in South Africa to ameliorate the condition of black workers.[16]

Jackson maintained that U.S. policy was riddled with contradictions; sanctions were right for Nicaragua and Poland, but not for South Africa. Moreover, the MPLA should be pressed to include UNITA in the Angolan government, but no pressure should be put on South Africa to include the ANC in the Pretoria government. He also believed that it made no sense to apply sanctions against South Africa and at the same time cut aid to Zimbabwe and support UNITA rebels in Angola, which strengthened South Africa. In Jackson's view, U.S. policy had actually exacerbated problems in the region by encouraging and indulging the white regime's divide-and-rule tactics and leading that regime, its victims, and the international community to believe that whatever the rhetoric emanating from Washington, the U.S. supported the Pretoria government.

With a base of support for his Africa policies coming overwhelmingly from his African American constituency, Jackson was determined to find a solution to apartheid in South Africa and to end South African regional aggression. During the 1984 presidential election campaign, Jackson advocated a strategy that would couple sanctions with a comprehensive program of reconstruction in the neighboring states to strengthen them against South African retaliation and reduce their economic dependence on South Africa. Nevertheless, the Reagan administration retained its policy of constructive engagement.

## Impetus and Motivation for Diplomacy

The mission was precipitated by the ongoing crisis in South Africa and in the region. In 1985, Pretoria continued to disregard the rights of the black majority in the region by intensifying its repressive efforts to end unrest and refusing to negotiate unconditionally with credible black leaders. As Pretoria increased its attacks upon its neighbors, the Frontline States became more desperate to promote their cause internationally.

The opportunity presented itself in 1986 at the UN International Seminar for Sanctions against South Africa held in Paris, where African American anti-apartheid activists (such as Ronald Walters, a Howard University Political Science professor invited to testify on military and security issues, and Harry Belafonte, invited to give a keynote address) were asked to participate. Jesse Jackson, who had been invited as a major speaker, held a meeting with all the foreign ministers of African states in attendance. It was during that meeting that the foreign ministers extended an invitation to Jackson to visit Africa. The ministers believed that Jackson could popularize the idea of sanctions and bring attention to the problems in the region.[17] The proposed journey was disclosed in the United States at a time when TransAfrica and other African American leaders condemned the slow pace of the U.S. Senate in voting for sanctions against South Africa.

The overriding purpose of the mission was to help forge a comprehensive and humane U.S. policy for the Southern African region. The goals centered on fact finding and seeking information that could persuade the United States and South Africa to modify their policies. The fact-finding goals were to ascertain the impact of the apartheid system and South African destabilization activities on its neighbors; determine the potential impact of the proposed U.S. sanctions against South Africa; determine the minimum conditions and parameters under which a meaningful dialogue between the South African regime and the black majority could be conducted; inquire as to how the international community could best assist in achieving racial and social justice in South Africa; share this information with the U.S. public and government officials; make a moral appeal that would focus world attention on the views of the Frontline States leaders—to give them a forum to state what *they* believe. Policy goals were to forge closer relationships between Africans and African Americans; build momentum for the passage of the 1986-Sanctions Bill; help improve relations between the United States and the Frontline states; persuade the United States to recognize Angola (only the United States and South Africa refused to recognize the legitimacy of Angola); and put pressure on the United States to reverse its policy of supporting UNITA.[18] Other objectives were to meet with government officials, the academic community, and independent organizations and individuals to address and exchange constructive dialogue regarding the aforementioned concerns.

Specifically for Jackson, the tour also served as an early start to another bid for the Democratic presidential nomination. Traveling to the region would provide Jackson the chance to gain firsthand knowledge of Pretoria's geo-economic grip on the area and would place the Rainbow Coalition firmly astride the apartheid issue. With the insights he would gain and the public endorsement of all the black leaders in the region, Jackson would be able to significantly contribute to and shape the debate on apartheid.

## The Delegation

The delegation consisted of individuals who could benefit from a firsthand understanding of the situation in Southern Africa and address those issues upon their return. Hence, the delegation consisted of an interracial group of individuals who were involved in the anti-apartheid movement, including university experts on Southern Africa, Operation PUSH members, Rainbow Coalition members, U.S. policy-makers, business and political supporters, and friends. Among them were Clark Johnson, director of the Department of Human Relations, International Association of Machinists and Aerospace Workers, AFL-CIO; Ken Zinn, international representative of the United Mine Workers; Gene Wheeler, president of the Associated Health Systems, Los Angeles; George E. Johnson, president of Johnson Products; Professors Ronald Walters of Howard University, Gail Ganhardt of Columbia University, and Tom Karis of New York University; Robert Farrell, Los Angeles city councilman and president of the National Association of Local Black Elected Officials; Dick Griffrey, president of Solar Records; and Eugene Jackson, president of the National Black Radio Network. In addition, two U.S. farmers were included as members of the delegation for their agricultural expertise and knowledge of the U.S. food market. Jackson believed that U.S. agriculture could benefit from a relationship with Southern Africa, and, in turn, U.S. surpluses could help wipe out African famine.[19]

## Diplomacy in Southern Africa

With air transportation provided by the Nigerian government, the seventeen-day, eight-nation tour to Nigeria, Congo, Angola, Botswana, Mozambique, Zambia, Tanzania, and Zimbabwe was scheduled for August 13 through 28, 1986. Members of the delegation met with the presidents of the six frontline nations and with key political leaders in Nigeria and the Congo. The group also met with the leadership of African liberation organizations, such as Oliver Tambo, president of the ANC and Sam Nujoma, leader of SWAPO. The Jackson group was barred from entering South Africa.

In each of the eight countries visited, Jackson identified himself with African blacks and pledged to support them in their fight against South Africa. He also presented himself as an advocate of an alternate U.S. foreign policy toward the region and offered himself as someone who could help African leaders publicize their message in the United States.

The response everywhere was enthusiastic, partly because Jackson stressed his ethnic connection and partly because of the messages he conveyed. In addition to the mass rallies and fact-finding ventures, in each country, Jackson held long, private conversations with heads of state and other leaders. In almost every case, after these meetings a question-and-answer session was held with journalists.

The delegation first stopped in London where it visited the statue of famous ANC political prisoner Nelson Mandela and participated in demonstrations against apartheid. The diplomatic mission to Southern Africa began with a brief stop in Nigeria where the delegation met with President Ibrahim Babangida, who furnished the jet plane and staff for the tour, and with other officials, including the chief of staff of the armed forces. The group also held a briefing at the Institute for International Relations.

After the stop in Nigeria, the delegation traveled to the Congo for a courtesy visit to President Denis Sassou Nguesso, the elected chairman of the Organization of African Unity. As with most stops throughout the mission, a reception was held at the airport for the delegation and press statements were issued on the purpose and goals of the diplomatic endeavor. In the Congo, a tremendous state dinner was held in the delegation's honor at the U.S. embassy, which the entire diplomatic corps attended. Jackson met with members of the ruling Marxist-Leninist Central Committee and held a private meeting with President Denis Sassou Nguesso on issues of apartheid, Southern Africa, and the Frontline States.[20]

After leaving the Congo, the delegation traveled to Gaborone, the capitol of Botswana. Jackson met with H. E. Quett K. J. Masire, president of the Republic of Botswana and held meetings with the foreign minister as well as with other officials. More than 1,000 people crammed into a hall on the University of Botswana campus one night to hear Jackson speak.[21]

The first joint communique of the mission was issued between President Masire and Jesse Jackson. It stated among other things that: apartheid was the root cause of the problems both in South Africa and in Southern Africa; more concerted pressure was necessary to bring about conditions that would lead to genuine negotiations; UN Resolution 435, designed to bring about Namibian independence, be implemented without the linkage of the withdrawal of Cuban troops from another country; the international community should support SADCC's programs; and in light of South Africa's threat to increase sanctions on the Frontline States if United States sanctions were implemented, "the world community should carefully consider increased economic support for the [Frontline] States."[22]

The Jackson delegation then traveled to Angola for a three-day visit. Angola was considered a very important stop because Jackson aimed to improve United States-Angolan relations and persuade the United States to establish diplomatic relations with the Luanda government. U.S. talks with Angola had broken off the previous year in disagreement over the framework by which Cuban troops would withdraw from Angola and South African troops would withdrawn from Namibia. Jackson also wanted to address Angolan views on U.S. aid to UNITA and South African destabilization activities.

On the first day, a private meeting was held with Angolan President José Eduardo Dos Santos, who hosted a dinner in Jackson's honor. Jackson also had meetings with other officials, including Angolan Foreign Minister Afonso Van-Dunem, who said that his country was ready to establish diplomatic relations with the United States, despite the Reagan administration's hostility. Foreign Minister Van-Dunem told Jackson that Angola had excellent trade ties with the United States and he saw no reason why it should not have friendly political ties. To show the Jackson delegation an example of South African aggression, they were taken to a prison in Luanda to visit South African prisoner Captain Wunand du Toit, who had been captured while trying to blow up a U.S.- owned oil installation in Angola's northern province of Cabinda, 2,000 miles from the South African border. The delegation also traveled to Lubango, Angola, to visit an orphanage.

On the second day in Angola, the delegation visited the northern province of Cabinda where the U.S. oil company Chevron and Angola's state-run oil firm Sonangol operated a joint venture. Jackson told U.S. oilworkers employed in Cabinda that their country should recognize Angola and that flourishing bilateral trade showed that friendly ties were possible. Jackson said, "I want to send a message to the American people that if the Angolans are good enough for us to work and trade with, they should be good enough to have diplomatic relations with."[23] Oil officials said that Angola sold 65 percent of its oil to the United States and that Cabinda Gulf was responsible for 70 percent of Angola's 280,000 barrels per day (BDP) output.

While visiting the Gulf Oil/Chevron facility at Cabinda, the delegation discovered that the black workers there lived in a state of near apartheid. Environmental conditions were hazardous, and the wages were so low that the workers often accepted beer and cigarettes instead of money. In addition, the company made little investment in the surrounding community and since 1974 only nine black Angolans had technical training. Moreover, African American workers apparently were not recruited for work since there was only one employed out of 150 American employees. The reason given for the disparity was the lack of initiative by African Americans to seek jobs in the industry. However, there was also "no evidence that there was an affirmative action program in place for such lucrative jobs." When the Jackson delegation returned to the United States, information on the deplorable conditions at Cabinda was disseminated to interested congressional members. However, those efforts did not result in any discernible action, primarily because the Cuban issue prevented any serious dialogue on how to handle the problems in the northern province.[24] Ironically, the Cubans were assigned to protect the Angolan-American oil enterprise.

An important commentary on the leverage wielded by the Jackson delegation related to their abilities to suspend racist customs by their very presence. One example occured when the group was eating dinner on the lawn in Cabinda, they invited black Angolan employees gathered at the edge of the area to join them. The delegation was told by the employees that there was a rule against their association with white employees. The delegation responded by insisting that they join their group and demanded service for them.[25]

The proposed Angola Communique was so important to Jackson that he discontinued plans for a trip to Namibia, which already had been thwarted by South Africa's refusal to grant visas to the group. Jackson ultimately persuaded Dos Santos to extend an "olive branch" to the United States. In the communique Dos Santos indicated a willingness to go beyond mere contacts with the State Department to a full-fledged discussion on the various impediments that existed to normal relations. The communique also stated that current U.S. support for UNITA impeded the search for peace both in Angola and in Namibia; that the importance should be placed on Namibia's independence; and that the final settlement should involve discussions that included the United Nations, the United States, and South Africa, and would require the withdrawal of all foreign troops from Angola.[26] Angolan leaders also requested a meeting with Reagan to discuss ways of resolving tensions between the two nations. As a result of the Jackson delegation's witnessing the devastating effects of South Africa's destabilization policies, Dick Griffrey of Solar Records started a "Fund for a Free Africa," to assist those Angolans who were suffering and the surviving family members of relatives slain by UNITA.

In Mozambique, Jackson was treated as a visiting head of state and a royal reception was held in his honor. President Samora Machel greeted Jackson at his palace where they discussed South African destabilization in the region and in Mozambique through RENAMO.[27]

In Lusaka, Zambia, Jackson held a two-hour meeting with exiled leaders of the ANC and indicated that President Reagan should do the same to help avoid a bloodbath inside South Africa. ANC General Secretary Alfred Nzo, who described the Reagan administration as a friend and supporter of South Africa said of Jackson, "It is very inspiring for us to know that there is another America which has nothing to do with the program of those in power and which understands this region."[28] This statement indicates that he considered Jackson and his supporters allies inside the United States.

In Zambia, the delegation visited a UN refugee camp outside Lusaka that had been bombed by South African planes. Jackson also addressed the Institute for Namibia, a UN research agency on Namibia, where his message was that continued U.S. obstruction of an independent settlement in Namibia by linking it to the withdrawal of Cuban troops from neighboring Angola typified the administration's "inconsistency" because it eased the pressure on South Africa.[29] Jackson's appeal brought tears to the eyes of Zambian President Kenneth Kaunda, who stated as he rose to deliver a responding speech, "This young man has made me weep because I have been warning that unless the western powers do something we are going to have a catastrophe in this region in which hundreds of thousands will die."[30]

As Jackson traveled farther into the region, he was told how the Pretoria-backed rebels had severed the landlocked Frontline States' alternative transportation routes to the sea through Mozambique and Angola, forcing them into greater dependence on South Africa's transportation network. By that time, South Africa had applied a partial blockade on those routes in retaliation for the Frontline States' support of a Commonwealth sanctions package. According to press reports, it was then that Jackson named South Africa an "evil empire." Jackson also began to stress the urgency for a comprehensive U.S. policy that would couple sanctions with an aid plan for the Frontline States to help them defend their alternative transportation routes and to strengthen their defenses against South African attacks.[31]

In Tanzania, Jackson met with Tanzanian President Ali Hassan Mwinyi and traveled to a remote village in the poorest part of the country to meet with the former president, Julius K. Nyerere, the continent's most respected elder statesman. Nyerere told Jackson that the United States could score a diplomatic coup in Africa by reversing linkage of Namibian independence to the Cuban pull out of Angola.

In Harare, Zimbabwe, Jackson met with Prime Minister Robert Mugabe, the incoming chair of the 101-nation Nonaligned movement. Mugabe told Jackson that he and other leaders of the Frontline States hoped to use Jackson as "a channel of communication" to persuade the United States to give them stronger support in the struggle against apartheid. Mugabe labeled President Reagan and British Prime Minister Margaret Thatcher racists because of their refusal to ostracize South Africa. "Those in power in South Africa are white and Margaret Thatcher in my opinion is a racist. I would want to say the same about the present administration in Washington."[32] The prime minister said that he hoped Reagan would accept a request from the Frontline States leaders for a meeting, either in Africa or in Washington.[33]

Mugabe strongly endorsed Jackson's call for stiffer sanctions and support for the Frontline States to bolster them against retaliatory action from Pretoria. Mugabe said that the Frontline States needed U.S. development aid and military equipment, which would enable them to reduce dependence on South Africa's transportation network and would help them defend against South Africa-backed rebels in the region. After their talks, which lasted nearly two hours, Mugabe and Jackson visited the ANC house in Harare that had been demolished by South African raiders. Pretoria claimed that the house was used as a base for guerrillas, but Mugabe said that it housed civilian refugees.[34]

Ultimately, Mugabe accepted Jackson's invitation to visit the United States in September to brief the United States on why he and other leaders in the region viewed Reagan's policies with such contempt. Jackson offered to orchestrate Mugabe's visit to achieve maximum impact by arranging for him to meet with the House and Senate Foreign Affairs Committees, the State Department, mayors, labor leaders, and church and civil rights organizations, and for him to appear on television and address mass rallies. They considered that Mugabe's visit would be a forerunner of other tours by African leaders.

Jackson said in an interview that the information he had gained during his tour about the extent of South Africa's geoeconomic stronghold on the region and how Pretoria used it to reinforce its neighbors' dependence was very significant. In response to what he had learned, Jackson stated that a program modeled after the Marshall Plan is the type of initiative that the United States should adopt for Southern Africa. He said the program should be based on five themes: respect for the region's African leaders and people, which he said is lacking at present; aid based on the region's needs; favorable trade agreements; long-term aid, rather than just year-to-year; and development and defense assistance.[35]

Before returning to the United States, the delegation stopped in Lagos, Nigeria, where at a news conference Jackson urged President Reagan to meet with the leaders of the Frontline States and the leaders of rebel groups in order to hear their views on apartheid, sanctions, and destabilization. He also called for increased aid, trade, and investment with the Frontline states and urged the administration to impose economic sanctions on South Africa to force an end to apartheid. Jackson promised the African leaders that he would attempt to marshal public and government support in the United States to help them repel countersanctions and aggression by South Africa. He also said he would organize meetings with labor groups, civil-rights groups, members of Congress, and the public, if Reagan refused their request for a summit meeting.[36]

## Effectiveness of the Diplomatic Mission

As in the previous cases discussed, Jackson was successful in using citizen diplomacy as an alternate avenue to participate in the international arena. In bypassing conventional mechanisms for participation in foreign affairs, Jackson and his delegation traveled abroad and met with foreign officials to discuss their mutual concerns. The initial accomplishments of the mission were that Jackson: (1) gained insight into the extent of South Africa's geoeconomic stronghold on the region and how Pretoria used it to reinforce its neighbors' dependence and took that information home to the U.S. public; (2) opened lines of communication to a region of the world often ignored in the United States; (3) established personal relationships with leaders in the region; (4) issued joint communiques with each leader, which set forth their views on the nature of problems in the region and the most efficacious solutions; and (5) gained credibility in the region, which was evidenced by the signing of agreements by all six Frontline States leaders.

Upon his return, Jackson held a press conference at the National Press Club to report his findings. He also discussed the issues raised during his tour of Southern Africa with State Department officials, some of whom he found receptive. During his meeting with Undersecretary of State Michael H. Armacost and Chester A. Crocker, Jackson informed them that President Kaunda would issue a formal invitation to Reagan for a meeting with the presidents of the Frontline States. State Department officials seemed interested in the idea but made no commitment. With regard to Angola, Crocker said he was "willing to talk to Angola" and agreed to meet with Jackson again on the subject.[37]

However, Jackson was unsuccessful in persuading the Reagan administration to alter its policies. First, Jackson's request for a meeting with President Reagan and Secretary of State George Schultz was denied. Then Reagan declined to meet with the Frontline States leaders for scheduling reasons. Irate, Jackson responded, "He's had time to host Mr. Peres, he's had time to host Mrs. Aquino and King Carlos, referring to Israeli Prime Minister Shimon Peres and Philippine President Corazon Aquino, with whom Reagan met at the White House last week, and to King Juan Carlos of Spain, whom Reagan met Monday while in New York to address the United Nations. He's had time to host who's important to him. African people and African Americans are not important to him."[38] Jackson also declared that Reagan's refusal to meet with the Frontline States leaders was further evidence of his "race-conscious policies toward Africa and American blacks."[39]

Jackson learned of Reagan's decision not to meet with the African heads of state during a telephone conversation with Zimbabwean Prime Minister Robert Mugabe, who was scheduled to address the UN the following week in New York. Jackson said he would speak to Mugabe before then and try to persuade him to take the Frontline States leaders' case directly to the U.S. public. Jackson also began to arrange for the Frontline States leaders to visit the United States before November, stating, "I'm putting together an invitation from a group of congressmen, civil rights and church organizations, the Rainbow Coalition and labor unions, inviting the front-line states' presidents to come here." Jackson intoned, "Mr. Reagan may choose not to see them, but the congressmen who support sanctions will receive them, the Rainbow Coalition will receive them, labor will receive them, urban America will receive them. They will be received."[40]

In his continuing effort to bolster support for the Comprehensive Sanctions Bill, Jackson testified before the House Banking International Development Subcommittee. In his statement, Jackson referred to South Africa as "an octopus with tentacles that have a suffocating stranglehold on the economies of all of the states in Southern Africa" and he said that the United States must provide economic and military aid to those nations.[41]

In August 1986 the Senate voted for a modified and limited version of the Sanctions Bill.[42] Although President Reagan vetoed it, on October 2, Congress overrode the president's veto. For the first time, official U.S. policy toward South Africa included substantive sanctions.

Jackson praised those who helped override President Reagan's veto. He also argued that sanctions by themselves were not sufficient and that a new policy of sanctions combined with aid, trade, development, and defense for the Frontline States was required. Jackson urged Congress to consider giving military aid to those nations to help them prevent South African sabotage of their railroads, depots, and highways.[43]

This case suggests, as in the Central American case, that it is very difficult to persuade the United States to negotiate its policy position when it lacks the will to do so, despite the concessions made. The Reagan administration's refusal to meet with the Frontline States leaders was clear evidence that it had no intention of altering its policies toward nations in the region. Actually little change occurred in U.S. official policy toward the southern African region throughout the remainder of Reagan's term, especially regarding the issues of apartheid, U.S. recognition of Angola, and South African destabilization of its neighbors. However, Jackson scored with the legislative branch of government. The attention focused on Southern Africa as a result of Jackson's foray contributed to increased knowledge about the region and therefore increased pressure on Congress by interest groups and other concerned citizens.[44] It also contributed to the passage of the Comprehensive Sanctions Bill.

Later, other accomplishments of the trip were realized. For instance, Pan-Africanism, as a legitimate framework to help unify the African "world" gained more salience. The notion that African Americans should seek ways to contribute to the development of Africa also recieved increased attention. These ideas were put into practice as relationships flourished between African American and African leaders. For instance, since 1986, Jackson and other prominent African Americans have hosted several African dignitaries in the United States, most notably, President Kenneth Kaunda of Zambia and Sam Nujoma, leader of SWAPO and now President of Namibia. Since then, when many African leaders travel to the United States they "touch base" with African American leadership and often African Americans provide assistance in terms of political and economic contacts. Finally, Jackson has been invited several times to various African nations to discuss U.S. policy in Africa and African American perspectives on Africa.

As with the previous missions, this one, too, engendered sharp criticisms. However, issues of race were more salient in the attacks on Jackson's travels—even more so than in the Goodman case. In one instance, Jackson was compared to more moderate African American leaders such as Andrew Young, who was viewed as understanding how African Americans should behave abroad. In the *Atlanta Journal Constitution*, one writer asserts:

> Jackson should take a cue from Atlanta Mayor Andrew Young, who holds similar views and has enormous popular appeal in Africa, but who makes a point of operating within the framework set up by the State Department when he goes abroad. Even when Young is sharply critical of U.S. policy, as he was earlier this week during a visit to Marxist Angola, there is no doubting his motives. First, Young had legitimate business in Africa. Second, it was not for self-aggrandizement that he spoke out but, rather, to prick U.S. consciences despite the damage it might do him politically. He has not made a career of rubbing our noses in foreign soil.[45]

This mission also sparked criticisms from some African Americans who maintained that not all African Americans were opposed to U.S. policy in the region. For instance, conservative Republican Dr. Maurice Dawkins, creator of Black Americans for a Free Angola and supporter of UNITA, held a press conference upon Jackson's return where he stated that although his organization agreed with Jackson on civil rights, employment issues, and racism, it considered his position flawed on the issue of Angola. This group, in support of UNITA, also embarked upon a fact-finding mission to Angola.[46]

## U.S. Official Involvement and Citizen Diplomacy

As in the previous missions, the State Department provided logistical assistance, briefed Jackson and members of his delegation, and upon his return, were made privy to the information Jackson had acquired. However, despite its assistance to the diplomatic endeavor and Jackson's debriefing, the executive branch refused to seriously consider any policy change. On the other hand, the legislative branch considered the information resulting from the diplomatic effort. This scenerio again demonstrates that although

Jackson bypassed conventional processes to inject his concerns into international politics and U.S. foreign policy processes, ultimately the system expanded to include some of his interests.

## Summary

The motivation for the venture to Southern Africa was humanitarian and centered on concerns of morality in U.S. policy. Jackson's policy interests were to forge closer relations between the United States and black Africans and to shift U.S. policy away from assisting Pretoria. His personal interest of strengthening the relationships between Africans and African Americans was also a strong motivation for diplomacy.[47] The mode consisted mainly of fact finding and negotiations in order to bring information to the U.S. public and government officials on pertinent issues in the region and to set forth an African African's views on how to solve problems. Jackson's efforts were instrumental in providing to the U.S. public firsthand information on South African aggression within its borders and in the region and was instrumental in providing additional information to Congress for decision-making on the 1986 Sanctions Bill.

Jackson's efforts in Southern Africa had the potential to open lines of communication between the U.S. executive branch, Frontline State-leaders, and rebel leaders. However, the Reagan administration, interested neither in any meaningful dialogue with these parties nor in modifying its policies in the region, ignored Jackson's efforts. The outcome of the diplomatic effort in Southern Africa, as in the case of Central America, demonstrates that citizen diplomacy can result in policy change when the citizen's interests are congruent with official foreign policy objectives.

# Conclusion

Citizen diplomacy can provide an alternate route for private citizen participation in U.S. foreign affairs and international politics. In each of the cases examined, U.S foreign policy processes expanded to address many of the concerns of Reverend Jesse Jackson and his constituencies.

Citizen diplomacy acknowledges that "participation in conventional politics without recourse to unconventional methods promises little payoff for powerless minorities."[1] It also addresses a key element of the pluralist model of democracy, which is the assumption that there are multiple access points to power. A well-known example of this multiplicity at work is how advocates of civil rights effectively used the courts when other access points were closed. In addition, embodied in democratic theory is the idea that groups excluded from the normal political arena may gain entry by engaging or threatening to engage in abnormal political activity.[2] In Jackson's case, unconventional modes of political activity were used to focus attention on his international concerns. One result was that he acquired legitimacy for his activities, not only from U.S. officials, but also from dignitaries abroad. Hence, citizen diplomacy opened U.S. foreign policy processes by including previously excluded ideas, individuals, and activities.

## The Logan Act

Potential ramifications of the Logan Act do present problems for the overall theses and creates a dilemma for democratic participation. By its very nature this act threatens to negate citizen participation in the international arena in an area of dispute between the United States and a foreign nation. Nevertheless, it must be pointed out that since its enactment, the Logan Act has never been enforced. The failure to enforce the act not only nullifies questions regarding its constitutionality, which certainly would be challenged on First Amendment grounds, but also denies serious credence to the argument that citizen diplomacy cannot be participatory by its existence. However, enforcing the Logan Act would set forth challenges to democratic theory for the reason that it would place limits on citizens' activities in the international sphere. The fact that the Logan Act was not enforced in Jackson's endeavors upholds the argument that Jackson's diplomacy provided a viable alternative route for participation. If, on the other hand, the Logan Act had been enforced in any of the cases discussed, then a reevaluation of the central argument in this book would be necessary.

At this juncture in history, there needs to be serious discussion relating to the existence of the Logan Act. Not only has the act failed to deter individuals from engaging in the action that it prohibits, but there is a strong degree of unwillingness to enforce the act because of a sure constitutional challenge. Furthermore, "maintaining a criminal statute in the face of visible nonenforcement against arguable violations weakens the overall fabric of criminal law."[3] In view of these facts, ultimately, the act should be repealed.

## The Nature of a Citizen Diplomat

Before moving on to other important issues and questions, this discussion on democratic participation and citizen diplomacy requires acknowledgment of E. E. Schattsneider's argument that pluralism is heavily biased toward elites. Schattsneider's criticism also has implications for citizen diplomacy, which also favors elites or those who have attained notoriety, such as former attorney general Ramsey Clark and W. E. B. DuBois. Jesse Jackson personifies the necessary characteristics of citizen diplomats. He is a well-known figure, is respected by a large segment of the American population, has a history of challenging conventional wisdom, and understands how to get the attention of policy-makers. Individuals lacking these attributes will find it very difficult to meet with high-ranking foreign officials, much less presidents of nations. Hence, the international activities of those citizens without such distinction society are usually relegated to "people-people contact," or they must gain influence and access not individually, but as members of powerful interest groups. This implies that not all citizens will be able to engage in citizen diplomacy, and thus participation in the international arena for those citizens must be accessed through other channels.

## Motivation, Mode, and Effectiveness

With respect to the question of the motivation for citizen diplomacy, the various approaches that were highlighted in chapter 2 and Jackson's efforts in Syria, Central America and Cuba, and Southern Africa underscore the point that the motivations are not only numerous and varied, but without ideological bounds. With regard to Jackson's initiatives, in Syria the underlying motive was humanitarian; in Central America, the primary motives were humanitarian, to promote peace, and to focus on issues of morality in U.S. foreign policy; and in Southern Africa, the motives were humanitarian, to promote pan-Africanism, and to focus on morality in foreign policy. Jackson's personal concerns were also motivating factors—particularly those issues rooted in African American political culture and the African American Christian tradition, such as fairness, justice and racial equality.

The 1984 and 1988 presidential election campaigns also factored into Jackson's international initiatives. Engaging in his own brand of personal diplomacy helped Jackson demonstrate to the U.S. electorate that he is a respected world leader with leverage in the international arena and that he is capable of conducting international diplomacy. The diplomatic initiatives also gained him favor with voters who were concerned with specific international issues. In the case of Syria, Jackson was able to demonstrate to the people of New Hampshire that he was concerned with one of their own, and nationally he was able to solidify his African American base. He was also able to galvanize support among other voters who were opposed to Reagan's foreign policies. In Central America, Jackson used his diplomacy to gain favor with the Hispanic American electorate, which wields power in several significant states, such as California, Texas, and New York. With regard to Southern Africa, Jackson was able to energize African American voters and demonstrate that he was a candidate with intricate knowledge of the issues in the region and also one who possessed real solutions to the problems there.

With respect to strategy, the citizen diplomat maintains relations both with nation-states and with nonstate actors. When citizen diplomats enter the international arena, they represent their own constituencies. Passing messages, negotiating, bargaining, conciliating, and exchanging information with foreign leaders are the methods most often used by citizen diplomats to accomplish goals and/or influence policy. Although there are attempts to influence U.S. policy, those attempts are most often directed at contacting foreign officials to persuade them to act in a fashion that will force a desired response from the United States. Upon return, many citizen diplomats hold meetings with government officials to report on their missions and to offer suggestions on how to resolve conflicts.

Jackson employed most of the aforementioned techniques in his diplomatic efforts. For example: in Syria the emphasis was on negotiations; in Central America, the methods used were negotiating, bargaining, and exchanging information; in Southern Africa, Jackson was primarily interested in gathering information and promoting dialogue between U.S. officials and Frontline State officials. Jackson, as do many other citizen diplomats, notified the State Department of his intended mission and held briefing sessions with officials. While abroad, logistical assistance was provided to Jackson and his delegations, and upon return a debriefing with State Department officials and/or testimony before congressional committees occurred.

It is important to evaluate effectiveness, not only in relation to issues of democratic participation in the U.S. policy processes, but also in relation to the goals of the actual missions. On the interrelationship between citizen diplomacy and U.S. foreign policy processes, Jackson's efforts proved to be successful in establishing citizen diplomacy as an alternate approach for private citizen participation in the international arena. In each case study, Jackson was successful in "opening" up international processes to address his concerns and those of his constituency. He discussed with U.S. and foreign officials areas of interest between nations and set forth his views on the resolution of international conflicts. Hence, by engaging in citizen diplomacy, Jackson was able to overcome the statutory and functional limitations placed on private citizens who seek to influence U.S. foreign policy and establish relationships with international leaders.

Jackson had two sets of goals for each mission: fact-finding and policy goals. Of course, the fact-finding goals are the least difficult to achieve when a citizen diplomat has the support of the host country, which Jackson normally had. The policy goals were usually divided into two areas: (1) goals to influence the policy of the host government, usually to persuade it to modify its position on certain issues in order to make it easier for the United States to concede to negotiations; and (2) goals that were geared toward persuading the United States to alter its policies. Jackson was more effective at persuading the host country to modify its policies than he was in his efforts toward his home nation. In the case of Southern Africa, the SADCC states were vulnerable to the United States, and hence from a power position, the United States saw no reason to concede to negotiations. The same can be said about those governments and rebel parties in Central America who had not gained the support of the United States. Syria was different in that the goal of Jackson's mission was not based primarily on U.S. action. The ultimate withdrawal of U.S. troops from Lebanon occurred because the United States was interested in easing its way out of a dangerous situation in the Middle East.

The question of effectiveness is a difficult one. How do we measure effectiveness considering that the outcome of a situation can be attributed to many variables and that the measurement of influence is elusive when the individual attempting to influence policy has no official standing? The foremost question is whether or not influence is only measured by policy change, or does having input and consideration in the decision-making process satisfy influence? There are several ways to consider Jackson's effectiveness.

First, if success is measured by having input into the policy process, then Jackson was successful in all three endeavors.

Second, if success is only measured by persuading the United States to alter its policies toward governments, then success in Syria (the release of Lt. Goodman) and Southern Africa (providing information that assisted in the passage of the 1986 Comprehensive Anti-Apartheid Act) is evident. With regard to Central America, the United States failed to recognize Jackson's efforts in Nicaragua and El Salvador. And, even in Cuba where the United States was able to use Jackson's efforts to achieve its goal of sending undesirable Mariel boat people back to Cuba, it ignored Jackson's pleas to use that opportunity to work toward normal relations.

Third, if success is measured by persuading the foreign governments and rebel leaders not in favor with the United States— namely Angola, Cuba, and Nicaragua—to modify their policies toward the United States, then success again is evident. An exception is El Salvador, which held to its position on the terms for dialogue with rebel groups. Notwithstanding, Jackson's efforts did play a role in starting a dialogue between rebel groups and the government in El Salvador, which led to later negotiations.

Fourth, if success is measured by modifying policies that led to serious negotiations with the United States in order to normalize ties, then only the Syrian mission can be considered successful, and it only moderately so.

Because effectiveness can have various meanings, for the purposes of this discussion, if the goal was ultimately accomplished or Jackson was able to make a meaningful contribution to the output of a situation, then Jackson's diplomacy is considered effective. In Syria, Jackson's successful rescue of Lt. Goodman set off a chain of events that not only led to the reestablishment of communications between the United States and the Syrian government and to an easing of tensions, but it also played a significant role in the eventual pull-out of U.S. Marines from Lebanon and therefore a shift in U.S. policy. In Central America and Southern Africa, where the goals were more grandiose and where Jackson's attempts to persuade the United States to alter its policies failed, it is more difficult to discern a modification in U.S. policy. In Southern Africa, there was congressional support for Jackson's efforts which was manifested in the passage of the 1986 Anti-Apartheid Act. In main, in Central America and Cuba and Southern Africa, Jackson's efforts were met with more enthusiasm by foreign officials than by those at home. And even in Cuba, where Jackson was able to bridge a communication gap between the United States and Cuba on the issue of the Mariel boatlift rejects, the United States already had expressed an interest in pursuing that line of communication.

Although Jackson did not accomplish all of his objectives, he was still able to inject his views into the decision-making arena. Interest-group support for his efforts, congressional support, and executive branch participation demonstrate that Jackson's efforts were not futile. Kenneth Bleakly, former deputy chief of mission to

El Salvador, stated that Jackson's trip to El Salvador was an important part of the process and that "Jackson helped move the process along."[4]

It is also important to note that given the personal nature of citizen diplomacy, the basis for evaluating each mission should also include the nonsystemic, autonomous goals of the citizen diplomat, such as establishing personal or business relationships with foreign leaders. Although Jackson did not couch his efforts in terms of personal goals, it is clear that he sought not only to articulate the concerns of African Americans, but also to be considered a key player in international affairs—especially the affairs of people of African descent. In this regard, Jackson's missions and the publicity surrounding each gave him the credibility and legitimacy necessary to be perceived as someone that should be consulted on international affairs. Hence, Jackson was also successful at building new forms of diplomatic relations.

Several factors contributed to the success or failure of Jackson's missions. In the Syria case, one can speculate that Jackson's prior positive contacts with President Assad and other regional leaders, as well as Assad's desire to benefit from the release (the least of which was to bring pressure on the Reagan administration to stop reconnaissance flights over his territory), were important determinants of the outcome. In Central America, key actors, such as the Sandinista and Castro governments, were interested in normalizing relations with the United States which could have boosted their economic and political standing immensely. Rebel organizations not in good standing with the United States were also interested in taking their plight to the U.S. public. Even in the case of Southern Africa, the Frontline States were interested in communicating with U.S. policy-makers and were therefore willing to grant concessions and/or alter their own policies. Essentially, those parties that had the most to gain from having better relations with the United States were most interested in granting concessions.

## Citizen Diplomacy and the Presidential Election Campaign

With regard to the presidential electoral campaigns, reliable data on minority support for Jackson's 1984 bid shows that among Hispanics, Jackson received 33 percent of the Puerto Rican vote and

17 percent of the Mexican American vote in California and New York. It is estimated that he received 35 percent of the Asian vote in New Jersey and 20 percent in California. Jackson received only 5 percent of the Jewish vote in New York and 8 percent in California. Arab Americans voted for Jackson overwhelmingly.[5] Jackson received 77 percent of the black vote. He received only 5 percent of the white vote, but white votes accounted for 22 percent or approximately 788,000 of Jackson's total votes.[6]

Jackson also made serious inroads into winning the support of America's ethnic and racial groups. For instance, Dr. James Zogby, one of Jackson's five deputy campaign managers, served as coordinator of efforts among Arab Americans.[7] Cesar Chavez, the farm labor leader, sought to forge a statewide Hispanic-black coalition to press a "Hispanic-black agenda" before the Democratic National Convention's 1984 platform committee, and Jackson had the support of the LULAC leadership.[8] Ethnic groups also formed their own associations, for example, Latinos for Jackson chapters and Asian Americans for Jackson. No doubt, Jackson's policy positions on foreign affairs issues contributed to his appeal among ethnic groups.

## Citizen Diplomacy and Foreign Policy Processes

Other questions regarding citizen diplomacy were answered as a result of this investigation. A key concern was whether or not Jackson's citizen diplomacy provided an alternate channel for citizen participation in international affairs. As mentioned previously, the traditional modes of participation for private citizens in the international arena are voting, interest-group participation, and contacting officials. Citizen diplomacy allows citizens the opportunity to interact in a domain that has primarily been reserved for U.S. officials. Operating outside the existing national foreign policy-making system, they travel abroad and meet with foreign officials themselves in order to achieve a specific objective or to influence policy.

Another significant question was how does citizen diplomacy fit into the foreign policy-making system and process. The evidence resulting from the investigation demonstrates that citizen diplomacy does operate outside of the official process set up for citizen participation, and it is therefore an alternate system. However, the official system can opt to include citizen diplomats by authorizing official representatives of the system to assist their efforts. A discussion with Kenneth Bleakly, the deputy chief of mission in El Salvador during the time of Jackson's 1984 visit, illuminates this phenomenon.[9] By asserting that the State Department considered it beneficial to seek cooperation from private citizens, and by stating that they had decided early on to endorse the efforts of Jackson, as a nationally known leader seeking peace, he agreed that the views of private citizens are valued by the executive branch. This perhaps may occur because citizen diplomacy has proven to be a useful source of information for U.S. foreign policy elites, as in the cases of Tom Hayden and Ramsey Clark in Vietnam. Ultimately, cooperating with citizens whose proclivity is to reject or bypass official policy provides the illusion that U.S. democracy is definitely more participatory than it was established to be.

With regard to the issue of citizen diplomacy as a significant challenge to the executive and legislative branches' authority over foreign affairs, this investigation indicates that it is not. However, various presidential administrations and their foreign policy establishments have proven to be savvy enough to use the activities of citizen diplomats to their advantage. When those administrations found that they could not use those activities to further their own interests, they simply ignored the citizen diplomat's accomplishments. For example, in the case of Syria, President Reagan used Jackson's success to his benefit by endorsing the release publicly and sending his envoy to follow up on the doors opened by Jackson. However, in the cases of Fidel Castro in Cuba and Jose Eduardo Dos Santos in Angola, although Jackson was able to persuade both leaders to extend an olive branch to the United States, Jackson's accomplishments were ignored. This proves that the ultimate power remains with the government and that citizen diplomacy does not represent a serious challenge to the system.

This does not suggest that the citizen diplomat cannot create problems for a particular administration. On the contrary, the citizen diplomat can publicize within the United States and abroad the fallacies of a particular policy and can align himself or herself ideologically with a foreign nation or with international consensus. For instance, in the case of Nicaragua, where the issue of U.S. funding of the Contras was already controversial, the media attention provided to it as a result of Jackson's travels intensified the pressure for Reagan to stop funding the Contras.

The citizen diplomat can also create problems for a particular branch of government when he or she is aligned with a different branch. For instance, as in Southern Africa, where the executive branch opposed the Anti-Apartheid Act, Jackson's efforts helped to galvanize enough support in Congress to secure its passage. It appears that a citizen diplomat could align him or herself with the executive branch to bring about similar problems for Congress. Thus, ultimately, the challenge is there but it has not been significant enough to warrant serious concern.

## Citizen Diplomacy and Race

This investigation found that race as a significant factor in Jackson's diplomatic forays was dependent upon the issue area of concern. On the question of race as a motivating factor for Jackson's diplomacy, this examination found that humanitarian objectives and objectives that were centered around the elections were primary motives—not race. However, the variable of race was perhaps most salient in the case of Southern Africa, where Jackson was interested in establishing closer ties between African Americans and black South Africans based upon their similar experience and ethnic affinity.

On the question of effectiveness and race, Jackson's prior history with foreign leaders, the goals and objectives of foreign officials, and Jackson's status as a leading figure and negotiator on the world stage were instrumental in facilitating his diplomacy. Race may have factored into a foreign government's decision about meeting with Jackson, especially if it attempted to reach out to those considered outside of the U.S. foreign policy establishment. However, if Jackson's race factored into the decisions it was not publicly evident.

It is argued by many that race played a factor in U.S. actions. Some African American leaders believe that the United States did not vigorously attempt to win the release of Lt. Goodman because he is an African American.[10] Similar notions were postulated regarding South Africa, where African Americans have consistently argued that if South Africa was a black-majority regime oppressing its white citizens and neighbors, the United States would not have advocated a policy based on forging closer relations and sanctions would not have been a controversial issue.

In the cases of Angola, Central America, and Syria, ideological issues and concerns were most salient in U.S. decision-making. U.S. policies toward Cuba, Angola, Nicaragua, and the insurgents in El Salvador were based upon their socialist leanings and close relationship with the Soviet Union. The United States refused to alter its policies until those adversaries changed their idological perspective and relationship with the Soviet Union. As discussed earlier, the United States found some benefit for altering its policies in Syria. However, those decisions had little to do with race, but more with President Reagan's political objectives. Hence, if race did play a role in those situations, it appears that it was only minor and indiscernible.

It can be argued, however, that race was present even when the nations involved in Jackson's diplomatic effort were not considered African or "black." For example, even though race was not obvious in Jackson's ventures into the Middle East, it remained salient in the sense that the foreign circumstances were not seen as justifying "black" intervention; and thus Jackson's endeavor aggravated relations between American Jews and African Americans and those between African Americans and Israelis.

## Citizen Diplomacy and African American Politics

With respect to Jackson's citizen diplomacy and its effects on African American politics, Jackson demonstrated that African American politics is international in scope. By illuminating the views of many African Americans, and particularly Southern Africa, Jackson ultimately moved African Americans one step closer to other blacks in the world. In focusing his attention on other areas in the world, such as his trip to Armenia during the earthquake of 1989 and his efforts in the Soviet Union, he shared with other nations and peoples the support and viewpoints of African Americans. In addition, he spoke to an African American foreign policy that is embodied in a third world approach, one that sees the world through the eyes of those who have been excluded from full participation in the American political economic and social system. The citizen diplomacy of Jackson was reflected in this perspective. It is likely that the diplomatic efforts of African Americans will continue in this mode.[11]

## Postscript

The support Reverend Jesse Jackson received in his 1988 presidential bid increased substantially from 1984. Having set out to broaden his base, Jackson more than doubled his primary vote in 1988 from 3.3 to 6.7 million, constituting 29 percent of the total primary vote. He nearly tripled the number of his delegates at the national convention, from 384 in 1984 to 1,122 in 1984. Jackson delegates constituted a force of 29 percent at the 1988 convention. While he ran a distant third in 1984, he placed second out of a field of eight in 1988.[12]

Jackson faired better in 1988 for several reasons. First, the front runner Gary Hart dropped out of the race, after his extramarital affair with model Donna Rice made headlines. Jackson remained the only presidential contender who had also run in 1984. Second, he was not competing against nationally established Democratic leaders such as Walter Mondale. Third, with the exception of Illinois Senator Paul Simon, Jackson was the only Democratic contender who represented and espoused traditional liberal Democratic policies and values.[13] In 1984, half of the contenders, including the front runner, Mondale, had been traditional Democrats. Fourth, in 1988, Jackson campaigned on a broader set of issues and themes. For instance, Jackson avoided the two issues he identified as priorities in 1984, namely the primary threshold rule and run-off primaries. Fifth, Jackson hired more experienced and politically seasoned managers to run his 1988 campaign. Finally, in 1988, the threshold for winning delegates was reduced from 29 percent to 15 percent. This change also may have helped Jackson win more delegates in 1988.[14]

Jackson was also more successful in influencing the platform process on foreign affairs issues. For instance, Jackson and Democratic nominee Michael Dukakis reached agreement before the convention on designating South Africa as a terrorist state. However, several sensitive issues continued to divide Jackson and the Democratic nominee. For example, Jackson supporters brought to the floor two amendments to the party platform. The first was a

U.S. pledge against first use of nuclear weapons. The second was self-determination for the Palestinians. The "no first use" pledge was defeated by a 2 to 1 margin, while the issue of Palestinian self-determination was never voted on.[15]

Since the 1988 presidential election campaign, Jackson has continued to influence U.S. foreign policy and international affairs. Changes in the international political climate, the election of a Democrat to the White House, and Jackson's continued visibility and popularity are responsible for his increased success.

On Middle East issues, Jackson began to reap benefits from his earlier initiatives. In particular was the peace agreement between Israel and the PLO, which vindicated Jackson's call for communication and mutual recognition in 1979.

On September 13, 1993, more than three thousand guests were invited by President Clinton to a White House ceremony to witness the signing of the peace agreement between Israel and the PLO. Jackson was invited to witness the signing based on his longstanding involvement in the peace effort. The fifty African Americans who attended the event also included figures such as Joint Chiefs of Staff Chairman General Colin Powell, Commerce Secretary Ron Brown, and Representative Charles Rangel of New York.[16]

Since the signing of the peace agreement, Jackson's involvement with peace efforts in the Middle East has continued. For instance, at the invitation of Israel and the PLO, Jackson traveled to Israel to address a conference marking the thirtieth anniversary of the founding of the PLO in April 1994. During the visit, however, conflict between the two parties emerged as a result of an Arab suicide bomb attack which killed several people in Afula and the killing of thirty Palestinian worshippers by a Jewish settler in Hebron. Jackson met with PLO Chairman Yasser Arafat, Israeli Prime Minister Yitzhak Rabin, and Israeli Minister of Foreign Affairs Shimon Peres to urge them to continue peace talks. He also persuaded Arafat to condemn publicly the massacre in Afula as a step toward reconciliation.[17]

Following the "Hymie incident," Jesse Jackson has specifically reached out to the Jewish community. For instance, Jackson met with the Syrian ambassador to the United States regarding exit visas for Syrian Jews. In addition, Jackson is considered to have given more favorable speeches toward Israel and Zionism.[18]

Jackson's earlier work on issues of South Africa and apartheid also signalled the role that he would play in the transition to majority rule there. An invitation was issued to Jackson by the South Africa Council of Churches to visit South Africa in 1990. The invitation was prompted by President De Klerk's decision to lift the ban on the ANC and other anti-apartheid organizations, to ease restraints on black political activity, and to release political prisoner Nelson Mandela. During Jackson's 1988 presidential election bid, the South African government denied him a visa. However, after strong support was given to Jackson's application by Piet G. J. Koornhof, the South African ambassador to Washington, Jackson finally was issued a visa for a twelve-day visit. This was Jackson's first visit to South Africa in eleven years.

Jackson wanted to focus attention on the recent changes in South Africa. During his five-city tour, he met with clergy, anti-apartheid leaders, and trade union officials, and held rallies in Cape Town and Johannesburg. Three of the most influential black leaders in the country held a news conference with Jackson—Walter F. Sisulu, a recently freed leader of the ANC; Reverend Frank Chikane of the South African Council of Churches; and Reverend Allan Boesak of the United Democratic Front.[19] Jackson also met briefly with Nelson Mandela after his release. From South Africa, Jackson flew to Namibia, where he addressed the Constituent Assembly and met with Sam Nujoma, Namibia's first elected president.

After his release from prison, Nelson Mandela returned the support given to him by African Americans. For instance, during a visit to the United States in 1990, Mandela paid homage to those who had given their lives fighting for civil rights. He also attended the annual NAACP meeting to receive the W. E. B. Du Bois Medal that was awarded to him in 1986—four years before his release.[20]

Democrat Bill Clinton's election to the presidency also shaped Jackson's international activity. Clinton's call for diversity in government and attempts to reach out to the African American community made room for Jackson and other African Americans to play a larger role in U.S. foreign affairs. For instance, President Clinton selected Jackson to lead the official U.S. delegation to observe South Africa's first all-race elections. The new parliament dominated by black South Africans unanimously elected Nelson Mandela as the first democratically elected president on May 9, 1994. Clinton also included Jackson in a forty-four-member delegation to represent the United States at the ceremony marking Mandela's inauguration as president of South Africa. The delegation included Vice President Al Gore and his wife, Tipper Gore; the first lady, Hillary Rodham Clinton; musician Quincy Jones; Coretta Scott King; Colin Powell; NAACP Director Ben Chavis; Assistant Secretary of State for Africa George Moose; and several Congressional Black Caucus members.[21] The inclusion of prominent African Americans in the U.S. delegation symbolizes the distinguished role that African Americans have played in South African affairs.

President Clinton continued to give credence to African American participation in developing and implementing U.S. foreign policy toward Africa when he selected Jackson as a quasi-envoy to Nigeria in July 1994 to engage in conflict resolution. The crisis in Nigeria stemmed from the military government of General Ibrahim Babangida's nullification of elections held in June 1993. The opposition leader, Mashood Abiola, was widely believed to have won the presidential contest. However General Sani Abacha was given control over the government. Abacha dissolved almost all of the country's democratic institutions, put many opposition leaders in jail, and banned newspapers critical of his regime. Later, Abiola was charged with treason and arrested after he declared himself president on the first anniversary of the June 1993 election.

As a result of the Nigerian government's policies, protests and riots broke out in its capitol Lagos, and in other cities. Oil workers began a strike aimed at forcing the government to free Abiola.

In hopes of thwarting a potential civil war and to help facilitate the return to democracy, President Clinton sent Reverend Jackson to Nigeria. Jackson's duties were to meet with the government and opposition leaders in order to find ways to end the conflict. He also delivered a letter from President Clinton to General Abacha in which Clinton asked that votes from the aborted Nigerian elections of June 1993 be tabulated and announced. The letter also said that any military-sponsored conference on the future shape of a Nigerian government would be considered illegitimate unless the results of the 1993 elections were taken into account.[22] During meetings with the parties involved in the conflict Jackson set forth Clinton's position that military rule is unacceptable to Nigeria's friends and trading partners abroad.[23] Jackson also urged the government to free political prisoners and lift the ban on the outlawed newspapers as a first step toward peace.

Jackson's mediation efforts were unsuccessful. In his assessment of the mission, Jackson said he saw little hope for compromise. Abiola was committed to the election, while Abacha wanted to convene a constitutional conference to draw up a new political agenda. Jackson feared that tensions would continue to escalate which would raise the possibility of a civil war.[24]

Another reason for the failure of the mission was the lack of support for Jackson's efforts by leading Nigerian opposition organizations and prominent individuals. For instance, political activist and Nobel Prize winner Wole Soyinka and members of the Campaign for Democracy contended that Jackson's role in the mediation effort was not objective and that Jackson is not trusted by prodemocracy groups. The charge was based on a previous donation made by Abiola of $250,000 to a Jackson-backed campaign to build business links between Africans and African Americans and the fact that Jackson borrowed an airliner from military ruler Ibrahim Babangida to travel in Africa during his 1986 visit. They were also upset about the praise that Jackson gave to General Babangida's transition program, which they considered fraudulent.[25] Many of those opposed to Jackson's mission wrote letters to President Clinton and Secretary of State Warren Christopher asking that Jackson be replaced with a U.S. government envoy. It was also rumored that the Nigerian government objected to Jackson's mediation efforts. However, that charge was denied by Minister for Foreign Affairs Anthony Ani, who said that Nigeria did not refuse Jackson's visit, but needed more time to prepare for it.[26]

Upon his return, Jackson urged President Clinton to appoint a new envoy to Nigeria. Jackson said that he was not interested in serving as envoy but offered to assist the Clinton administration in any future mediation efforts. Jackson also suggested that the United States and other countries begin assertive, aggressive diplomacy to Nigeria in order to prevent a civil war. The military government in Nigeria has taken steps to resolve the conflict, such as convening a constitutional conference. However, the government still has not adequately addressed the military's exit from politics. To this day the Nigerian crisis remains unresolved.

Although the Clinton administration is more compatible with Jesse Jackson on foreign affairs issues than the Reagan and Bush administrations, significant differences remain. The crisis in Haiti illustrates Jackson's and Clinton's continued divergent policy perspectives.

The crisis in Haiti was spurred by a military coup that ousted President Jean-Bertrand Aristide less than eight months after he was democratically elected on September 30, 1991. After the ouster of Aristide, the military regime began to brutalize and terrorize the people of Haiti into submission to its rule. Citing fear of growing violence, the United States recalled its ambassador. However, it sent back thousands of Haitians fleeing to the United States on unsafe boats, disregarding the same fears that propelled it to bring back its own ambassador from Haiti. The Bush administration claimed that the Haitians were leaving for economic rather than political reasons, which disqualified them for political asylum. Jackson accused President Bush of engaging in "race-based selective immigration," especially considering that Cubans fleeing Fidel Castro's rule were almost guaranteed political asylum.[27] Jackson called for economic sanctions against Haiti and the use of military power, if necessary, to restore Aristide to power.

While running for president in 1992, candidate Bill Clinton had also criticized George Bush for his policy regarding the Haitian refugees. Clinton said the Bush policy was illegal and immoral, adding that he feared a huge loss of life amongst Haitians.[28] However, once in office, the Clinton administration lawyers asked the Supreme Court to uphold the Bush policy of forcing Haitians sailing to the United States to return home. Jackson opposed Clinton's policy and stated, "We want President Clinton to take the same position as candidate Clinton."[29]

In January 1993, Jackson went to Haiti on a nonofficial visit. The purpose was to find ways to restore Aristide to power. Although Jackson was not representing the Clinton administration, he met with Warren Christopher before he left. Jackson believed that the military would be willing to talk as soon as the Clinton administration sent a clear signal to them. Christopher assured him that the Clinton administration intended to restore Aristide to power.[30]

During the two-day visit, Jackson met with military rulers, Haitian government officials, diplomats, and opposition leaders. Jackson appealed to General Raoul Cedras, leader of the military coup, to step down. Although the meeting produced no breakthrough regarding Aristide's return to power, Cedras told Jackson that his government would participate in UN-brokered talks on restoring democracy and would let a team of civilian observers monitor human rights conditions in Haiti. However, the military government, reneged on this agreement as well as on others that promised Aristide's return.

Jackson, along with other African American organizations and prominent individuals, led an intense fight against the repatriation of Haitians and the refugee camps set up for them at the U.S. Naval Base in Guantanamo Bay, Cuba. Randall Robinson of TransAfrica staged a hunger strike to protest Clinton policies of returning the Haitians, and human rights activists filed cases in court in protest. On March 20, 1993, Jackson and Congressman Charles Rangel of New York led an entourage to visit the Haitians at the Naval base.[31] Court decisions and Randall Robinson's hunger strike are often attributed to the Clinton administration's change in policy toward the refugees. The new policy required that fleeing Haitians be interviewed at sea to determine who would be granted asylum, departing from the previous position of sending all Haitians back.[32]

The pressure to restore Aristide to power also continued. At a news conference in November 1993 hosted by TransAfrica, the Congressional Black Caucus, Jesse Jackson, and others urged the international community to broaden the scope of sanctions. In a statement signed by forty-three prominent African Americans the call was made for UN sanctions against Haiti to be expanded beyond the ban on oil and weapons. However, the signatories were concerned that necessities, such as food and medicine, continue to be allowed. Although the statement did not explicitly call for the use of force, it said that strong punitive sanctions should be imposed on countries found to be violating the embargo.[33]

In response to the barrage of criticism from African Americans and the realization that his Haiti policy was not effective, President Clinton appointed William Gray special adviser to Haiti on May 8, 1994. The former congressman of Philadelphia and current head of the United Negro College Fund helped to persuade President Clinton to stop the forced return of refugees, to freeze financial transactions between the United States and Haiti, and to freeze commercial flights between the United States and Haiti.[34]

The stalemate with the Haitian military ended when President Clinton sent former President Jimmy Carter, Senator Sam Nunn of Georgia, and retired General Colin Powell to Haiti to negotiate a settlement. Under the threat of a military invasion, the military rulers agreed to restore power to President Aristide. President Aristide resumed power on October 15, 1994.

Although Africa and the Caribbean will remain the key areas of Jackson's international efforts, he will continue to address issues in other parts of the world. For instance, Jackson went on a six-day trip to the Soviet Union in January 1989 to help raise funds for the Armenians after the massive earthquake there. He also held meetings with human rights groups and Andre Sakarov, a leading Soviet dissident to explore the possibilities of developing closer ties between Americans and Soviets at the grassroots level.

Jackson's efforts will also remain controversial. He will continue to receive criticism from those who believe that U.S. foreign policy should be insulated from citizen diplomacy and from those who oppose his international intervention on ideological grounds. It is also likely that African and Caribbean leaders will begin to speak out against the intervention of private individuals in their countries' affairs when they perceive that the person is self-interested. Despite the opposition, Jesse Jackson's international efforts have given high visibility to citizen diplomacy and its potential.

# NOTES

## Foreword

1. The writer was deputy campaign manager for issues at the time.

2. Ronald W. Walters, "The Black Initiatives in the Middle East," *Journal of Palestine Studies,* 10, 2 (Winter, 1981):3–14.

3. Thomas A. Bailey, *A Diplomatic History of the American People* (New York: Appleton-Century-Croft, 1964), 96.

4. David Hoffman, "President Eases on Jackson," *The Washington Post,* July 10, 1984, 1. Also, Richard Cohen, "The Jackson Trip," *The Washington Post,* July 7, 1984, A15.

5. Ronald Walters, "The Issue Politics of the Jesse Jackson Campaign for President in 1984," in *The Social and Political Implications of the 1984 Jesse Jackson Presidential Campaign* ed. Lorenzo Morris (New York: Praeger, 1988), 18.

6. Roger D. Hatch and Frank E. Watkins, eds., *Straight from the Heart* (Philadelphia: Fortress Press, 1987), 85.

7. Ronald Walters, "African American Influence on U. S. Foreign Policy toward South Africa," in *Ethnic Groups and U.S. Foreign Policy* ed. Mohammed Ahrari (Westport, Ct: Greenwood Press, 1987), 65–81.

## Chapter One

1. In Marshall Frady, "Without Portfolio," *The New Yorker,* February 17, 1992, 68. For additional information on Jesse Jackson and the Persian

Gulf crisis, see "Jesse Jackson Visits Jordan on Way to Meet Iraqi Chief," *New York Times,* August 29, 1990, and Greg McDonald, "Jesse Jackson on a 'Journalistic Mission,' *Houston Chronicle,* August 29, 1990.

2. The trip was partially paid for by "Inside Edition," a syndicated King World Productions television program, and was described as a journalistic mission. However, Marshall Frady claimed it was calculated on Jackson's part to obtain the release of hostages.

3. Reverend Jesse Jackson, telephone interview by author on October 25, 1996, Washington, D.C.

4. Frady, "Without Portfolio," 59.

5. Ibid., 63.

6. In *Leaf Chronicle* (Clarksville, TN), September 5, 1990.

7. See "Jackson's Role Isn't Negotiations," *Chicago Sun-Times,* September 5, 1990; Ann Hodges, "Jesse Jackson May Be Playing a Risky Game," *Houston Chronicle,* September 5, 1990, 1D and 5D.

8. Two books that objectively address African American involvement in international affairs are Elliot Skinner, *African-Americans and U.S. Policy toward Africa 1850–1924* (Washington, DC: Howard University Press, 1992), and Ronald W. Walters, *Pan-Africanism in the African Diaspora* (Detroit: Wayne State University Press, 1993).

9. Legitimacy, as it is related to a contender for the U.S. presidency, includes many variables such as resources, base of support, character, organization, press coverage, endorsements, and approval—particularly by party leaders and mainstream institutions—participation in major presidential candidates' forums, such as the debates and showing in polls and primaries. For instance, in 1984, Jackson participated in all seven of the nationally televised debates involving the Democratic candidates and received endorsements and resources overwhelmingly from key institutions in the African American and religious community. He also received support from key leaders of other ethnic groups and peace and environmental groups. On that basis his diplomacy in 1984 was selected for scrutiny. See Ronald Walters, *Black Presidential Politics in America* (Albany: State University of New York Press, 1988), 163–72, for a detailed discussion on credibility and the 1984 Jackson campaign.

10. John Spainer and Eric Uslander, *How American Foreign Policy Is Made* (New York: CBS College Publishing, 1982), 5.

11. Articles 1 and 2 of the Constitution are the authoritative statements on government control of foreign affairs.

12. Charles W. Keggley, Jr., and Eugene R. Wittkopt, *American Foreign Policy: Pattern and Process* (New York: St. Martin's Press, 1987), 415–59.

13. John W. Spanier and Eric Uslaner, *American Foreign Policy Making and the Democratic Dilemmas* (New York: MacMillan Publishing Company, 1994), 29.

14. While Spanier and Uslaner use the term *personal diplomacy* in their hierarchical model, they fail to adequately explain what the term means. For information on the problem of definition and nomenclature, see the section "What Is Already Known about Private Citizens in International Affairs," in chapter 1 of this book.

15. Citizen diplomacy is distinguished from traditional/official diplomacy which is the conduct of foreign policy by representatives of government to reach official agreements with other nation-states and nonstate actors within a given framework of policy. Citizen diplomacy should not be confused with private diplomacy, which is official diplomacy concealed from the public. Public diplomacy which is also distinguished from citizen diplomacy, is an instrument of official foreign policy and encompasses the dissemination of information abroad.

16. The case studies referred to are found throughout the book, especially those discussed in chapter 2.

17. See William Davidson and Joseph Montville, "Foreign Policy according to Freud," *Foreign Policy* (Winter 1981–82): 145–57.

18. See James L. Hickman and James A. Garrison, Jr., "Psychological Principles of Citizen Diplomacy," in *Private Diplomacy with the Soviet Union,* ed. David Newsom (Lanham: University Press of America, 1987), 1930.

19. For instance see Maureen R. Berman and Joseph E. Johnson, eds., *Unofficial Diplomats* (New York: Columbia University Press, 1977); Adam Curle, *Making Peace* (London: Tavistock Publications, 1977); Harry Ashmore and William C. Baggs, *Mission to Hanoi: A Chronicle of Double-Dealing in High Places* (New York: Putnam, 1968).

20. William D. Davidson and Joseph Montville, "Foreign Policy according to Freud," 145–57.

21. For a detailed discussion on interest group activity see Norman J. Ornstein and Shirley Elder, *Interest Groups, Lobbying and Policymaking* (Washington, DC: Congressional Quarterly Press, 1978).

22. See U.S. Code 1988 Title 18 Section 953 for the act in its present form.

23. Curtis C. Simpson III, "The Logan Act of 1799: May It Rest in Peace," *California Western International Law Journal* 10 (Spring, 1980): 365–85.

## Chapter Two

1. See U. S. Code 1988 Title 18 Section 953.

2. Treaty of Amity, Commerce and Navigation, November 19, 1794, United States–Great Britain, 8 Stat. 116–29, T.S. no. 16.

3. George Logan's diplomatic efforts in Europe are recorded in Frederick Tolles, *George Logan of Philadelphia* (New York: Oxford University Press, 1953).

4. Ibid., 167.

5. See Annals of Congress, 5th Congress, 3rd Session, 2203–2206.

6. Ibid., 285.

7. Ibid., 288.

8. Ibid., 293.

9. Ibid., 298.

10. See Daniel Berrigan, *Night Flight to Hanoi* (New York: Macmillan, 1968), especially xi–xii.

11. Quoted in the *Washington Post*, March 15, 1990, B1, col. 1.

12. Ibid.

13. Quoted in the *Washington Post*, March 1, 1990, B2.

14. Ibid.

15. Quoted in the *Washington Post*, March 15, 1990, B1, col. 1

16. For additional information on Anderson's release, see *Time Magazine*, December 16, 1991, especially 16–29.

17. Fred Halstead, *Out Now: A Participant's Account of the American Movement against the Vietnam War* (New York: Monad Press, 1978), and Tom Gitlan, *The Sixties: Years of Hope, Days of Rage* (Toronto: Bantam Books, 1987).

18. Straughton Lynd and Tom Hayden present a description of their ten-day trip to Hanoi during the Vietnam War in Straughton Lynd and Tom Hayden, *The Other Side* (New York: The New American Library, 1966).

19. Clark's statement on his preconditions for traveling to Hanoi was recorded in *The New Yorker* 48 (September 2, 1972):17–18.

20. Ibid.

21. This statement was quoted in the *New York Times*, August 16, 1972, 6.

22. See *New York Times*, August 13, 1972, 2, and August 15, 1972, 1.

23. A brief discussion of Clark's citizen diplomacy is outlined in the *Los Angeles Times*, February 18, 1990, E1, col. 1.

24. See the *Boston Globe*, February 8, 1991, p. 6, col. 6, and the *Christian Science Monitor*, February 19, 1991, p. 7, col. 3, for further details of Clark's assessment of the U.S. bombing of Iraq.

25. John Reed, *Ten Days That Shook the World* (New York: Boni and Liveright, 1919).

26. For further information on Reed's second trip to the Soviet Union, see Robert Rosenstone, *Romantic Revolutionary: A Biography of John Reed* (Cambridge: Harvard University Press, 1990), 361–70.

27. Information about Owen's involvement with North and the Contras can be found in the *Chicago Tribune*, February 25, 1989, sec. 1, p. 3, col. 1. For further information on contributions to the Contras through Oliver North, see the *Chicago Tribune*, May 22, 1987, sec. 1, p. 1, col. 3, and Joseph Foote, "Contra-Productive," *Foundation News* 29, no. 2, (March/April 1988): 28–30.

28. See The Boland Amendment—Defense Appropriations Act, P.L. 97–377, § 793, and see Senators William S. Cohen and George J. Mitchell, *Men of Zeal* (New York: Penguin Books, 1989).

29. For a discussion on the impact of public opinion on the Vietnam War, see Robert Y. Shapiro and Benjamin I. Page, "Foreign Policy and Public Opinion," in *The New Politics of American Foreign Policy,* ed. David A. Deese (New York: St. Martin's Press, 1994), 230–33.

30. For additional information on Cuffe's emigration activities, see Mary Gage Atkin, *Paul Cuffe and the African Promised Land* (Nashville: Thomas Nelson, Inc., 1977).

31. See John Hope Franklin and Alfred A. Moss, *From Slavery to Freedom: A History of Negro Americans*, 6th ed. (New York: Alfred A. Knoff, 1988), 157.

32. Edwin Dorn and Walter C. Carrington, *Africa in the Minds and Deeds of Black American Leaders* (Washington, DC: Joint Center for Political and Economic Studies, 1991), 10.

33. See Theodore G. Vincent, *Black Power and the Garvey Movement* (San Francisco: Ramparts Press, 1971), 13–30, for a discussion on Garveyism and the UNIA.

34. C. Eric Lincoln, "The Race Problem and International Relations," in *Racial Influences in American Foreign Policy,* ed. George W. Shepard (New York: Basic Books, Inc. 1970), 51.

35. Edwin Dorn and Walter C. Carrington, *Africa in the Minds and Deeds of Black American Leaders,* 13. For additional information on Paul Robeson's international activities, see Martin Bauml Duberman, *Paul Robeson* (New York: Alfred A. Knopf, 1988).

36. Ibid, and see Ronald W. Walters, *Pan Africanism in the African Diaspora* (Detroit: Wayne State University Press, 1993), 108.

37. Robert G. Weisbord, *Ebony Kinship: Africa, Africans, and the African American* (Westport: Greenwood Press, Inc. 1973), 187.

38. Ibid., 210–11.

39. See Martin Luther King, Jr., *Where Do We Go from Here: Chaos or Community?* (New York: Harper & Row, 1967), 133–35, 173–74, 182–90.

40. See *Malcolm X: The Man and His Times,* ed. John Henrik Clarke (Toronto: The McMillan Company, 1969), 253–55.

41. Robert Weisbord, *Ebony Kinship,* 208.

42. Ibid., 216.

43. Edwin Dorn and Walter C. Carrington, *Africa in the Minds and Deeds of Black American Leaders,* 15.

44. African American internationalism encompasses a broad range of goals and strategies, some of which are not discussed here. For instance, many African Americans embrace passivism as a strategy for achieving international objectives. In particular, the ideas of Mohandas Gandhi are embraced by many African Americans. See Benjamin Rivlin, ed., *Ralph Bunche: The Man and His Times* (New York: Homes and Meier, 1990), 59, and Martin Luther King, Jr., *Stride toward Freedom* (San Francisco: HarperSanFrancisco 1986), 96–98.

45. See Allison Blakely, *Russia and the Negro* (Washington, DC: Howard University Press, 1986), 147.

46. Harry Haywood, *Black Bolshevik: An Autobiography of an Afro-American Communist* (Chicago: Liberator Press, 1978).

47. James Foreman, *Self-Determination: An Examination of the Question and Its Application to the African-American People* (Washington, DC: Open Hand Publishing, 1984), 39–46.

48. Ibid., 43–46.

49. Ibid.

50. Ibid., 50.

51. Ibid., 479.

52. For information on the constituency of the American Communist parties see, Philip J. Jaffe, *The Rise and Fall of American Communism* (New York: Horizon Press, 1975), 9–15 and Harvey Klehr, *The Heyday of American Communism* (New York: Basic Books, Inc., Publishers, 1984), 3–10.

53. As defined by Jack C. Plano and Milton Greenberg, *The American Political Dictionary* (New York: Holt Rinehart and Winston Inc. 1989), 498, nationalism can be viewed as "social and psychological forces that spring from unique cultural and historical factors to provide unity and inspiration to a given people through a sense of belonging together and of sharing values. Nationalism binds together people who possess common cultural, linguistic, racial, historical, or geographical characteristics or experiences and who give their loyalty to the same political group."

54. See Gale Warner and Michael Shuman, *Citizen Diplomats: Pathfinders in Soviet-American Relations and How You Can Join Them* (New York: Continuum, 1987), 329, for a brief discussion of Singer's activities.

55. See Martin Weil, "Can Blacks Do for Africa What the Jews Did for Israel?" *Foreign Policy* (Summer 1974): 109 for a discussion of the attempts by Polish and Irish U.S. citizen's to influence U.S. policy toward their homelands.

56. Martin Weil, "Can Blacks Do for Africa What the Jews Did for Israel?" 109, and Kenneth Longmeyer, "Black American Demands," *Foreign Policy* 60 (Fall 1985):3–17.

57. Note that African Americans are usually excluded from the discourse on private citizens' diplomacy. See Maureen R. Berman and Joseph E. Johnson, eds., *Unofficial Diplomats*; Michael Shuman and Gale Warner, *Citizen Diplomacy*; or John W. McDonald and Diane Bendahmane, eds. *Conflict Resolution: Track Two Diplomacy* (Washington, D.C.: Foreign Affairs Institute, U.S. Department of State, 1987). Jackson's efforts are also

alluded to in Curtis C. Simpson III, "The Logan Act of 1799: May It Rest in Peace."

58. Elliot Rudwick, *W. E. B. Du Bois: Voice of the Black Protest Movement* (Chicago: University of Illinois Press, 1982), 208.

59. Ibid.

60. Ibid., 212.

61. *Crisis*, 35 (1928): 134.

62. See James Turner, "Sixth Pan African Congress: A Briefing Paper," *Black World* (March 1974): 6, for discussion on the fourth PAC. Also see Elliot Rudwick, *W. E. B. Du Bois: Voice of the Black Protest Movement*, 231–32.

63. See P. Olisanwuche Esedebe, *Pan-Africanism: The Idea and Movement 1776–1963* (Washington, DC: Howard University Press, 1982), especially chapter 4.

64. W. E. B. Du Bois, *The Autobiography of W. E. B. Du Bois* (International Publishers, Co. Inc., 1968), 351.

65. Ibid., 356.

66. Elliot Rudwick, *W. E. B. Du Bois* 294–95.

67. Allison Blakely, *Russia and the Negro,* 102.

68. W. E. B. Du Bois, *The Autobiography,* 11.

69. See *Kent Dulles,* 357 U.S. 116 (1958) and Aptheker V. *Secretary of State,* 378 U.S. 500 (1964).

70. See Malcolm X (edited with prefatory notes by George Breitman), *Malcolm X Speaks* (New York: Merit Publishers, 1966), 62–63.

71. Malcolm X and Alex Haley, *The Autobiography of Malcolm X* (New York: Grove Press, Inc., 1965), 356.

72. Malcolm X and Alex Haley, *The Autobiography of Malcolm X,* 359–60.

73. Ibid., 362.

74. Ruby M. and E. U. Essien-udom, "Malcolm X: An International Man," in *Malcolm X: The Man and His Times*, 255.

75. For instance, see George Breitman, ed., *By Any Means Necessary: Speeches, Interviews, and a Letter by Malcolm X* (New York: Pathfinder Press, 1970), 113–26, 167–74.

## Chapter Three

1. This information on Jackson's personal and public life was provided by a combination of sources, including an interview with Reverend Jesse Jackson on September 25, 1996. Publications include "Biography—Jesse L. Jackson, Candidate for the 1984 Democratic Nomination for President," 1984, *Campaign Document*; Barbara Reynolds, *Jesse Jackson: The Man, the Movement, the Myth* (Chicago: Nelson-Hall, 1975); Elizabeth O. Colton, *The Jackson Phenomenon: The Man, the Power, the Message* (New York: Doubleday, 1989); Thomas Landess and Richard Quinn, *Jesse Jackson and the Politics of Race* (Ottawa, Illinois: Jameson Books, 1985); Manning Marable, *Black American Politics: From the Washington Marches to Jesse Jackson* (London: Verso, 1985).

2. Jesse Jackson, "The New Spirit of '76," in *What Black Politicians Are Saying*, ed. Nathan Wright (New York: Hawthorne Books, 1972) : 60–61.

3. Barbara Reynolds, *Jesse Jackson: The Man, the Movement, the Myth*, 36.

4. Ernest R. House, *Jesse Jackson & the Politics of Charisma* (Boulder: Westview Press, Inc., 1988), 7.

5. Ibid., 8–9.

6. Elizabeth Colton, *The Jackson Phenomenon*, 7.

7. Ernest House, *Jesse Jackson and the Politics of Charisma*, 92.

8. Emily Rovetch, ed., *Like It Is: Arthur E. Thomas Interviews Leaders on Black America* (New York: E. P. Dutton, 1981), 159.

9. Thomas E. Cavanaugh and Lorn S. Foster, *Jesse Jackson's Campaign: The Primaries and Caucuses* (Washington DC: Joint Center for Political Studies 1984), 2.

10. Matthew Holden, Jr., *The Politics of the Black Nation* (New York: Chandler Publishing Co., 1973).

11. Charles P. Henry, *Culture and African-American Politics* (Bloomington: Indiana University Press, 1990), 11.

12. Barbara Reynolds, *Jesse Jackson: The Man, the Movement, the Myth*, 39.

13. See Ernest House, *Jesse Jackson and the Politics of Charisma*, 15–16.

14. David Howard-Pitney, *The Afro-American Jeremiad: Appeals for Justice in America* (Philadelphia: Temple University Press, 1990), 5.

15. Ibid., 186.

16. Ibid., 189.

17. Ibid., 190.

18. Quoted in Ibid.

19. Martin Luther King, Jr. *Where Do We Go from Here: Chaos or Community?* 96.

20. Ira G. Zepp, Jr., *The Social Vision of Martin Luther King, Jr.* (New York: Carlson Publishing, Co. 1989), 207.

21. David A. Coolidge, Jr. "The Reverend Jesse Jackson and the Palestinian Question," in *The Social and Political Implications of the 1984 Jesse Jackson Presidential Campaign,* ed. Lorenzo Morris (Westport, CT: Praeger, 1990) 161–65.

22. Barbara Reynolds, *Jesse Jackson: The Man, the Movement, the Myth,* 281.

23. Ibid.

24. Ibid., 282.

25. "Jesse, Daley Meet to Seek Famine Aid," *Chicago Tribune,* July 25, 1973, sec. 3, p. 16, col. 3.

26. Ibid., 281.

27. See "Jackson Rips U.S. for Silence on Famine Aid," *Chicago Tribune,* September 8, 1973, sec. 26, p. 1A, col. 8, and "PUSH Campaign: 92,000 Collected for African Relief," *Chicago Tribune,* September 24, 1973, sec. 3, p. 1, col. 5.

28. George Goodman Jr., "Jackson exhorts 1,600 at a Memorial for Dr. King," *New York Times,* April 5, 1972, sec. L, p. 49.

29. See *Chicago Tribune,* June 13, 1974, sec. 2, p. N4A, col. 5.

30. Thomas A. Johnson, "U.S. Blacks Meet on South Africa," *New York Times,* August 24, 1976, p. L7.

31. See "S. Africa's Blacks Hail Jesse Jackson," *Chicago Tribune,* July 25, 1979, sec. 1, p. 6, col. 2.

32. See *Chicago Tribune,* July 25, 1979 sec. 1, p. 6, col. 2, and *Chicago Tribune,* August 3, 1979, sec. 1. p. 11, col. 3.

33. Joseph Egelhot, "A 'Delighted' Jackson Returns from South Africa," *Chicago Tribune,* August 3, 1979, sec. 1, p. 11. col. 3.

34. Eddie Stone, *Jesse Jackson* (Los Angeles: Holloway House Publishing Company, 1979), 234.

35. *Chicago Tribune,* December 4, 1977, sec.1, p. 40, col. 2.

36. "Influx of Viets Ripped by Jackson," *Chicago Tribune*, May 5, 1975, sec. 3, p. 1, col. 1.

37. "Jesse Hosts U.S. Arab Leaders," *Chicago Tribune,* December 16, 1974, sec. 2, p. 1, col. 6.

38. See Thomas Landess and Richard Quinn, *Jesse Jackson and the Politics of Race,* ch. 5.

39. The relationship between the PUSH trip to Lebanon in 1979 and Andrew Young's meeting with PLO representative Terzi is set forth in David Coolidge, "Jesse Jackson and the Palestinian Question," 157–58, and is based on an interview between Coolidge and Jack O'Dell.

40. See Eddie Stone, *Andrew Young: Biography of a Realist* (Los Angeles: Holloway House Pub. Co., 1980), 136-142. Stone contends that Young's meeting with Terzi was to discuss a procedural issue regarding an upcoming U.N. vote, and therefore not in violation of America's policy not to negotiate with the PLO.

41. Quoted in Thomas Landess and Richard Quinn, *Jesse Jackson and the Politics of Race,* 131.

42. Ibid., 130.

43. See Jack O'Dell and James Zogby, eds., *Afro-Americans Can Stand Up for Middle East Peace* (Washington, DC: Palestine Human Rights Campaign, 1980), 13.

44. Thomas Landess and Richard Quinn, *Jesse Jackson and the Politics of Race,* 137.

45. Ibid.

46. Ibid., 144.

47. Ibid., 145.

48. Ibid., 144.

49. "Jackson Accuses Begin of Racism," *Chicago Tribune,* September 26, 1979, sec. 1, p. 3.

50. Thomas Landess and Richard Quinn, *Jesse Jackson and the Politics of Race,* 149.

51. For instance, see *Chicago Tribune*, September 30, 1979, sec. 1, p. 2.

52. For more information on these incidents, see Landess and Quinn, *Jesse Jackson and the Politics of Race* 146–47 and *Atlanta Constitution,* October 23, 1979, 5A.

53. Thomas Landess and Richard Quinn, *Jesse Jackson and the Politics of Race,* 151.

54. Ibid., 150–51. No date for the poll was indicated. However, it is safe to assume that it was conducted soon after Jackson's return.

55. See Ernest House, *Jesse Jackson and the Politics of Charisma,* 50.

56. For additional information on symbolic capital as a source of political power, see Pierre Bourdieu, *Outline of a Theory of Practice* (Cambridge: Cambridge University Press, 1987), and Julie M. Feinsilver, "Cuba as a World Medical Power," *Latin American Research Review* 24 (1989): 2.

## Chapter Four

1. E. E. Schattsneider, *The Semi-Sovereign People* (New York: Holt, Reinhart & Winston,1960), 141.

2. Ibid., 29–31, 141.

3. Ronald W. Walters, "The Emergent Mobilization of the Black Community in the Jackson Campaign for President," in *Jesse Jackson's 1984 Presidential Campaign*, eds. Lucius Barker and Ronald W. Walters (Chicago: University of Illinois Press, 1989), 35.

4. Robert Smith, "From Insurgency toward Inclusion: The Jackson Campaigns of 1984 and 1988," in *The Social and Political Implications of the Jesse Jackson Presidential Campaign*.

5. Sheila Collins, *The Rainbow Challenge: The Jackson Campaign and the Future of U.S. Politics* (New York: Monthly Review Press, 1986), 107–10.

6. See Charles H. Wesley, "Negro Suffrage in the Period of Constitution Making, 1787–1865, in his *Neglected History* (Ohio: Central State College Press, 1965).

7. See John Hope Franklin, *From Slavery to Freedom: A History of Negro Americans*, third edition, (New York: Vintage Books Edition, 1969), 331–32, and Rutherford W. Logan, *The Betrayal of the Negro: From Rutherford B. Hayes to Woodrow Wilson* (New York: Collier Books, 1965), 23–30.

8. See Hanes Walton, Jr., "Black Presidential Participation and Critical Election Theory," in *The Social and Political Implications of the 1984 Jesse Jackson Presidential Campaign,* 54–62 for a historical account of African American participation in presidential elections.

9. See Manning Marable, *Black American Politics,* 231, and Frank Clemente and Frank Watkins, *Keep Hope Alive,* 5.

10. Frank Clemente and Frank Watkins, *Keep Hope Alive: Jesse Jackson's 1988 Presidential Campaign* (Boston: South End Press, 1989), 5–6.

11. The purpose of the plan was to develop a more effective response to the crisis in the black community. For more information see *The Black Leadership Family Plan for the Unity, Survival and Progress of Black People* (Washington, D.C.: The Black Leadership Forum and the Black Leadership Roundtable, 1982).

12. The People's Platform (1984) was published by the Black Coalition for the 1984 campaign in cooperation with the National Black Leadership Roundtable. The National Black Coalition was started by Joseph Lowery of the SCLC and included civil rights leaders and politicians who supported both the Mondale and the Jackson campaigns.

13. Collins, *The Rainbow Challenge,* 174.

14. Smith "From Insurgency toward Inclusion: The Jackson Campaigns of 1984 and 1988," 215.

15. Lucius Barker "Jesse Jackson's Candidacy in Political-Social Perspective: A Contextual Analysis" in *Jesse Jackson's 1984 Presidential Campaign,* 9.

16. Roger D. Hatch and Frank Watkins, eds., *Straight from the Heart* (Philadelphia: Fortress Press, 1987), 8.

17. Sheila Collins, *The Rainbow Challenge,* 107–10.

18. See Manning Marable, *Black American Politics,* 267–70, and Sheila Collins, *The Rainbow Challenge,* 173–74.

19. Manning Marable, *Black American Politics,* 274.

20. "Jesse Jackson's Philosophy" (campaign position paper, 1984).

21. Sheila Collins, *The Rainbow Challenge,* 171.

22. Manning Marable, *Black American Politics,* 271–72.

23. Ronald Walters, "The Issue Politics of the Jesse Jackson Campaign for President in 1984," in *The Social and Political Implications of the 1984 Jesse Jackson Presidential Campaign*, 21.

24. Ibid., 18.

25. Sheila Collins, *Rainbow Challenge*, 202.

26. See Armando Gutierrez, "The Jackson Campaign in the Hispanic Community: Problems and Prospects for a Black-Brown Coalition," in *Jesse Jackson's 1984 Presidential Campaign*, 114–15.

27. Lorenzo Morris and Linda Williams, "The Coalition at the End of the Rainbow," in *Jesse Jackson's 1984 Presidential Campaign*, 240–41.

28. Elliot Skinner, "African American Perspectives," unpublished paper, Columbia University, n.d.

29. See Harvey Klehr, *Far Left of Center: The American Radical Left Today* (New Brunswick: Transaction Books, 1985), and Arch Puddington, "Jesse Jackson, the Blacks and American Foreign Policy," *Commentary* 77, April 1984, especially p. 26.

30. Harvey Klehr, *Far Left of Center: The American Radical Left Today*, 172.

31. Elliot P. Skinner, "The Jesse Jackson Campaign and U.S. Foreign Policy," in *The Social and Political Implications of the 1989 Jesse Jackson Presidential Campaign*, ed. Lorenzo Morris, 172.

32. The third world includes the Americas south of the United States and most of Africa and Asia. According to Christopher Clapham, what is distinguishing about the third world is its economic peripherality and its subordination to the dominant industrial economics that have developed in Europe and North America. See Christopher Clapham, in *Third World Politics: An Introduction* (Madison: The University of Wisconsin Press, 1985), pp. 1–3.

33. Quoted in Morton Kondrake, "The Jacksonian Persuasion: He Too Has Ideas and They Should Be Examined," *New Republic*, April 30, 1984, 15.

34. Roger D. Hatch and Frank Watkins, *Straight from the Heart*, 224–25.

35. Frank Clemente and Frank Watkins, *Keep Hope Alive*, xix.

36. "The Middle East," Jackson campaign position paper, 1984.

37. Roger D. Hatch, *Beyond Opportunity: Jesse Jackson's Vision for America* (Philadelphia: Fortress Press, 1988), 70.

38. "New Directions Platform of the Jesse Jackson Campaign for President," Jesse Jackson for President Committee, Washington, D.C., n.d., p. 6.

39. David A. Coolidge, Jr., "The Reverend Jesse Jackson and the Palestinian Question," 163.

40. Frank Clemente and Frank Watkins, *Keep Hope Alive*, 9.

41. Armando Gutierrez, "The Jackson Campaign in the Hispanic Community: Problems and Prospects for a Black-Brown Coalition," in *Jesse Jackson's 1984 Presidential Campaign*, 113.

42. Reverend Jesse Jackson's speech before the African heads of states at the United Nations, "Foreign Policy—But Not Foreign Values," January 27, 1984, pp. 8–9.

43. Walters, *The Issue Politics of the Jesse Jackson Campaign for President*, 33. Also see Elliot Skinner, *Beyond Constructive Engagement: United States Foreign Policy toward Africa* (New York: Paragon House Pub., 1986), ix–x for a discussion of other presidential candidates' attempts to ignore the problem of South Africa during the debates.

44. Morton Kondrake, "The Jacksonian Persuasion," *Conservative Digest*, July 1984, 11.

45. For a partial list of peace leaders who supported Jackson, see the 1984 campaign pamphlet *Jesse Jackson: Study War No More.*

46. "Promoting Real Security," in Frank Clemente and Frank Watkins, *Keep Hope Alive*, 193–94.

47. Manning Marable, *Black American Politics*, 304.

48. See Elliot Skinner, "The Jackson Campaign and U.S. Foreign Policy," 282, for additional information on Jackson and the debates.

49. Curtina Moreland Young, "A View from the Bottom: A Descriptive Analysis of the Jackson Platform Efforts," in *Jesse Jackson's 1984 Presidential Campaign*, 154.

50. See "Two Mississippi Democrats Tugged Over Party Platform," *Clarion Ledger*, June 25, 1984, B-2 and Curtina Moreland Young, *A View from the Bottoms*, 155.

51. Ronald Walters, *Freeing South Africa*, unpublished paper, Howard University, March 1986, 5.

## Chapter Five

1. This information on U.S. policy in the Middle East and the rescue of Lieutenant Goodman was provided by several sources, including Congressional Quarterly, *The Middle East* (Washington, DC: Congressional Quarterly Press, 1990); Larry L. Fabian, "The Middle East," *Foreign Affairs* 62 (1983): 632–58; Bob Faw and Nancy Skelton, *Thunder in America* (Texas: Texas Monthly Press, 1986); Stephen Ambrose E., *Rise to Globalism: American Foreign Policy Since 1938* (New York: Penguin Books, 1985); and Wyatt Tee Walker, *The Road to Damascus* (New York: Martin Luther King Fellows Press, 1985).

2. Congressional Quarterly, *Middle East*, 42.

3. Ibid., 39.

4. Ibid., 73–74, for the text of the Camp David accords.

5. Ibid., 57.

6. See Zeev Schiff, "Dealing with Syria," *Foreign Policy* (Summer 1984): 92–112.

7. Stephen Ambrose, *Rise to Globalism*, 327.

8. Ibid., 328.

9. Ibid., 330.

10. Robert G. Newmann, "Assad and the Future of the Middle East," *Foreign Affairs* 63 (Winter 1983/1984): 237–57.

11. Bob Faw and Nancy Skelton, *Thunder in America*, 40.

12. Ibid., 41.

13. Roger Hatch, *Beyond Opportunity*, 70.

14. *Chicago Tribune*, December 26, 1983, sec. 1, p. 29.

15. A detailed account of the Jackson venture into Syria is detailed in Walker, *Road to Damascus*, 5.

16. Ronald Walters, "The Issue Politics of the Jesse Jackson Campaign," 24.

17. *Chicago Tribune*, December 26, 1983, sec. 1, p. 29.

18. Ibid., December 29, 1983, sec. 1, p. 3.

19. For instance, see George F. Will's editorial, "Jesse Jackson Travels Light," *Washington Post*, January 12, 1984, A19; an editorial in the *Washington Post*, January 4, 1984, A16; and Tom Morganthal, et. al., "Appointment in Damascus," *Newsweek* (January 9, 1984), 21.

20. See Wyatt Tee Walker, *The Road to Damascus*, 6–7.

21. *Chicago Tribune*, December 26, 1983, sec. 1, p. 29.

22. William Raspberry, "He Rescued Ronald Reagan," *Washington Post*, January 7, 1984, A-1, 22.

23. *Chicago Tribune*, December 31, 1983, sec. 1. p. 2., col. 1.

24. Wyatt Tee Walker, *Road to Damascus*, 10–13.

25. *Jet*, January 29, 1984, 55.

26. *Chicago Tribune*, December 30, 1983, sec. 1, p. 1.

27. Ibid., December 31, 1983, sec.1, p. 2.

28. Ibid., 1.

29. Ibid.

30. Wyatt Tee Walker, *Road to Damascus*, 43.

31. Ibid., 44.

32. *Washington Post*, January 2, 1984, sec. A, p. 14.

33. James Kelly, "Looking for a Way Out," *Time* (January 16, 1984):11, and Wyatt Tee Walker, *Road to Damascus*, 79–81.

34. Wyatt Tee Walker, *Road to Damascus*, 51.

35. Ibid., 57.

36. Ibid., 65.

37. For further details of the meeting, see Walker, *Road to Damascus*, 93.

38. See Congressional Quarterly, *The Middle East*, 282, for further details of the treaty.

39. Quoted from Faw and Skelton, *Thunder in America*, 43.

40. Michael Cheers, "Untold Story of How Jesse Jackson Won Navy Flyer's Freedom," *Jet* (January 23, 1984):14.

41. In Wyatt Tee Walker, *Road to Damascus*, 103.

42. Ibid., 3.

43. Ibid., 115.

44. Quoted in James Kelly, "Looking for a Way Out," 10.

45. Ibid.

46. Ronald Walters, "The Issue Politics of the 1984 Jackson Campaign," 25.

47. Bernard Weinraub, "Risk of War Rises Mondale Asserts," *New York Times*, January 4, 1984, A7.

48. Howell Raines, "Jackson Coup and '84 Race," *New York Times*, January 4, 1984, A8.

49. Elliot Skinner, "The Jesse Jackson Campaign and U.S. Foreign Policy," 172.

50. See James Kelly, "Looking for a Way Out," 10.

51. *Yonkers' Herald Statement*, "Opportunism in Damascus," January 3, 1984. This article was reprinted in Wyatt Tee Walker, *Road to Damascus*, 154.

52. *Chicago Tribune*, December 26, 1983, sec. 1, p. 29.

53. Wyatt Tee Walker, *Road to Damascus*, 18–20.

54. Thomas Landess and Richard Quinn, *Jesse Jackson and the Politics of Race*, 204.

55. For more detailed information on Reagan's statements after the release, see Department of State, *American Foreign Policy*, 1984, Document 243, Washington, D.C., taken from the weekly compilation of President Documents, January 9, 1984, 1.

56. James Kelly, "Looking for a Way Out," 11.

57. Ronald Smothers, "Jackson Urges U.S. Not to 'Shun' Direct Talks with Syrians," *New York Times*, January 6, 1984, A6.

58. Cass Peterson, "Navy Scuttles Jackson's Plan for a Rally Featuring Goodman," *Washington Post*, January 7, 1984, sec A, p. 2.

59. See James Kelly, "Looking for a Way Out," 10–11.

60. Milton Coleman, "Jackson Calls for Protests of U.S. Military Moves," *Washington Post*, February 6, 1984, A2.

61. See Stephen E. Ambrose, *Rise to Globalism*, 330–32.

## Chapter Six

1. Tom Barry and Deb Preusch, *The Central American Fact Book* (New York: Grove Press Inc., 1986), 4.

2. See Walter Le Feber, *The American Age* (New York: W. W. Norton & Company, 1989), 677–87 for a discussion on the Reagan Doctrine and its application in Latin America.

3. Robert S. Leiken and Barry Rubin, eds., *The Central American Crisis Reader* (New York: Summit Books, 1987). See document no. 10, "Secretary of State Philander Knox: The Monroe Doctrine and the Caribbean" (1912), 63–72.

4. A brief history of U.S. intervention in Central America is provided in Charles Maechling, Jr., "Washington's Illegal Invasion," *Foreign Policy* (Summer 1990): 113–15.

5. John Spanier, *American Foreign Policy Since World War II* (Washington: Congressional Quarterly Press, 1988), 121.

6. Ibid., 124, and Walter Le Feber, *The American Age*, 268, 557–61.

7. Alfred Stephan, "U.S.-Latin American Relations," *Foreign Affairs* (1979): 686.

8. See *American Foreign Policy*, 1984, Document 560, U.S. Cuban Agreement on Immigration and Refugee matters, 1128.

9. Walter Le Feber, *The American Age*, 657–58.

10. See Viron Vaky, "Positive Containment in Nicaragua," *Foreign Policy* (Fall 1987):50, for a discussion on the idea of containment and Reagan's policies in Nicaragua.

11. Ibid., 43.

12. The text of the act can be found in Leiken and Rubin, *The Central American Crisis Reader*, 577–78.

13. Nina M. Serafino, *Nicaragua: Conditions and Issues for U.S. Policy* (Washington, D.C.: Library of Congress Issue Brief # IB82115), 5.

14. Tom Barry and Deb Preusch, *The Central American Fact Book*, 200.

15. Ibid., 202.

16. See Tom Barry and Deb Preusch, *The Central American Fact Book*, 206.

17. See *Congressional Research Service* "El Salvador Aid: Congressional Action, 1981–1986 on President Reagan's Requests for Economic and Military Assistance for El Salvador." Report No. 87-230 F.

18. For a detailed account of Panama and the 1903 Canal Treaty with the United States see David McCollough, *The Path between the Seas* (New York: Simon & Schuster, 1977), especially pages 361–402.

19. Tom Barry and Deb Preusch, *The Central American Fact Book*, 301–02.

20. Ibid., 303.

21. Information on the Contadora group and its activities can be found in Helen Schooley's *Conflict in Central America* (United Kingdom: Longmon Group, 1987), 294–301, and Adolfo A. Zinser "Negotiations in Conflict: Central America and Contadora," in *Crisis in Central America*, ed. Nora Hamilton, et. al. (Boulder: Westview Press, 1988), 97–115.

22. Adolfo Zinser, "Negotiations in Conflict," 102.

23. Ibid., 105.

24. Ibid., 107.

25. The information on Jackson's ventures in Mexico and Central America was provided by Armando Gutierrez both by phone interview and in his article "The Jackson Campaign in the Hispanic Community: Problems and Prospects for a Black-Brown Coalition," in Barker and Walters, eds., *Jesse Jackson's 1984 Presidential Campaign*. For quote see pages 112–13.

26. Bill Richardson "Hispanic American Demands," *Foreign Policy* 60 (Fall 1985): 30–39; see pages 32–33 for demographic information on the Hispanic population and electorate.

27. See Armando Gutierrez, "The Jackson Campaign in the Hispanic Community," 117.

28. Jackson campaign document, speech made at Cento De Estudios Fronterizos Del Norte De Mexico (CEFNOMEX), May 14, 1984, Tijuana, Mexico.

29. Ronald Walters, "The Issue Politics of the Jesse Jackson Campaign," 25.

30. Armando Gutierrez, "The Jackson Campaign in the Hispanic Community," 118.

31. Jackson Campaign Document, *Return to New Mexico from Mexico City*, May 29, 1984, 1–2.

32. Armando Gutierrez, "The Jesse Jackson Campaign in the Hispanic Community," 120.

33. Ibid., 122.

34. Ibid., 113.

35. Jackson press statement, Panama City, Panama, June 23, 1984.

36. For Jackson's testimony before Congress, see the *Congressional Record—Extension of Jesse Jackson's Remarks*, June 29, 1984, vol. 130, no. 92, part 15, 98th Congress 2nd Session p. 20431.

37. Deputy Coordinator of Bureau of International Commerce and Information, Kenneth Bleakly, U.S. Department of State, telephone interview by author, June 2, 1992.

38. Jackson press statement in Managua, Nicaragua, June 28, 1984—Jackson campaign document.

39. Tom Barry and Deb Preusch, *The Central American Fact Book*, 283.

40. Armando Gutierrez, senior policy adviser to the 1984 Jackson Campaign, Albuquerque, New Mexico, telephone interview by author from Washington, D.C., March 11, 1992.

41. For more information on the controversy over Farrakhan's statements, see Milton Coleman and Martin Schram, "Jackson Denounces Farrakhan," *Washington Post*, June 29, 1984, A4.

42. Statement by the Reverend Jesse Jackson, campaign document, June 28, 1984.

43. Armando Gutierrez, telephone interview by author, March 11, 1992.

44. Associated Press wire, Wednesday, June 27, 1984, 4:48 P.M.—Betty Ann Williams, p. 2.

45. Ibid, 2.

46. Ibid., 1.

47. Jackson press statement, United States, July 5, 1984, campaign document.

48. For instance, in an agreement made between Jackson and high-ranking officials in the Sandinista government, the Sandinistas conceded to a meeting with the Catholic and Protestant churches of Nicaragua to work out differences. See Juan Williams, "Jackson Arrives in U.S. with Freed Prisoners," *The Washington Post*, June 29, 1984, A1 and A24.

49. See Lou Harris and Associates Poll (The Harris Survey), 1984, No. 58, Study Title: "Reagan's Lead Over Mondale Narrows," where 57% of the respondents stated that Reagan and Shultz should have talked with Jackson after the mission to Central America.

50. The *Washington Post*, June 29, 1984, sec. A, pp. 1, 24; and July 1, 1984, A. 1.

51. Betty Ann Williams, Associated Press Wire, June 27, 1984, 1.

52. Ibid., 1.

53. Department of State, *American Foreign Policy 1984*, document 560.

54. Tom Barry and Deb Preusch, *The Central American Fact Book*, 212.

55. Ronald Walters, "The Issue Politics of the Jesse Jackson Campaign for President," 22.

56. Ibid., 26.

57. See Armando Gutierrez, "The Jackson Campaign in the Hispanic Community," 123.

58. Ibid.

59. Betty Ann Williams, Associated Press wire, June 27, 1984, 2.

60. Jackson press statement, United States, July 5, 1984, campaign document.

61. *The Economist*, July 7, 1984, p. 21.

# Chapter Seven

1. United States Department of State, *A U.S. Policy toward South Africa: The Report of the Secretary of State's Advisory Committee on South Africa*, January 1987, 19.

2. See Joseph Hanlon, *Beggar Your Neighbors: Apartheid Power in Southern Africa* (Bloomington: Indiana University Press, 1986), 139–50, for a discussion of the MNR, and 154–65 for a discussion of UNITA.

3. Joseph Hanlon, *Beggar Your Neighbors,* 7.

4. Ibid., 2.

5. Ibid., 1.

6. Ibid., Appendix 1. Also see Phyllis Johnson and David Martin, *Frontline Southern Africa: Destructive Engagement* (New York: Four Walls Eight Windows, 1988). See note 1 and page xxii.

7. Olajide Aluko and Timothy M. Shaw, *Southern Africa in the 1980s* (London: George Allen and Unwin Publishers Ltd, 1985), 23. For additional information on the origin and activities of the Frontline States and SADCC, see Carol B. Thompson, *Challenge to Imperialism: The Frontline States in the Liberation of Zimbabwe* (Boulder: Westview Press, 1985).

8. Stephen R. Lewis, Jr., Georgetown University Center for Strategic and International Studies (CSIS) "Southern African Interdependence" *Africa Notes* (March 27, 1986).

9. Robert M. Price, "U.S. Policy toward Southern Africa," in *International Politics in Southern Africa,* ed. Gwendolyn M. Carter and Patrick O'Meara (Bloomington: Indiana University Press, 1982), 45–54.

10. See Gwendolyn Carter, "United States Policies toward South Africa and Namibia," in Elliot Skinner, *Beyond Constructive Engagement: United States Foreign Policy Toward Africa* (New York: Paragon House Publishing, 1986), 228–35, and TransAfrica, Washington, D.C., *United States Foreign Policy and the Black World: Proposals for a New Relationship,* Four Sets of Recommendations by Black National Organizations, May 1988, 5.

11. See Joseph Hanlon, *Beggar Your Neighbors,* 27–28.

12. U.S. Department of State, *A U.S. Policy toward South Africa,* 37.

13. Phyllis Johnson and David Martin, *Frontline Southern Africa,* 423.

14. For information on the dependence of neighboring countries to South Africa and U.S. arguments on this issue see U.S. Department of State, Bureau of Public Affairs, "Meaning of Sanctions and Countersanctions for South Africa's Neighbors," *Gist,* August 1986.

15. Ibid., 431.

16. Elliot Skinner, "The Jackson Campaign and U.S. Foreign Policy," 175.

17. Ronald Walters, Ph.D., Professor of Political Science at Howard University, interview by author on March 5, 1992, Washington, D.C.

18. Ronald Walters, Ph.D., interview by author, March 5, 1992, and Jackson staff memorandum, July 31, 1986, on the mission to Southern Africa.

19. *Afro-American,* August 23, 1986, 1.

20. *Chicago Tribune,* August 17, 1986, sec. 1, p. 3, col. 4.

21. Scott Kraft, "Jesse Jackson in Africa—An Eye-Opening 2 Weeks," *Los Angeles Times,* September 14, 1986, sec. 1, p. 34, col. 1.

22. Ronald Walters, "Beyond Sanctions," *World Policy Journal* (Winter 1986–87):104.

23. *Chicago Tribune,* August 18, 1986, sec. 1, p. 6, col. 3.

24. Ronald Walters, Ph.D., interview by author May 28, 1992.

25. Rainbow Coalition, Frontline States tour document.

26. Ronald Walters, *Beyond Sanctions,* 101–102.

27. Scott Kraft, "Jesse Jackson in Africa—An Eye-Opening 2 Weeks," 34.

28. Allister Sparks, "Jackson Calls for Support of South Africa's Neighbors," *Washington Post,* August 24, 1986, A26.

29. Ibid.

30. Ibid.

31. Allister Sparks, "Jackson Scores Points in Africa," *Washington Post,* September 1, 1986, A27.

32. Quoted in Allister Sparks, "Mugabe Sees Role for Jackson," *Washington Post,* August 28, 1986, A29.

33. Ibid.

34. Ibid.

35. Allister Sparks, "Jackson Calls for Support of S. Africa's Neighbors," A26.

36. Nathaniel Sheppard, Jr., "Jackson Vows Push for African Summit," *Chicago Tribune,* August 29, 1986. sec. 1, p. 14, col. 1.

37. Joanne Omang, "Jackson, U.S. Aides Meet on African Summit Idea", *Washington Post,* September, 10, 1986, A34.

38. George E. Curry, "Jackson to Invite African Leaders to U.S.," *Chicago Tribune*, September 24, 1986, sec. 1, p. 10, col. 1.

39. Ibid.

40. George Curry, "Jackson to Invite African Leaders to the U.S.," 10.

41. See Jackson's testimony before the Subcommittee on International Development Institutions and Finance of the Committee on Banking, Finance and Urban Affairs, October 7, 1986. Serial No. 99-99 U.S. Government Printing Office, Washington, D.C.: 1986.

42. Comprehensive Anti-Apartheid Act., Oct. 2, 1986, 22 U.S.C. 5001-5116 (Supp. 4 1986).

43. *Big Red News*, October 18, 1986, 30.

44. A Gallup Poll released October 6, 1986 shows that American citizens' sympathy with black South Africans increased from 63% in October 1985 to 73% in September 1986.

45. *Atlanta Constitution*, August 15, 1986, sec A. p. 22, col. 3.

46. *Washington Inquirer,* September 12, 1986, vol. 6, no. 37, pp. 1, 7.

47. Ronald Walters, Ph.D., interview by author, March 5, 1992.

## Chapter Eight

1. Edward S. Greenberg, "Models of the Political Process: Implications for the Black Community," in *Black Politics: The Inevitability of Conflict/Readings,* ed. Edward Greenberg, Neal Milner, and David Olson (New York: Holt, Rinehart and Winston, Inc., 1971), 3.

2. Robert Dahl, *Preface to Democratic Theory,* 138

3. Curtis Simpson, "The Logan Act of 1799: May It Rest In Peace," 379.

4. Kenneth Bleakly, deputy coordinator director of Bureau of International Commerce and Information, U.S. Department of State, telephone interview by author, June 2, 1992.

5. Lorenzo Morris and Linda F. Williams, "The Coalition at the End of the Rainbow," in *Jesse Jackson's 1984 Presidential Campaign,* 233.

6. Joint Center for Political Studies, *Blacks and the 1988 Democratic National Convention* (Washington, DC, 1988), 28; Lorenzo Morris, L. F. Williams, and Acie Byrd, "Preliminary Review of Highlights of Rainbow Voter Participation in the Jackson Campaign," unpublished paper, Washington, DC, July 7, 1984.

7. Joe Pichirallo and Mary Thornton, "Arab-Americans Play Major Role in Jackson Drive," *Washington Post* May 21, 1984, A3.

8. See Armando Gutierrez, "The Jackson Campaign in the Hispanic Community," 233.

9. Kenneth Bleakly, Department of State, telephone interview by author, June 2, 1992.

10. See Ronald Walters, "The Issue Politics of the Jesse Jackson Campaign for President," 24.

11. See Alfred Hero Jr., "American Negroes and U.S. Foreign Policy," in *The American People and South Africa*, ed. Alfred O. Hero, Jr., and John Barratt (Lexington: Lexington Books, 1981), for a discussion on the liberal foreign policy views of African Americans; Philip White, "The Black American Constituency for Southern Africa, 1940–1980," in *The American People and South Africa*, ed. Alfred Hero and John Barratt.; Jill Nelson, "International: The Middle East, South Africa and Parity with the Soviets Are among the Issues We're Determined to Influence," *Black Enterprise* 11 (August 1980): 58–62; Frederick Harris and Linda Williams, "JCPS/Gallup Poll Reflects Changing Views on Political Issues," *Focus* 14 (October 1986): 3–6; *Gallup Report* "Threat of War, International Tensions Viewed as Most Important Problems Facing the Nation," report no. 219, (December 1983) for a discussion of African-Americans views on President Reagan's foreign policies; and Milfred C. Fierce, "Black and White American Opinions towards South Africa, *The Journal of Modern African Studies* 20 (December 1982): 669–87.

12. *Congressional Quarterly,* vol. 46, July 9, 1988, p. 1892, and vol. 46, July 2, 1988, p. 1800.

13. J. Owens Smith, Mitchell F. Rice, and Woodrow Jones, Jr., *Blacks and American Government* (Iowa: Kendall/Hunt Publishing Company, 1991), 107–113.

14. *Congressional Quarterly,* vol. 46, March 19, 1988, pp. 740–741, and vol. 46, July 21, 1988. pp. 1799–1801.

15. *Congressional Quarterly,* vol. 46, July 23, 1988, p. 2012.

16. *Jet* (September 27, 1993): 4.

17. See "Observers Arrive in Hebron," *Dallas Morning News*, April 12, 1994, 13A, and "BBC Summary of World Broadcasts," *The British Broadcasting Corporation*, April, 13, 1994.

18. Sue Fishkoff, "US Syrian Jews Hope Exodus Will Continue," *The Jerusalem Post,* January 1, 1993, and; *Jerusalem Post,* April 18, 1994.

19. Susan Hack, "Jackson's South Africa Mission," *Newsday*, February 8, 1990, 7.

20. Muriel L. Whetstone, "Mandela in America," *Ebony* (August 1994): 48.

21. Lerone Bennett, Jr., "15 Days That Shook the World," *Ebony* (August 1994): 60–80.

22. George White, "Jackson Cites Perils in Nigeria Deadlock," *Los Angeles Times,* July 31, 1994, A, 28.

23. Paul Adams, "Unions Stand Firm in Countdown to Confrontation," *Financial Times,* August 2, 1994, 6.

24. *Atlanta Journal and Constitution* July 29, 1994, A, 12.

25. Diana Walker, "Inside Lagos: Jesse's Troubled Trip to Nigeria," *Time,* August 1, 1994, 11.

26. Toye Olori, "Nigeria: Political Crisis Deepens," *Interpress Service Global Information Network,* July 22, 1994.

27. Betsy Ward, "Jackson Faults Bush on Haitian Policy," *Newsday,* November 25, 1991, 6.

28. Bill Nichols, "Clinton Flip-Flops on Haiti Issue," *USA Today*, March 3, 1993, 4A.

29. Ibid.

30. Marie O'Conner, "Jackson Visits Haiti, Finds Military Open to Exiled President's Return," *Atlanta Journal and Constitution,* January 24, 1993, B, 7.

31. Ron Howell, "Haitian Refugees or Prisoners," *Newsday*, March 21, 1993, 13.

32. Bill Nichols and Bruce Frankel, "Ruling to Free Haitians Is Yet Another Problem," *USA Today,* June 9. 1993, 11A, and Karen De Witt, "Hunger Strike on Haiti: Partial Victory at Least," *New York Times*, May 9, 1994, 1.

33. Franki Ransom, "Jesse Jackson Urges Invasion to Save Haiti," *Atlanta Journal and Constitution*, November 11, 1993, D, 6.

34. Derrick Z. Jackson, "Bill Gray's Eminence," *The Baltimore Sun,* October 31, 1994, 11.

# BIBLIOGRAPHY

## Books

Aluko, Olajide, and Timothy M. Shaw. *Southern Africa in the 1980s.* London: George Allen and Unwin Publishers Ltd, 1985.

Ambrose, Stephen E. *Rise to Globalism: American Foreign Policy Since 1938.* New York: Penguin Books, 1985.

Ashmore, Harry S., and William C. Baggs. *Mission to Hanoi: A Chronicle of Double-Dealing in High Places.* New York: G. P. Putnam's Sons, 1968.

Atkin, Mary Gage. *Paul Cuffe and the African Promised Land.* Nashville: Thomas Nelson Inc., 1977.

Barry, Tom, and Deb Preusch. *The Central American Fact Book.* New York: Grove Press Inc., 1986.

Benson, Mary. *Nelson Mandela: The Man and the Movement.* New York: W. W. Norton and Company, 1986.

Berrigan, Daniel. *Night Flight to Hanoi.* New York: MacMillan, 1968.

Berry, Jeffrey M. *The Interest Group Society.* Boston: Little Brown, 1984.

"Black Leadership Family Plan for the Unity and Survival and Progress of Black People." Washington D.C.: The Black Leadership Forum and the Black Leadership Roundtable, 1982.

Blakely, Allison. *Russia and the Negro.* Washington, D.C.: Howard University Press, 1986.

Bourdieu, Pierre. *Outline of a Theory of Practice.* Cambridge: Cambridge University Press 1977.

Branch, Taylor. *Parting the Waters: America in the King Years 1954-1963.* New York: Simon and Schuster, 1988.

Briggs, Ellis. *Anatomy of Diplomacy.* New York: David McKay Company, Inc., 1968. Stanford University Press, 1974.

Caute, David. *The Year of the Barricade: A Journey through 1968.* New York: Harper & Row Publishers, 1988.

Cavanaugh, Thomas E., and Lorn S. Foster. *Jesse Jackson's Campaign: The Primaries and Caucuses.* Washington, D.C.: Joint Center for Political Studies. 1984.

Clapham, Christopher S. *Third World Politics: An Introduction.* Madison: The University of Wisconsin Press, 1985.

Collins, Sheila D. *The Rainbow Challenge: The Jackson Campaign and the Future of U.S. Politics.* New York: Monthly Review Press, 1986.

Colton, Elizabeth O. *The Jackson Phenomenon: the Man, the Power, The Message.* New York: Doubleday, 1989.

Congressional Quarterly. *The Middle East.* Washington, D.C.: Congressional Quarterly Press, 1990.

Curle, Adam. *Making Peace.* London: Tavistock Publications, 1971.

Dahl, Robert. *Pluralist Democracy in the United States: Conflict and Consent.* Chicago: Rand McNally, 1967.

———. *A Preface to Democratic Theory.* Chicago: University of Chicago Press, 1956.

———. *Who Governs.* New Haven: Yale University Press, 1961.

Democratic National Committee. "Summary of the Report of the Fairness Commission of the Democratic National Committee." *Fairness Commission of the Democratic National Committee.* Washington, D.C. n.d..

Dorn, Edwin, and Walter C. Carrington. *Africa in the Minds and Deeds of Black American Leaders.* Washington, D.C.: Joint Center for Political and Economic Studies, 1991.

Du Bois, W. E. B. *The Autobiography of W. E. B. Du Bois.* International Publishers, Co. Inc., 1968.

———. *The Souls of Black Folk.* New York: New American Library, 1969.

Faw, Bob, and Nancy Skelton. *Thunder in America.* Austin: Monthly Review Press, 1986.

Foreman, James. *Self-Determination: An Examination of the Question and Its Application to the African-American People.* Washington, D.C.: Open Hand Publishing, 1984.

Franklin, John Hope. *From Slavery to Freedom: A History of Negro Americans.* Third Edition. New York: Vintage Books Edition, 1969.

Franklin, John Hope, and Alfred A. Moss, Jr. *From Slavery to Freedom: A History of Negro Americans.* Sixth Edition. New York: Alfred A. Knoff, 1988.

Gitlin, Todd. *The Sixties: Years of Hope, Days of Rage.* Toronto: Bantam Books, 1987.

Goldberg, David Howard. *Foreign Policy and Ethnic Groups: American and Canadian Jews Lobby for Israel.* New York: Greenwood Press, 1990.

Halsted, Fred. *Out Now! A Participant's Account of the American Movement Against the War.* New York: Monad Press, 1978.

Hanlon, Joseph. *Beggar Your Neighbors: Apartheid Power in Southern Africa.* Bloomington: Indiana University Press, 1986.

Hatch, Roger D. *Beyond Opportunity: Jesse Jackson's Vision for America.* Philadelphia: Fortress Press, 1988.

Hayden, Tom. *Reunion: A Memoir.* New York: Random House Inc., 1988.

Haywood, Harry. *Black Bolshevik: An Autobiography of an Afro-American Communist.* Chicago: Liberator Press, 1978.

Henry, Charles P. *Culture and African-American Politics.* Bloomington: Indiana University Press, 1990.

Hitchcock, David I. *U.S. Public Diplomacy.* Washington D.C.: The Center for Strategic and International Studies, 1988.

Holden, Matthew, Jr. *The Politics of the Black Nation.* New York: Chandler Publishing Co., 1973.

House, Ernest R. *Jesse Jackson and the Politics of Charisma.* Boulder: Westview Press, Inc., 1988.

Howard-Pitney, David. *The Afro-American Jeremiad: Appeals for Justice in America.* Philadelphia: Temple University Press, 1990.

Hughes, Barry B. The Domestic Context of American Foreign Policy. San Francisco: W. H. Freeman and Company, 1978.

Jackson, Jesse L. *Straight from the Heart.* Philadelphia: Fortress Press, 1987.

Janda, Kenneth, Jeffrey M. Berry, and Jerry Goldman. *The Challenge of Democracy.* Boston: Houghton Mifflin Company, 1989.

Johnson, Phyllis, and David Martin. *Frontline Southern Africa: Destructive Engagement.* New York: Four Walls Eight Windows, 1988.

King, Martin Luther, Jr., *Stride toward Freedom.* San Francisco: Harper San Francisco, 1986).

———. *Where Do We Go from Here: Chaos or Community?* New York: Harper & Row, 1967.

Klehr, Harvey. *Far Left of Center: The American Radical Left Today.* New Brunswick: Transaction Books, 1985.

Landess, Thomas, and Richard Quinn. *Jesse Jackson and the Politics of Race.* Ottawa: Jameson Books, 1985.

Le Feber, Walter. *The American Age.* New York: W. W. Norton and Company, 1989.

Litt, Edgar. *Beyond Pluralism: Ethnic Politics in America.* Glenview, Illinois: Scott Foresman, 1970.

Logan, Rutherford, W. *The Betrayal of the Negro: From Rutherford B. Hayes to Woodrow Wilson.* New York: Collier Books, 1965.

Lynd, Straughton, and Tom Hayden. *The Other Side.* New York: The New American Library, 1966.

McCollough, David. *The Path between the Seas.* New York: Simon & Schuster, 1977.

McGhee, George C., ed. *Diplomacy for the Future.* Lanham: University Press of America, 1987.

Marable, Manning. *Black American Politics: From the Washington Marches to Jesse Jackson.* London: Verso Press, 1985.

Morris, Aldon. *The Origins of the Civil Rights Movement.* New York: The Free Press, 1984.

National Black Leadership Roundtable, *People's Platform.* Washington, D.C.: 1984.

Newsom, David D. *Diplomacy and the American Democracy.* Bloomington: Indiana University Press, 1988.

————, ed. Private Diplomacy with the Soviet Union. Lanham: University Press of America, 1987.

Ornstein, Norman J., and Shirley Elder. *Interest Groups, Lobbying and Policymaking.* Washington D.C.: Congressional Quarterly Press, 1978.

Plano, Jack C., and Milton Greenberg. *The American Political Dictionary.* New York: Holt, Rinehart and Winston, Inc., 1989.

Rauschenbusch, Walter. *Dare We Be Christians?* Boston: Pilgrim Press, 1914.

————. *The Belated Races and the Social Problems.* New York: American Missionary Association, 1914.

Reed, Adolph L., Jr. *The Jesse Jackson Phenomenon.* New Haven: Yale University Press, 1986.

Reed, John. *Ten Days That Shook the World.* New York: Boni and Liveright, 1919.

Reynolds, Barbara A. *Jesse Jackson: the Man, the Movement, The Myth.* Chicago: Nelson-Hall, 1975.

Rivlin, Benjamin, ed. *Ralph Bunche: The Man and His Times.* New York: Holmes and Meier, 1990.

Rosenstone, Robert. *Romantic Revolutionary: A Biography of John Reed.* Cambridge: Harvard University Press, 1990.

Rudwick, Elliot. *W. E. B. Du Bois: Voice of the Black Protest Movement.* Chicago: University of Illinois Press, 1982.

Schattsneider, E. E. *The Semi-Sovereign People.* New York: Holt Press, 1960.

Schooley, Helen. *Conflict in Central America.* United Kingdom: Longmon Group, 1987.

Smith, J. Owens, Mitchell F. Rice, and Woodrow Jones, Jr. *Blacks and American Government.* Iowa: Kendall/Hunt Publishing Company, 1991.

Spanier, John W. *American Foreign Policy since World War II.* Washington, D.C.: Congressional Quarterly, 1988.

Spanier, John W., and Eric Uslander. *American Foreign Policy Making and the Democratic Dilemmas.* New York: MacMillan Publishing Company, 1994.

————. *How American Foreign Policy Is Made*. New York: CBS College Publishing, 1982.

Stone, Eddie. *Jesse Jackson*. Los Angeles: Holloway House Publishing Company, 1979.

Thompson, Carol. *Challenge to Imperialism: The Frontline States in the Liberation of Zimbabwe*. Boulder: Westview Press, 1985.

Tolles, Frederick B. *George Logan of Philadelphia*. New York: Oxford University Press, 1953.

TransAfrica. *United States Foreign Policy and the Black World: Proposals for a New Relationship*. Washington, D.C., May 1988.

Truman, David B. *The Governmental Process*. New York: Knopf, 1951.

Verba, Sidney, and Norman H. Nie. *Participation in America*. New York: Harper and Row Publishers, 1972.

Vincent, Theodore G. *Black Power and the Garvey Movement*. Berkeley: Ramparts Press, 1971.

Walker, Wyatt Tee. *The Road to Damascus*. New York: Martin Luther King Fellows Press, 1985.

Walters, Ronald W. *Black Presidential Politics in America: A Strategic Approach*. Albany: State University of New York Press, 1988.

Warner, Gale, and Michael Shuman. *Citizen Diplomats: Pathfinders in Soviet-American Relations and How You Can Join Them*. New York: Continuum, 1987.

Westoby, Adam. *The Evolution of Communism*. New York: The Free Press, 1989.

X, Malcolm, and Alex Haley. *The Autobiography of Malcolm X*. New York: Grove Press, Inc., 1965.

Young, Oran R. *The Intermediaries: Third Parties in International Crises*. Princeton: Princeton University Press, 1967.

Zepp, Ira G., Jr. *The Social Vision of Martin Luther King Jr.* New York: Carlson Publishing Co., 1989.

## Journal and Magazine Articles

Bennett, Lerone, Jr. "15 Days That Shook the World." *Ebony* (August 1994): 60–80.

Bird, Kai. "The Very Model of an Ex-President." *The Nation* 251 (November 12, 1990): 545, 560, 562–564

Bolling, Landrum R. "Private Interventions in Foreign Policy." *Kettering Review* (Winter, 1983): 39–41.

Cheers, Michael. "Untold Story of How Jesse Jackson Won Navy Flyer's Freedom," *Jet* (January 3, 1984): 14.

Cobb, Roger W., and Charles D. Elder. "The Politics of Agenda Building: An Alternative for Modern Democratic Theory." *Journal of Politics* 33 (1971): 892–915.

Congressional Quarterly, vol. 46, March 19, 1988; July 9, 1988; July 23, 1988.

Congressional Quarterly Weekly Report. "Convention '88: The Democrats." 46 (July 1988): 1797–1807 and 1871–1900.

Congressional Quarterly Weekly Report. "The Jackson Mystique: Emotion, Ambition." 42 (January 1984): 9–12.

*Congressional Record.* "Extension of Jesse Jackson's Remarks." Vol. 130, no. 92, part 2, 98th Congress., second sess., June 29, 1984.

*Crisis* 35 (1928): 134.

Davidson, William D., and Joseph Montville. "Foreign Policy according to Freud." *Foreign Policy* (Winter 1981/82): 145–57.

*Economist.* (July 7, 1984): 24.

Fabian, Larry L. "The Middle East." *Foreign Affairs* 62 (1983): 632–58.

Feinsilver, Julie M. "Cuba as a World Medical Power." *Latin American Research Review* 24 (1989): 2.

Fierce, Mildred C. "Black and White Opinions towards South Africa." *The Journal of Modern African Studies* 20 (December 1982): 669–87.

Foote, Joseph. "Contra-Productive." *Foundation News* 29 (March/April 1988): 28–30.

Gamson, William. "Stable Unrepresentation in American Society." *American Behavioral Scientist* 12 (November-December 1968).

Harris, Frederick, and Linda Williams. "JCPS/Gallup Poll Reflects Changing Views on Political Issues." *Focus* 14 (October 1986): 3–6.

Kearney, Kevin M. "Private Citizens in Foreign Affairs: A Constitutional Analysis." *Emory Law Journal* 36 (Winter 1987): 285–355.

Kelly, James. "Looking for a Way Out." *Time* (January 16, 1984): 10–11.

King, Wayne. "Carter Redux." *The New York Times Magazine* (December 10, 1989): 38–41.

Kondrake, Morton. "The Jacksonian Persuasion: He Too Has Ideas and They Too Should Be Examined." *New Republic* (April 30, 1984): 13–16.

Kopkind, Andrew. "The Sixties and the Movement." *Ramparts* (February 1973).

Lewis, Stephen R., Jr. "Southern African Interdependence." *Africa Notes* (March 27, 1986) Georgetown University Center for Strategic and International Studies (CSIS).

Longmeyer, Kenneth. "Black American Demands." *Foreign Policy* 60 (Fall 1985): 3–17.

Maechling, Charles, Jr. "Washington's Illegal Invasion." *Foreign Policy* (Summer 1990): 113–31.

Morganthal, Tom, Elizabeth Colton, and Thomas M. DeFrank. "Appointment in Damascus," *Newsweek* (January 9, 1984): 20–21.

Nelson, Jill. "International: The Middle East, South Africa and Parity with the Soviets Are Among the Issues We're Determined to Influence." *Black Enterprise* 11 (August 1980): 58–62.

Newmann, Robert G. "Assad and the Future of the Middle East." *Foreign Affairs* 63 (Winter 1983/1984): 237–57.

*New Yorker,* (September 2, 1972): 48.

Parenti, Michael. "Power and Pluralism: A View from the Bottom." *Journal of Politics* 32 (1970): 501–30.

Puddington, Arch. "Jesse Jackson: The Blacks and American Foreign Policy." *Commentary* 77 (April 1984): 19–27.

Richardson, Bill. "Hispanic American Demands." *Foreign Policy* (Fall 1985): 30–39.

Schiff, Zeev. "Dealing with Syria." *Foreign Policy* (Summer 1984): 92–112.

Simpson, Curtis C., III. "The Logan Act of 1799: May It Rest in Peace." *California Western International Law Journal* 10 (Spring 1980): 365–85.

Skocpol, Theda, and Margaret Somers. "The Uses of Comparative History in Macrosocial Inquiry." *Comparative Studies in Society and History* 22 (April 1980): 174–97.

Stephan, Alfred. "U.S.-Latin American Relations." *Foreign Affairs* 58 (1979): 659–92.

*Time Magazine* (December 16, 1991).

Turner, James. "Sixth Pan African Congress: A Briefing Paper." *Black World* (March 1974).

Vaky, Viron. "Positive Containment in Nicaragua." *Foreign Policy* (Fall 1987): 42-58.

Walker, Diana. "Inside Lagos: Jesse's Trip to Troubled Nigeria." *Time* (August 1, 1994):11.

Walters, Ronald W. "Beyond Sanctions." *World Policy Journal* (Winter 1986/87): 91–110.

Weil, Martin. "Can Blacks Do for Africa What the Jews Did for Israel?" *Foreign Policy* 15 (Summer 1974): 109–130.

Wesley, Charles H. "Negro Suffrage in the Period of Constitution Making, 1787–1865." Neglected History. Ohio: Central State College Press, 1965.

Whetstone, Muriel L. "Mandela in America." *Ebony* (August 1994): 46–50.

# Edited Volumes

Barker, Lucius J., and Ronald W. Walters, eds. *Jesse Jackson's 1984 Presidential Campaign: Challenge and Change in American Politics.* Urbana: University of Illinois Press, 1989.

Berman, Maureen R., and Joseph E. Johnson, eds. *Unofficial Diplomats.* New York: Columbia University Press, 1977.

Bracy, John. H., Jr., August Meier, and Elliot Rudwick, eds. *Black Nationalism in America.* Indianapolis: The Bobbs-Merrill Company, Inc. 1970.

Breitman, George, ed. *By Any Means Necessary: Speeches, Interviews, and a Letter by Malcolm X.* New York: Pathfinder Press, 1970.

Carlson, Don, and Craig Comstock, eds. *Citizen Summitry: Keeping the Peace When it Matters Too Much to Be Left to Politicians.* Los Angeles: Jeremy P. Tarcher, Inc., 1986.

Chittick, William O. ed. *The Analysis of Foreign Policy Outputs.* Columbus: Charles E. Merrill Publishing Company, 1975.

Clarke, John Henrik, ed. *Malcolm X: The Man and His Times.* New York: The MacMillan Company, 1969.

Clemente, Frank, and Frank Watkins, eds. *Keep Hope Alive: Jesse Jackson's 1988 Presidential Campaign.* Boston: South End Press, 1989.

Leiken, Robert S., and Barry Rubin, eds. *The Central American Crisis Reader.* New York: Summit Books, 1987.

McDonald, John W., and Diane B. Bendahmane., eds. Conflict *Resolution: Track Two Diplomacy.* Washington D.C.: Foreign Affairs Institute, U.S. Department of State, 1987.

Madison, James, Alexander Hamilton, and John Jay. *The Federalist Papers.* Edited by Clinton Rossiter. New York: New American Library, 1961.

Morris, Lorenzo, ed. *The Social and Political Implications of the 1984 Jesse Jackson Presidential Campaign.* New York: Praeger Press, 1990.

O'Dell, Jack, and James Zogby, eds. *Afro-Americans Can Stand Up for Middle East Peace.* Washington, D.C.: Palestine Human Rights Campaign, 1980.

Rovetch, Emily, ed. *Like It Is: Arthur E. Thomas Interviews Leaders on Black America.* New York: E. P. Dutton, 1981.

Skinner, Elliot, ed. *Beyond Constructive Engagement: United States Foreign Policy Toward Africa.* New York: Paragon House Publishing, 1986.

Tocqueville, Alexis de. *Democracy in America.* Edited by Richard D. Heffner, New York: Mentor Books, 1956.

## Articles within Edited Volumes

Barker, Lucius, "Jesse Jackson's Candidacy in Political-Social Perspective: A Contextual Analysis." Edited by Lucius Barker and Ronald W. Walters. *Jesse Jackson's 1984 Presidential Campaign.* Chicago: University of Illinois Press, 1989.

Bolling, Landrum R. "Strengths and Weaknesses of Track Two: A Personal Account." Edited by John W. McDonald and Diane Bendahmane. *Con-*

*flict Resolution: Track Two Diplomacy.* Foreign Service Institute, Washington, D.C.: U.S. Department of State, 1987.

Carter, Gwendolyn. "United States Policies toward South Africa and Namibia." Edited by Elliot Skinner. *Beyond Constructive Engagement.* New York: Paragon House Publishing, 1986.

Cohen, Bernard C. "The Influence of Non-Governmental Groups on Foreign Making." Edited by Douglas M. Fox. *The Politics of U.S. Foreign Policy Making.* Pacific Palisades, California: Goodyear Publishing Company, Inc., 1971.

Collier, David. "New Perspectives on the Comparative Method." Edited by Dankwart A. Rustow and Kenneth Paul Erickson. *Comparative Political Dynamics: Global Research Perspectives.* New York: HarperCollins Publishers, 1991.

Connolly, William. "The Challenge to Pluralist Theory." Edited by William Connolly. *The Bias of Pluralism.* New York: Atherton Press, 1969.

Coolidge, David. "The Reverend Jesse Jackson and the Palestinian Question." Edited by Lorenzo Morris. *"The Social and Political Implications of the 1984 Jesse Jackson Campaign for the President.* New York: Praeger, 1990.

Essien-udom, E.U., and Ruby M. Essien-udom. "Malcolm X: An International Man." Edited by John Henrik Clarke. *Malcolm X: The Man and His Times.* Toronto: The MacMillian Company, 1969.

Fuchs, Lawrence H. "Minority Groups and Foreign Policy." Edited by Lawrence H. Fuchs. *American Ethnic Politics.* New York: Harper Torchbooks, 1986.

Greenberg, Edward S. "Models of the Political Process: Implications for the Black Community." Edited by Edward Greenberg, Neal Milner, and David Olsen. *Black Politics: The Inevitability of Conflict/Readings.* New York: Holt, Rinehart and Winston, Inc., 1971.

Gutierrez, Armando, "The Jackson Campaign in the Hispanic Community: Problems and Prospects for a Black-Brown Coalition." Edited by Lucius Barker and Ronald W. Walters. *Jesse Jackson's 1984 Presidential Campaign.* Chicago: University of Illinois Press, 1989.

Hero, Alfred O., Jr. "American Negroes and U.S. Foreign Policy." Edited by Alfred O. Hero Jr. and John Barratt. *The American People and South Africa.* Lexington: Lexington Books 1981.

Hickman, James L., and James L. Garrison, Jr. "Psychological Principals of Citizen Diplomacy." Edited by David Newsom. *Private Diplomacy with the Soviet Union.* Lanham: University Press of America, 1987.

Jackson, Jesse. "The New Spirit of '76'." Edited by Nathan Wright. *What Black Politicians are Saying.* New York: Hawthorne Books, 1972.

Lincoln, Eric C. "The Race Problem and International Relations." Edited by George W. Shephard. *Racial Influences on American Foreign Policy.* New York: Basic Books, Inc., 1970.

Litt, Edgar. "Distributive Democracy and American Politics." Edited by Edgar Litt and Michael Parenti. *Democracy's Ordeal in America: A Guide to Political Theory and Action.* Hinsdale, Illinois: The Dryden Press, 1973.

Montville, Joseph V. "The Arrow and the Olive Branch: A Case for Track Two Diplomacy." Edited by John W. McDonald and Diane Bendahmane. *Conflict Resolution: Track Two Diplomacy.* Washington D.C.: Foreign Service Institute, U.S. Department of State, 1987.

Morris, Lorenzo, and Linda Williams. "The Coalition at the end of the Rainbow." Edited by Lucius Barker and Ronald Walters. *Jesse Jackson's 1984 Presidential Campaign: Challenge and Change in American Politics.* Urbana: University of Illinois Press. 1989.

Price, Robert M. "U.S. Policy toward Southern Africa." Edited by Gwendolyn M. Carter and Patrick O'Meara. *International Politics in Southern Africa.* Bloomington: Indiana University Press, 1982.

Saunders, Harold. "When Citizens Talk: Nonofficial Dialogue in Relations between Nations." Edited by John W. McDonald and Diane Bendahmane. *Conflict Resolution: Track Two Diplomacy.* Washington D.C.: Foreign Service Institute, U.S. Department of State, 1987.

Shapiro, Robert Y., and Benjamin I. Page. "Foreign Policy and Public Opinion. Edited by David A. Deese. *The New Politics of American Foreign Policy.* New York: St. Martin's Press, 1994.

Skinner, Elliot, "The Jesse Jackson Campaign and U.S. Foreign Policy." Edited by Lorenzo Morris. *The Social and Political Implications of the 1984 Jesse Jackson Presidential Campaign.* New York: Praeger, 1990.

Smith, Robert. "From Insurgency toward Inclusion: The Jackson Campaigns of 1984 and 1988." Edited by Lorenzo Morris. *The Social and Political Implications of the Jesse Jackson Presidential Campaign.* New York: Praeger, 1990.

Stewart, Philip D. "Informal Diplomacy: The Dartmouth Conference Experience." Edited by David Newsom. *Private Diplomacy with the Soviet Union.* Bloomington: Indiana University Press, 1987.

Thompson, Robert J., and Joseph R. Rudolph, Jr. "Irish-Americans in the American Foreign-Policy-Making Process." Edited by Mohammed E. Ahrari. *Ethnic Groups and U.S. Foreign Policy.* New York: Greenwood Press, 1987.

Walters, Ronald W. "The Emergent Mobilization of the Black Community in the Jackson Campaign for President." Edited by Lucius Barker and Ronald W. Walters. *Jesse Jackson's 1984 Presidential Campaign.* Chicago: University of Illinois Press, 1989.

———. "The Issue Politics of the Jesse Jackson Campaign for President in 1984." Edited by Lorenzo Morris. *The Social and Political Implications of the 1984 Jesse Jackson Presidential Campaign.* New York: Praeger Press, 1990.

Walters, Ronald W., Daryl Harris, and Karin Stanford. "African-Americans and the Political System: Parameters of Internal and External Struggle." Edited by Michael L. Conneff, Thomas J. Davis, and Shiame Okunor. *African-American Civilization*. New York: St. Martin's Press, 1994.

Walton, Hanes, Jr. "Black Presidential Participation and Critical Election Theory." Edited by Lorenzo Morris. *The Social and Political Implications of the 1984 Jesse Jackson Presidential Campaign*. New York: Praeger Press, 1990.

White, Philip. "The Black American Constituency for Southern Africa 1940–1980." Edited by Alfred O. Hero, Jr., and John Barratt. *The American People and South Africa*. Lexington: Lexington Books: 1981.

Young, Curtina Moreland. "A View from the Bottom: A Descriptive Analysis of the Jackson Platform Efforts." Edited by Lucius Barker and Ronald W. Walters. *Jesse Jackson's 1984 Presidential Campaign*. Chicago: University of Illinois Press, 1989.

Zinser, Adolfo A. "Negotiations in Conflict: Central America and Contadora." Edited by Nora Hamilton, *Crisis in Central America*. Boulder: Westview Press, 1988.

## Campaign Documents and Statements

Jesse Jackson campaign document. "Economic Policy Position Paper." 1984.

———. "Jesse L. Jackson, Candidate for the 1984 Democratic Nomination for President." 1984.

———. "Jesse Jackson's Philosophy." Campaign position paper, 1984.

———. "The Middle East." Campaign position paper, 1984.

———. "New Directions Platform of the Jesse Jackson Campaign for the President." Washington, D.C., 1984.

———. "Return to New Mexico From Mexico City." May 29, 1984.

———. "Statement by Reverend Jesse Jackson." June 28, 1984.

———. *Study War No More*. 1984.

Jesse Jackson press statement. Managua, Nicaragua. June 28, 1984.

———. Panama City, Panama. June 23, 1984.

———. United States. July 5, 1984.

Jesse Jackson speech. "Foreign Policy—But Not Foreign Values." January 27, 1984.

Rainbow Coalition. *Frontline States Tour Document*. 1986.

## Government Documents

Congressional Research Service. *El Salvador Aid: Congressional Action, 1981–1986 on President Reagan's Requests for Economic and Military Assistance for El Salvador*. Report No. 87-230.

Serafino, Nina M. *Nicaragua: Conditions and Issues for U.S. Policy.* Washington, D.C.: Library of Congress Issue Brief # IB821154.

U.S. Department of State. *American Foreign Policy.* 1984, Document 243. Washington, D.C., 1986.

———. *American Foreign Policy.* 1984, Document 560. Washington, D.C. 1986.

———. *A U.S. Policy toward South Africa: The Report of the Secretary of State's Advisory Committee on South Africa.* January 1987.

———. Bureau of Public Affairs. "Meaning of Sanctions and Countersanctions for South Africa's Neighbors." *Gist* (August 1986).

## Legal Cases

*Aptheker v. Secretary of State* 378 U.S. 500 (1964).

*Brown v. Board of Ed of Topeka,* Shawnee County, Kan., SC, VA, 73 Sct 1, 344 U.S. 1, 97

Led 3-App & E 818; Evid 43 (4).

*Kent v. Dulles,* 357 U.S. 116 (1958).

*Logan Act* U.S. Code 1988 Title 18, Section 953.

*Military and Paramilitary Activities in and against Nicaragua* (Nicar V.U.S.), Merits, 1986 ICJ Rep. 14 (Judgement of June 27).

## Treaties and Acts

Comprehensive Anti-Apartheid Act, Oct. 2, 1986, 22 U.S.C. 5001–5116 (supp. 4 1986).

The Logan Act, Annals of Congress, 15th Congress, 3rd session, or U.S.C. S 953 2203–2206 (1982) for act in its present form.

Treaty of Amity, Commerce and Navigation, November 19, 1794, United States–Great Britain, 8 Stat. 116–29, T.S. Mo. 16.

## Unpublished Papers

Morris, Lorenzo, Linda Williams, and Acie Byrd. "Preliminary Review of Highlights of Rainbow Voter Participation in the Jackson Campaign." Unpublished paper. Howard University: Washington, D.C., July 7, 1984.

Skinner, Elliot, "African American Perspectives." Unpublished paper. Columbia University, n.d.

Walters, Ronald W. "Freeing South Africa." Unpublished paper. Howard University, March 27, 1986.

# INDEX